Christianity
in the
ACADEMY

RenewedMinds

Christianity
in the
ACADEMY

Teaching at the Intersection
of *Faith* and *Learning*

Harry Lee Poe

A RenewedMinds Book

Baker Academic
A Division of Baker Book House Co
Grand Rapids, Michigan 49516

©2004 by Harry Lee Poe

Published by Baker Academic
a division of Baker Book House Company
P.O. Box 6287, Grand Rapids, MI 49516-6287
www.bakeracademic.com

Printed in the United States of America

Library of Congress Cataloging-in-Publication Data
Poe, Harry Lee, 1950–
     Christianity in the academy : teaching at the intersection of faith and learning / Harry Lee Poe.
          p.   cm.
     "A RenewedMinds book".
     Includes bibliographical references and index.
     Contents: A personal introduction : religion in higher education — The religious spectrum in higher education — The challenges of higher education — From modernity to postmodernity — A Christian worldview — The doctrines and the disciplines — Interdisciplinary dialogue — Asking the critical questions — Etcetera.
     ISBN 0-8010-2723-3 (pbk.)
     1. Universities and colleges—Religion. 2. Church and education. I. Title.
BV1610.P64 2004
230′.071′1—dc22   2003022929

This volume is respectfully dedicated to

Lewis A. Drummond,
Richard B. Cunningham,
Eric C. Rust, and
John Macquarrie,

who fostered in me an appreciation for philosophy.

Contents

Illustrations

8

Foreword

The unceasing human problem that lies back of the historical contrast between Athens and Jerusalem is the problem of *finding an adequate basis in knowledge for life*. Stated another way, it is the problem of *dealing with reality in terms of assuredly true beliefs*. This is usually understood to be a necessary condition for human prospering, if not of survival itself.

Athens and Jerusalem stand for importantly different ways of approaching this problem. Athens refers to the capacity of unaided human thought to grasp reality. It was among the Greeks of the ancient world that awareness most vividly arose of the human mind's ability to grasp (some) reality by thinking, and Athens symbolizes that world-shaping discovery. Jerusalem, by contrast, refers to the declaration of reality and the gift of knowledge from a supreme, personal divinity who cares about what happens in human life and intervenes to give direction and assistance to the human enterprise. Thus, it too implicates a specific form of culture and a corresponding historical tradition.

The overall tradition of the Western world within which the colleges and universities of Europe and the Americas arose was one in which the human capacities for thought and study were accepted as good and necessary things, though limited in what they could provide in the way of knowledge about reality and about human well-being and well-doing. They were, by and large, to be encouraged and cultivated, but only in proper subordination to the contents of the tradition of revealed truths—God-told truths—that make up what used to be called "the Judeo-Christian tradition." To see how that worked at its strongest, one need only consult the works of Thomas Aquinas or—in a rather different but no less forceful form—those of René Descartes. The weight of this

9

arrangement was institutionalized in law and culture and continued to exercise an overwhelming influence on society at large until the two world wars—long after the arrangement had lost its intellectual footing among many regarded as advanced thinkers by the intellectual elite.

No longer, of course. The social and institutional rejection of the arrangement reached flood tide around the middle of the twentieth century and continues today, primarily in the legal system and in the popular arts and media. Higher education is now committed to this rejection from the ground up. There is no area of specialization within the university that assumes any understanding of theology (as knowledge of God) as a prerequisite for the highest level of competence in the field. You would not want to assume that things stood otherwise in a divinity school. I am not saying that this is correct in any intellectually responsible sense. Just that it is so. Max Picard's book *The Flight from God*[1] is an indispensable source for understanding that "flight" as a social fact.

Professor Poe's book is, first of all, a striking portrayal of the disarray into which the enterprise of higher education has fallen since it lost its background assumptions in the Judeo-Christian worldview. One of his sentences captures most of the facts: "While the academy lacks a unifying theory of knowledge, it also lacks a basis for character." That is how it is. Knowledge and truth are talked about for public-relations purposes and sometimes in the context of official accreditation, but research, not knowledge, rules. We have research universities, but no knowledge universities, and there are very few professors who would talk about truth in their professional associations. Truth is actually something of a joke in those contexts.

And, of course, there is no cognitive basis for character formation that can actually be recognized as such; for morality, as it is now officially understood within the academy, simply is not a matter of knowledge ("research"). It has been defined out of knowledge. How this came about is solidly and strikingly demonstrated in Julie A. Reuben's recent, masterful work: *The Making of the Modern University: Intellectual Transformation and the Marginalization of Morality.*[2]

Of course, character continues to be formed in the young by faculty and the university environment and on the basis of assumptions about life and reality that no one defends because they constitute the secular orthodoxy that is now the authoritative worldview of the university as a social institution. It cannot be otherwise. Character *is* formed by the process of life and whatever governing assumptions prevail at the time.

Professor Poe's is an honest book. That is not easy. The university in general is not an honest place. But the book is also profoundly informed by his own experience through the years, from a student to a highly regarded and widely connected writer and leader. His description, in chapter 1, of his own experiences with his teachers in connection with religion and religious issues is a window on the prevailing process then and, even more so, now. That process is crazy and crazy making. It is little wonder that multitudes of students simply give up on education except as a formality for making it into a professional school or a career. They settle for "success"—which is, mainly, what higher education promises.

Perhaps most important for the future, *Christianity in the Academy* challenges Christians in higher education to be responsible to bring together in their own intellectual and academic work the cognitive and conational substance of their beliefs about God and humans and about their fields of concentration—including, of course, higher education itself.

We are, I believe, nearing the point where it must become painfully obvious to those in higher education that there simply is no longer a cognitive framework for education, higher or lower. It is one thing to reject the spiritual interpretation of life that characterized schools and universities through the centuries. It is quite another to replace that interpretation with another that is sufficient to the task, much less superior. As is made clear in this book, this has not been done and is not being done. One must give Nietzsche his due. He did recognize the problem. His suggestions of a solution are simply ludicrous. (Just try putting them into practice.) And, as recent decades have made clear, "Burn, baby, burn" is dramatic street noise, but you still have to have a place to live when it's all over. And that is the problem now facing the academy. What does it, will it, live by? Diversity, or pluralism, alone will not suffice. It derives from Christian ethical teachings, anyway, and has never been successfully rooted as a social force elsewhere. There is a place for diversity, of course, but with no *uni-*, diversity has no foundation and even now is losing the force it gained from a passing political negativity.

There is, then, a desperate need for the collaboration of biblical faith and higher education. But leaving that aside for the moment, the more pressing need is for coherence and mutual supplementation among *all* of the areas of life dealt with in the academic fields—and beyond. There is little point in discussing the integration of "faith and learning" when we can't even begin to deal with the integration of sociology and chemistry, or of economics and physics, or of business administration and ethics, or of sports and mental health, or of psychology and physiology.

In all of these vital respects and more, Professor Poe's book does much to point us in the right directions. There is serious intellectual work to be done, and no one is in a better position to grasp the nettle

than a Christian who has learned to trust truth because he or she knows
the God of truth, in relation to which every field actually does come
together. They have a place to stand to confront those from any quarter
who falsely contrast Athens and Jerusalem and who, in the name of "ac-
ceptability"—professional or otherwise—seek to shut down the avenues
of free and hopeful intellectual and creative activity.

Dallas Willard
Department of Philosophy
University of Southern California

Preface

Religion exist

This book has been a long time in the making but a short time in the writing. It is the result of many years of trying to understand how the gospel speaks to the issues in every sphere of life. I have learned from many people, too many to remember. Some intended to teach me something, while others had no idea they were teaching me anything at all. At first, my study focused on life outside the academy. On the surface it would seem that theology is the one discipline that can, without difficulty, be associated with faith. Sadly, too many theologians have never made the connection between faith and the study of religion.

Semantics is always a problem among professors. We create new names for things, like the ancients who believed that if they knew the name of something they had power over it. Different groups of Christian teachers debate the proper label for the subject of this book. Some agree on the integration of faith and learning. Others speak of scholarship from a faith perspective. One contingent likes the idea of the collaboration of faith and learning. Still others refer to the correlation of faith and learning. This book will please few who take a party line on this issue, because I do not mind speaking loosely about it. Whatever its name, this book concerns itself with what faith has to do with higher education.

This issue has its advocates in most Christian traditions, from Cardinal Newman as the Catholic patron to Abraham Kuyper as the Reformed patron. These nineteenth-century giants recognized a growing problem that would come to full measure by the second half of the twentieth century. The problem is the strange silence of Christians who teach in higher education. While any number of philosophical and ideological interpretations of reality abound in the academy, Christians seem somehow intimidated and reluctant to contribute a Christian perspective to the discussion.

In the last fifteen years, a number of books have been written that address the problem. Its historical roots have been analyzed. Its philosophical nature has been identified. The need for Christian scholarship has been advocated. The legitimacy of Christian scholarship has been defended. The lack of Christian scholarship has been berated. What seemed to be missing was a book that helped people go about "thinking Christianly" in relation to their discipline. It does no good to tell people they ought to do something if they do not know what you mean.

This book attempts to illustrate the kinds of issues that are about faith, issues that different academic disciplines regularly treat. A major part of the task is learning to recognize a faith issue. This book does not advocate the "add Jesus and stir" approach. (C. S. Lewis disapproved of such an approach, which typically imports theological issues or ideas that are not already present.) This book hopes to expose those most critical issues of faith that form the very substance of the academic disciplines. It also challenges readers to distinguish philosophical and other biases that may have been imported into their disciplines but are not intrinsic to those disciplines.

Some prefer to leave faith issues to the theologians and philosophers. Some of my best friends are theologians and philosophers, in fact, but I prefer not to entrust the future of the world to them. What those who defer to theologians and philosophers do not seem to realize is that rival ideas about the nature of reality go unchallenged because Christians in every discipline trust that their students will take a Bible course that will straighten them out. That will not happen. It is not necessary to become a credentialed theologian or philosopher, but it is necessary to be informed enough to defend one's own discipline. With that thought in mind, the discussion presented in this book has been kept simple. Suggestions for further reading are given at the end of each chapter, and these suggestions comprise books written in an accessible style (i.e., they are not for experts).

Because this book is written in a simple style, critics may charge that its treatment of individual disciplines is facile. The critics may be correct, but there is a reason I have described the disciplines and their work in their simplest form. Many of the disciplines are in a state of flux, and conflict exists over their nature. In these times Christians have their greatest opportunity to contribute to the conversation. A consensus will eventually emerge, but at that point it will be too late. While matters are fluid, however, no single point of view has privileged status.

I am indebted to a number of professors from different schools who helped me think through the disciplines, their subject matter and methodologies, and the values and philosophical foundations of each. Much of this research took place under the auspices of the Center for Faculty Development at Union University. I appreciate the invitation of Kina Mallard, the center's director, and Nan Thomas, who conducts the center's Collegium program, to help lead faculty discussions about the role of faith in their work. I have also benefited greatly from collaboration with Terry Morrison, director of InterVarsity's faculty ministry. In addition to the ongoing Union University faculty-development programs, the Center for Faculty Development hosted a new faculty workshop for the Council for Christian Colleges and Universities. At that workshop we were joined by Harold Heie, director of the Center for Christian Studies at Gordon College, and Don King, professor of English at Montreat College and editor of the *Christian Scholars Review.* These two men have been invaluable guides and partners in conversation. I am also indebted to Lee Royce, former president of Anderson College in South Carolina, who invited me to lead a weekend retreat for his faculty and in doing so gave me the first opportunity to present this material.

Among those faculty members who helped me understand their disciplines are Glen Marsh, David Ward, Jim Patterson, David Thomas, Mary Platt, Grace Aaron, John McIlwain, Gavin Richardson, Rose Mary Foncree, Randy Smith, Ervin Martin, Susan Jaspersen, Steve Strombeck, James Huggins, Wayne Wofford, Carol Weaver, Susan Jacob, Carla Sanderson, Toni Chiarelli, Steve Brinton, Earl Reed, Scott White, Betsye Robinette, Melinda Clarke, Randy Hollingsworth, Ralph Leverett, Ann Singleton, Camille Searcy, Michele Atkins, Ken Newman, Carrie Whaley, Sandra Hathcox, Aaron Lee Benson, Christopher Nadaskay, Michael Mallard, Jill Webb, Stephen Carls, and Marlyn Newhouse.

Since 1998 I have had the opportunity to work with the C. S. Lewis Foundation on several projects designed to encourage a renaissance of Christian scholarship and creativity among faculty members in the United States. As program director for the C. S. Lewis Summer Institute in Oxford and Cambridge, I enjoyed the fruits of my labors as we heard several dozen internationally recognized Christian scholars discuss their disciplines at the intersection of faith. None of these experiences, however, has been more valuable than the personal conversations and exploration of ideas with Stan Mattson, the president, and fellow board members Dallas Willard, Todd Pickett, Karen Mulder, Grady Spires, Gayne Anacker, and Nigel Goodwin.

Several years ago I began what has become a major project to explore science and faith with my colleague Jimmy Davis, professor of chemistry and associate provost at Union University. Along the way we have developed a course, written two books together, and established the Baconian Society to encourage the dialogue between science and faith. I am deeply indebted to Dr. Davis for his many hours of conversation, which have helped me gain an understanding of the intersection of science and faith. We also have had the opportunity to attend several conferences sponsored by the John Templeton Foundation, which have further contributed to my understanding of thinking critically about the philosophical influences on a discipline. While in Oxford we benefited greatly from the insight of Arthur Peacocke.

I have the advantage of a wife who also works in the academy. Mary Anne Poe serves as professor of social work and director of the social work program at Union University. She also has a graduate theological degree. The impact she has had on my own thought and understanding is immense. Her contribution to my thought has far exceeded my contribution to hers.

After serving in academic administration for ten years at three different schools, I stepped down (or up?) from a vice presidency at Union University to return to the classroom as professor of faith and culture. I am indebted to David S. Dockery for establishing this new position that allows me to teach across a variety of disciplines. I am further indebted to Charles Colson and the board of Prison Fellowship for funding my position as the Charles Colson Professor of Faith and Culture. This book is the first by-product of their confidence in me, and I hope it will prove helpful to others.

I wish to express my thanks to Marjorie Richard for her help in typing parts of this manuscript, and to Juanita Cotner, who produced several of the graphics for the book. Last, I wish to thank Bob Hosack, my acquisitions editor at Baker Academic, who recognized the value of this project and has helped to bring it to fulfillment, and to Wells Turner, my copyeditor, who did such a beautiful and professional job of turning the manuscript into a book.

Harry Lee Poe
Jackson, Tennessee

1

A Personal Introduction
Religion in Higher Education

Does religion have any place in the academy? Does it belong in colleges and universities that devote themselves to the deliberation of great ideas? When Paul visited Athens, the center of learning in the ancient world and the location of the original academy, he found that religion mattered to people. He encountered not only the Jews who studied the books of the Law and the Prophets but also members of the various schools of philosophy, including the Epicureans and the Stoics. Here were people interested in the latest ideas. Two thousand years later the academy continues its fascination with the latest ideas, the fads of thought that come and go. The old way of thinking is quickly forgotten when the next fad comes along. Fads affect not only what teenagers wear but also what scholars in the academic disciplines think about as well as how they think.

Paul did not bring religion or philosophy to Athens. They were already there as topics of concern. The Athenians, both the pagan worshipers and the philosophers, had a concern for the great issues of religion. I believe this aspect of the academy or urban life has not changed in two thousand years. The academy deals with religion.

While attending a secular university for my undergraduate education, I encountered a great deal of conversation about religion among faculty and students. My first English class was an honors course in which we pursued the question What does it mean to be an intellectual? Over the course of the semester, we read the first two volumes of Bertrand Russell's unfinished autobiography. Russell was a great hero of my English professor, who referred to Russell as "the grand old atheist." Russell, one of the leading mathematicians and philosophers of the twentieth century, had shown his courage by taking a stand and arguing that God does not exist. Russell stood in contrast to those who cling to the idea of God as an emotional crutch because they lack the courage to enter life, take it as it is, and then be done with it when it ends.

Another English professor, who was one of the great idols on campus, taught a course on the Victorian revolutionaries. He examined Freud, Darwin, William Morris, and the pre-Raphaelite artists and other great figures who forever changed the cultural landscape. He also taught a popular course on film. The class, an upper-level elective, met in one of the largest lecture halls at the university. One afternoon a friend drove the professor and a crowd of us to lunch in his 1948 Rolls-Royce. I recall the professor's immense pleasure and his chortling remark as we rolled merrily along: "It's amazing how shallow our convictions are." Over lunch that day, I also remember another comment he made. It was the kind of statement that punctuates campus conversation, usually lost somewhere in the mind, and yet helps to form the fabric of how we think. The remark, made casually to a group of students who drank in every word, would continue to affect the thinking of these people long after they left behind their sophomoric infatuations with a witty, young professor. While buttering a biscuit, he said, "The resurrection is the most pagan idea I have ever heard." The students, of course, nodded in agreement.

In sociology I had an Englishman for a professor. His authority came in great measure from his accent, in small measure from his peculiar goatee. He was a grand old atheist and spent the semester debunking Christian ideas. He particularly enjoyed debunking the idea of love. He argued that love amounts to little more than a contract or reciprocal agreement: you scratch my back and I'll scratch yours. At the time, this critique of love was a shocking idea to me. His logic seemed impeccable, and I found it devastating until I realized he was absolutely right in terms of how most people think about love. This common understanding of love, however, contrasts sharply with what Christ taught about love. Love is what you do in spite of what it costs you, not because of what it will gain for you.

During my first year in college, my political science professor scoffed at the idea of religion. It was a waste of time. It detracts from the more important issues of the day. He agreed with Marx that religion is the opiate of the masses and used by power structures to keep the mob in line. He had an urbane worldly wisdom that came out in various ways, a wisdom we would all understand when we were older.

In my freshman year, my Western civilization professor was a former Catholic priest who in leaving his order also left God behind. He spent that semester ridiculing all the religious ideas and personalities we came across. A study of Western civilization necessarily involves an examination of religion as practiced among the peoples of Europe. He did not import the discussion of religion into the course, but he certainly had a perspective from which he interpreted religion to the students. His perspective had nothing to do with scholarship and everything to do with his own emotions as well as earlier experiences and personal struggles.

While attending a prestigious private research university, my wife took an ethics course taught by a Hindu. He developed the ethics course around the Bhagavad Gita, which he believed expressed the highest ethic known to humanity. Over the course of the semester he elaborated on the superiority of the Bhagavad Gita's teachings, as compared with the inferiority of Jesus' teachings. This was not a religion course nor even a comparative religion course. It was not a course on Hinduism. Students signed up for the course to fulfill a part of the core curriculum. They knew only that they had enrolled in an ethics course.

A friend from my hometown went to a small women's college that was owned and operated by a Christian denomination but no longer identified itself as a Christian school. Although the college's many artifacts harkened back to its pietistic roots, its current mission and hiring policy had no connection with its past. Because of its past, however, many parents and students, as well as the public at large, continued to think of it as a Christian school. For many, a Christian school is a safe place to go. Its safety may have to do with protection from the temptations of alcohol, drugs, and sex, or it may have to do with protection from strange ideas. For some, the safety of a Christian school has to do with being able to rely on the curriculum being true.

Few Christian colleges are actually safe in any of these regards. I happened to be staying in a hotel near this Christian college during the weekend of its spring festival. A student and her boyfriend had the room next to mine and kept me awake all night. As for strange ideas and reliability, my friend had an English professor who taught that God is actually "the spirit of the age." In other words, *God* is merely a label for the prevailing mind-set. According to this professor, in literature of the romantic period, *God* simply expresses the way people thought about themselves in relation to nature. During the baroque period, people thought about themselves differently, also expressed as *God*. This explanation made perfect sense to my friend, an extremely intelligent woman who had never heard religion discussed intellectually before. Though raised in a Baptist church and involved in Sunday school, choir, and mission groups, she had no intellectual foundation for critically considering the questions of religion.

Religion is a matter of great interest to students and faculty across the United States. Religion, which addresses the great themes of life that bleed across the disciplines, is already established in the American academy and does not need to be imported. The great critical questions of life are religious issues. They provide the glue that holds together disciplines, now fragmented by specialization.

Years ago, when I was a student, I learned a valuable lesson about the presence of religion in the academy. I chaired the University Union's Films Committee, which had become the most extensive film program on any U.S. college campus. (This was in the days before VCRs, when films rented from companies in Atlanta and Los Angeles were shipped in and out every day.) The committee hosted a series that featured films all day long, every day, all semester. We screened classic films, foreign films, experimental films, and first-run blockbusters. A group of Marxists on campus asked the committee to show a series of Marxist films. (This all happened during the Vietnam War, the fall after some campus riots.) As the committee chair, I told them that we did not want to show political films in our series. The group's leader told me, bluntly, "All films are political films." At the time, his statement startled me, but I have since realized that he was quite right. By extension, I also now realize that all films are religious films. They may not teach doctrine or explain the Bible or the Bhagavad Gita, but they deal with the stuff about which religion is concerned. All films have a perspective that reflects a religious attitude. This attitude may be positive or negative, but religion is already there.

Likewise, all subjects are religious subjects. The ancients understood this unity of life. Indeed, they deified every aspect of life. They understood that no break or disjunction exists between the secular and the sacred. Paul observed this deification when he first arrived in Athens. He saw idols and temples that provided the means for recognizing the sacredness of every aspect of life, including buying and selling, drinking, making war and peace, establishing laws, and marriage. A deity oversaw each of these activities, and many more. At the very least, the Athenians recognized that religion is an aspect of what people are and what they do.

The postmodern world, whatever it shall be two or three hundred years from now, has reacted against the fragmentation of modernity. This fragmentation can easily be seen in the academy as disciplines split off and become increasingly rarified amid specialization. People experience this fragmentation in everyday life, feeling pulled apart by the demands and compartmentalization of the many different aspects of life. In this context the postmodern person craves wholeness. The idea of having things pulled back together is what Jesus referred to as *peace*. In the face of pressure and conflict, Jesus assured his disciples, "Peace I leave with you; my peace I give you. I do not give to you as the world gives. Do not let your hearts be troubled and do not be afraid" (John 14:27 NIV). Peace involves having all the pieces in place, everything related to each other.

The postmodern world has also recognized and acknowledged spiritual reality. The modern world was always antagonistic toward the idea of the spiritual and drawn more toward the material. It had a preference for the here and now. It paid attention to what could be heard, seen, smelled, touched, and tasted. Spirituality was tolerated so long as it could be isolated from the rest of life. In the inverse of the Christian college situation, where some seek safety from secular ideas, modernists wanted safety from consideration of the spiritual. Postmodernists, on the other hand, have a profound craving for the spiritual, and they pursue it in many ways. Through the spiritual, they apparently seek the solution to the problem of fragmentation. Modernists, by contrast, seek the solution to fragmentation through a better time-management system!

The postmodern world accepts the reality of the differences between people through what we call *pluralism*. Everybody seems to be different. This situation contrasts with the modern world, which was homogeneous. People were the same, which made it easier to choose sides between us and them. When I was a freshman, I had a math professor from China who was Buddhist. In my sophomore year, I had a Pakistani statistics professor who was Muslim. This pluralism of cultural and religious perspectives has multiplied manyfold since I was in college.

We do not have to bring religion to the contemporary academy any more than Paul had to bring religion to Athens. The issues of religion, the topics of conversation that are religious in nature, are already there. People already talk about them.

Philosophy

Alongside religion, philosophical ideas permeate the academy, although we are not always aware of their presence or impact. Religion and philosophy interact with and influence each other, although often unintentionally and unconsciously. Whether we are aware of it or not, philosophy runs through every discipline of the academy. Indeed, prevailing philosophies may so dominate disciplines that we identify the values of the philosophical position with the discipline. Ironically, the philosophy may be hidden under so many layers of "what everybody knows" that we do not even recognize its presence.

When Paul went to Athens, he found philosophy as pervasive as religion, and he engaged both equally. The philosophy of Athens had actually altered the religion of Athens. When Paul stood up to address Stoics and Epicureans in the Areopagus, he did not discuss the atonement or justification (Acts 17:16–34). He dealt with the philosophical and religious issues that the Athenians themselves grappled with. He addressed critical questions already present in the context. In stark contrast with the other sermons of the Book of Acts that explore the presuppositions of the Jews, Paul dealt with questions the Athenians wondered about: What kind of God exists? What kind of universe exists? What is the nature of humanity?

We tend to ignore the philosophy, or the worldview, out of which we operate, largely because we have grown so accustomed to it. Yet, worldview is a topic of conversation in which any Christian can freely and appropriately participate. The conversation is already going on; we do not have to introduce the conversation to the academy. If Paul had preached at Athens on the prophecies, as Peter had done on the day of Pentecost (Acts 2), or on the Law, as he had done at the synagogue in Antioch of Pisidia (Acts 13:16–41), he would have been introducing a new conversation. Instead, he addressed questions already in progress from his faith perspective.

Unfortunately, we all have our own set of philosophical assumptions and presuppositions that we may not have explored. These form the lens through which we understand our own faith. Though we may not have formally adopted a philosophy, the casual phrases we use in conversation and our methodology for going about life itself betray the philosophy we have uncritically bought into. "You can't argue with success" is the philosophy of pragmatism. "Seeing is believing" and "the proof of the pudding is in the eating" represent the philosophy of knowledge known as *empiricism.* "Beauty is in the eye of the beholder" represents relativism. "It all boils down to . . ." represents the approach of reductionism. To one degree or another, in different areas of our fragmented lives, we have bought into one or more particular philosophies that have been prevalent in the West during the modern period, but we have not necessarily done so critically. It has just happened.

In the marketplace of ideas, the fundamental assumptions (philosophies) to which people cling are the very things that Christ challenges. Every discipline of the academy makes enormous assumptions and goes about its business with untested and unchallenged presuppositions. We are used to this. Assumptions and presuppositions have become so much a part of the fabric of life that we do not notice the threads. These threads make up the worldview of the culture in which we live. They are the things "everybody knows" and that, therefore, go untested. They are so deeply ingrained in us that we are rarely even aware of them.

Consider how Christ challenged the teachers of his day. Remember that Jesus was not merely a faith healer and a miracle worker. As strange as it may seem to say, even from a faith perspective, he was not even merely the Son of God. Jesus was a member of the Jewish academy of his day. He was a rabbi, a teacher, a master, a doctor, a professor. The Jewish academy was not like the Greek academy, but it was an approach to higher education that went back to the Babylonian captivity, some five hundred years before Christ. As a rabbi, Jesus challenged the principles of interpreting the Law that prevailed in his guild (academic discipline). Notice that he did not merely disagree about interpretations. The rabbinic system relied upon disputation over the interpretation of the Law. Jesus disputed the underlying presuppositions governing what possible interpretations might be reached.

Jesus' challenge can be seen in how he approached the Law in the Sermon on the Mount (Matt. 5–8). Challenging the assumption that the law against murder was about only murder, Jesus argued, "If you are angry with a brother or sister, you will be liable to judgment" (Matt. 5:22 NRSV). He then proceeded to discuss how relationships with other people are damaged. Murder may be the ultimate end of a problem, but Jesus wanted to focus on the origin of the problem. Jesus also challenged the assumption behind the law against adultery, which everyone assumed was about adultery, when he said, "Anyone who looks at a woman lustfully has already committed adultery with her in his heart" (Matt. 5:28 NIV). Then he began to explore how actions result from something going on inside. Rather than dispute whether a particular act had violated the Law, Jesus approached the Law from the perspective of what it might teach us about ourselves.

Jesus also challenged the underlying presuppositions of the practice of piety when he said, "Beware of practicing your piety before others in order to be seen by them . . ." (Matt. 6:1 NRSV). In particular, he pointed out the problem of public prayer in Jewish culture at that time. Prayer was seen as good in and of itself, yet Jesus cautioned that prayer that draws attention to ourselves may actually cause spiritual damage. He suggested that the solemn ritual of prayer, as it had been practiced for more than a thousand years, could be bad! He further pointed out the problem of benevolence, claiming it is possible to give to the poor in such a way that it does spiritual damage. For example, we may receive a plaque from the Rotary club and yet jeopardize our good standing with God. Almsgiving was also not a good thing in and of itself. According to Jesus, it is possible to do a good deed yet receive no credit from God for it!

Jesus critiqued some of the basic understandings of good, evil, and the activity of God. He challenged the assumptions that underlay the prevailing interpretation of suffering within his culture. On one occasion the disciples asked Jesus, "Rabbi, who sinned, this man or his parents, that he was born blind?" (John 9:2 NIV). The people of his day believed that suffering proved the displeasure of God while wealth and health proved God's pleasure. Everybody knew it. This fundamental presupposition was a lens through which the people of that culture interpreted life. On another occasion Pilate killed some Galileans and had their blood mixed with their sacrifice. Jesus asked his disciples, "Do you think that these Galileans were worse sinners than all the other Galileans because they suffered this way?" (Luke 13:2 NIV). At the beginning of the Sermon on the Mount, Jesus turned these presuppositions on their head when he declared, "Blessed are the poor in spirit. . . . Blessed are those who mourn. . . . Blessed are the meek. . . . Blessed are those who are persecuted. . . ." (Matt. 5:3–5, 10 NIV). Jesus continually challenged the presuppositions and assumptions that served as a lens through which the people of his day interpreted Scripture.

If we intend to challenge the assumptions of those in the academic marketplace of ideas, then we must also be willing to examine our own assumptions. Just as Jesus Christ challenged the academy of his day, he continues to challenge his disciples. He is still our teacher.

A Public or Private Conversation?

For the last five hundred years in the West, the religious conversation in the marketplace of ideas has been a family feud, a conversation within the Christian community. During this time, the community has been fragmented; nonetheless, it is a family of people who acknowledge the Lord Jesus Christ.

In the nineteenth century in Tennessee, Kentucky, and Arkansas, the Baptists and the Churches of Christ fought over who was the true church. Only these two groups were involved because they both agreed that Methodists, Presbyterians, Episcopalians, and Catholics were not the true church. In the eighteenth century in England, the pedobaptists and the Anabaptists fought over the method and the mode of baptism. In the seventeenth century, the Presbyterians, the Congregationalists, and the Episcopalians fought over church government. In the sixteenth century, Lutherans, Calvinists, and Catholics fought over the Lord's Supper. Christians have always been able to find something to fight over.

In the twenty-first century a different conversation goes on within the academy, because it is no longer a homogeneous academy. Though it was created in the West as an institution to serve the church, the academy no longer has any tie to the Christian faith. Religious themes are not brought to the academy; religious themes are already being discussed within the academy, although not as they were discussed when the academy was a subdivision of the church. In fact, if we are not careful, the current discussion will not be perceived as religious. We have so accustomed ourselves to the way the discussion is supposed to go, the kind of vocabulary that should be used, the institutional and ritualistic accompaniments that must be acknowledged, and the tone of voice to be employed that we may not recognize the discussion as essentially religious in nature.

My university recently hosted a regional conference for new faculty at schools committed to teaching from a faith perspective. During the conference we explored many of the themes this book addresses. On Sunday we held a worship service, and our philosophy professor, an accomplished musician, played during the singing. He had chosen "Rock of Ages," but he played the tune differently than most people were accustomed to. The words were familiar, yet the participants had great difficulty singing. It did not sound right, we did not recognize it, it was not familiar, and we did not know how to take part. Perhaps we are so lost in our assumptions (what is familiar and thus sounds right) that we do not recognize religious themes being discussed in the academy.

Joining the Conversation

Paul challenged the religious ideas of pagan religion in Athens, but he also challenged the philosophical assumptions of the Stoics, who believed everything was "god," and the Epicureans, who believed in many gods and many universes but no creator. I have heard pastors and theologians argue that Paul was wrong to converse with the philosophers on their own turf. Furthermore, he was wrong to take the approach he did, as opposed to the traditional expository sermon. They point to Paul's failure on his mission in Athens as a sign that God was not pleased with what Paul did. Notice the method of argument. They bring to Scripture the philosophical position of pragmatism as the criterion for interpreting the text. That philosophical approach becomes the ultimate test, rather than faithfulness. Even in appealing to pragmatism, note the standard for evaluating success. Pentecost saw three thousand converts, therefore it was a success. Athens saw only a few converts, therefore it was a failure. By extension and with the same approach, we may conclude that since the disciples of Jesus betrayed and deserted him, resulting in his death, Jesus was a failure.

In applying the test of pragmatism and the American cultural love affair with large numbers as the final test, this particular subgroup of Christians manages to distort spiritual reality. They interpret success in terms of huge numbers and fail to recognize that the small group of people who did respond to the gospel in Athens constituted a major victory.

Like Paul, Christians today are called to go into the marketplace. For teachers, that means going into the marketplace of ideas. We are called to listen for religious themes that are being discussed. These themes may not be our issues, just as what kind of God exists was not an issue for Paul (his people had settled that issue centuries earlier), yet it was a key issue for the Athenians. Paul seemed to operate from the conviction that the Holy Spirit was already active in Athens ahead of him, busily convincing people of sin, righteousness, and judgment as Jesus had said. Nevertheless, the Holy Spirit dealt with the Athenians on the basis of who they were, rather than on the basis of who Paul was.

We may believe that the Holy Spirit is at work. Yet we do not notice it because the issues of religion do not sound like what we have heard before. The issues percolate up in the study and discussion of the disciplines, becoming the occasion more for conversation than for lecture. The standard model for religious conversation resembles a lecture (sermon). Everyone sits quietly and listens. There is no time for questions or disagreement because it is a holy time of worship, not to be profaned by conversation. If that is what is meant by Christianity coming into the marketplace, then the marketplace probably has no room for Christianity. On the other hand, if we can participate, as everyone else does, thinking and talking about the great themes of life, then we have a place in the marketplace. If we follow Paul's lead and engage the academy, we may not have instant success, but another voice will be heard—a voice that offers another way to make sense of the great issues of life.

At this point I should indicate one of my own presuppositions. I believe that Jesus Christ can hold his own if we can manage to strip enough of ourselves out of the way so that he can be seen. Scripture gives no instructions on how to stitch a shoe or raise a crop, though it talks about shoes and farming. It gives no directions on cooking or sewing, though it talks about cooking and sewing. It gives no instructions on building construction or musical composition, though it speaks of both of these activities. Indeed, the Bible speaks of biology, astronomy, and other branches of science, but one should not confuse the discussion with an instruction about the disciplines. Rather, the discussion indicates a point of intersection between faith and life. Faith cuts across all disciplines, even though all disciplines do not cut across one another.

Paul was not the only early Christian who considered the relationship between faith and learning in Athens. Tertullian, who was born about one hundred years after Paul visited Athens, did not think it was appropriate to mix Christian faith with the academy, lest the faith be contaminated. In his famous challenge to the philosophical center of the ancient world, Tertullian demanded, "So, then, where is there any likeness between the Christian and the philosopher? between the disciple of Greece and of heaven? between the man whose object is fame, and whose object is life?"[1] Elsewhere he asked, "What indeed has Athens to do with Jerusalem? What concord is there between the Academy and the Church? what between heretics and Christians?"[2] The attitude of Tertullian has survived well into the twenty-first century.

The Christian faith was never banished from higher education by vote of the faculty. Instead, it quietly stole away or went into dormancy; Christians still teach in colleges and universities in great numbers. Stan Mattson, president of the C. S. Lewis Foundation, has estimated that as many as fifty thousand Christians hold such teaching posts in the United States. Christians who teach in the academy do not have the same attitude toward learning that Tertullian had, but they may share the same reluctance to mix two different areas of life. To be a whole person, however, a Christian must have some kind of internal conversation. If only for peace of mind, it is important to engage the relationship between what one believes and what one teaches.

Part of the reluctance to deal with the issues may come from the inflammatory language some Christians use when describing the engagement of diverse views in American culture. The term *culture wars* does not tend to invite participation by Christians who hold faculty positions. Of course, as inflammatory a character as Paul could be when dealing with problems inside the church, he did not go to the Areopagus announcing a war. Instead, he invited conversation and agreed to discuss his ideas. This is the way of the academy.

In many cases, conversation can lead to clarity, even when it does not result in changing another person's beliefs. An example from the sciences will illustrate how latent philosophical ideas can distort and confuse a professional scholar's understanding of material fundamental to his or her own discipline. One of the most emotionally charged intellectual issues at the intersection of faith and scholarship is evolution. Unfortunately, many Christians who do engage the secular academy over this issue do so in an unconstructive way. They do not always recognize the distinction between the Bible and their interpretation of the Bible. The Bible must be interpreted just as the scientific data must be interpreted. An example of positive engagement, however, comes from the 1999 annual report of the American Scientific Affiliation, a national organization of scientists and theologians interested in the positive engagement of science and religion.

> For several years, ASA members have been attempting to remove philosophy masquerading as science from the biology curriculum. Perhaps the most glaring example of the abuse of science was NABT's [National Association of Biology Teachers] official 1995 statement on teaching evolution (*The American Biology Teacher*, Jan. 1996, pp. 61–62). Ideal material for a critical thinking skills essay, one section stated,
>
>> Evolutionary theory, indeed all of science, is necessarily silent on religion and neither refutes nor supports the existence of a deity or deities. Accordingly, the National Association of Biology Teachers, an organization of science teachers, endorses the following tenets of science, evolution and biology education: The diversity of life on earth is the outcome of evolution: an unsupervised, impersonal, unpredictable and natural process of temporal descent with genetic modification that is affected by natural selection, chance, historical contingencies and changing environments.
>
> Shortly after NABT's resolution appeared, Loren Haarsma and a dozen other ASA members submitted a scholarly critique to NABT. Their critique was ignored. On behalf of the Science Education Commission, letters exposing NABT's naturalistic philosophy masquerading as science were written and subsequently published in *Christianity Today* (Feb. 3, 1997), *Commentary* (Sept. 1996), and *First Things* (June–July, 1997). Following Philip E. Johnson's publication of the NABT's lack of understanding of the difference between philosophy and science in *Defeating Darwinism by Opening Minds,* his friends, Huston Smith and Alvin Plantinga, made a formal public protest to the NABT, on the basis that their statement went beyond the boundaries of empirical science.
>
> At their October 1997 meeting, the board of the NABT initially unanimously rejected Smith and Plantinga's critique. Three days later, upon the urging of Eugenie Scott, executive director of NCSE, the board unanimously reversed its position and deleted the words "unsupervised" and "impersonal" from its statement, citing public misunderstanding of its intent as the reason for the change.[3]

Notice the problem with definition. The Christian scholars objected, not to the idea of evolution, but to a definition that went beyond what science can assert. At the beginning of the statement, the NABT affirmed that science could not comment on God, but its definition did comment on God and introduced the concepts of supervision and personality. Once the NABT had done this, it had left science and proceeded to a philosophical view of God. Evolutionary research can describe changes in life forms and their context, but it cannot speak to such matters as cause, purpose, and goal. As soon as it mixes naturalism with science, it has entered the world of philosophy. It would not be an exaggeration to say that the majority of the academy's members today do not realize this distinction. Such a situation does not exist only with respect to evolution, however. Similar situations can be found in virtually every discipline of the university.

This book will suggest a way to go about thinking of one's discipline from a faith perspective. It by no means purports to be the only way, or even the best way. Rather, it seeks to stir the imagination enough that its own flaws become evident and the interested reader will move in entirely new directions. This book suggests several ways to begin thinking about how faith informs teaching:

1. Recognize the issues. We will explore the religious dimensions of life's everyday issues. I will suggest ways that the gospel engages these issues.
2. Examine higher education. We cannot assume the academy will continue in the form in which it has existed for centuries, for there are now tremendous pressures to change. Identifying these forces will help define the context in which teaching will take place in the future.
3. Recognize the opportunities created by postmodernity. Many cherished values and presuppositions have disappeared with the rise of postmodernity, but this "cleaning of the slate" has also brought fresh opportunities for the consideration of faith.
4. Critique the disciplines. It is important that one explores the scope, values, methodologies, and underlying philosophies behind the disciplines of the academy to identify where religious conversation is taking place. Likewise, one must explore the degree to which disciplines build upon, and contribute to, one another, resulting in the transference of unchallenged philosophical presuppositions from one discipline to the next.
5. Take off the theological lenses. Because we tend to confuse our culture, philosophy, and theology with Jesus Christ, we represent the greatest barrier to our participation in the religious conversation of the academy. Learning to distinguish our theology from our faith will help us learn to engage the actual questions.
6. Ask the critical questions. Critical questions arise within the different disciplines. Each discipline has its unique perspective, and for that reason no single discipline can adequately answer the questions of life.

Teaching from a faith perspective does not mean introducing something that is not already present in the discipline. Instead, one must build on the skills that academic types already possess. Good scholarship involves discovering and then interpreting what is already present.

Questions to Ponder

1. What does your discipline have to do with religious issues?
2. Did you ever study under a professor who discussed a religious issue? If so, how was it handled? Were you conscious about appropriate and inappropriate religious remarks? Appropriate or inappropriate remarks on subjects other than religion?
3. How would you be regarded by other faculty members within your discipline if they knew you discussed religious issues related to your discipline?
4. Is it possible to discuss a religious issue without most participants being aware that they are discussing a religious issue?
5. Is there a difference between teaching from a faith perspective and proselytizing?

Further Reading

The project to encourage the integration of faith and learning has become a minor industry in recent years, but several people deserve special attention because of the role they have played in stimulating the discussion. Some of the following books are out of print but are well worth the search.

Blamires, Harry. *The Christian Mind: How Should a Christian Think?* Ann Arbor, Mich.: Servant, 1963.

Holmes, Arthur F. *All Truth Is God's Truth.* Grand Rapids: Eerdmans, 1977.

Marsden, George M. *The Outrageous Idea of Christian Scholarship.* New York: Oxford University Press, 1997.

Noll, Mark A. *The Scandal of the Evangelical Mind.* Grand Rapids: Eerdmans, 1995.

Wolfe, David L., and Harold Heie. *Slogans or Distinctives: Reforming Christian Higher Education.* Lanham, Md.: University Press of America, 1993.

2

The Religious Spectrum in Higher Education

A discussion of the appropriate place of religion or faith in higher education poses a number of difficulties. Such a discussion veils conflicting assumptions, presuppositions, attitudes, prejudices, convictions, and motives from the varying perspectives of almost anyone who takes part in the discussion. Behind these conflicting dimensions lie all of the fears and other emotions that often animate academic conversation without awareness or acknowledgment.

As the first chapter suggested in anecdotal fashion, religion has a presence within the fabric of American higher education, though that presence often occurs accidentally rather than intentionally. The intentional presence of religion in higher education takes many forms, perhaps depending on the nature of an institution. One no longer expects to find religion at a state university, although the grand old state universities along the east coast still have their memorials from a time when faith had a synthesized relationship to education. The oldest building on the campus of the University of South Carolina (1803) houses its lovely old chapel. Once Mr. Jefferson was safely in his grave, the University of Virginia erected a massive gothic chapel on its campus. Similar campus tours will reveal old monuments to a former time when the relationship between faith and education seemed quite compatible.

All of the grand old colleges of Oxford and Cambridge have their own chapels, many dating from the time when they were established as religious institutions prior to the Reformation. Even though these colleges have long since ceased to have any official relationship with an ecclesiastical body, they continue to have a chaplain who conducts religious services. The tradition of male choirs and sung services has made these chapel services well known around the world. The choir of King's College, Cambridge, in particular, has achieved an international reputation for the consistently high quality of its music. Christ Church College in Oxford has a unique situation with its chapel and choir. Though the college has no official dependency upon the Church of England, the chapel of the college also serves as the cathedral for the diocese of Oxford.

Still, some of the younger Oxford colleges have a religious foundation and purpose long after their older sisters have severed those connections. A two-tier system of relationship exists within the loose confederation known as Oxford University. The top tier consists of the colleges, communities of higher learning governed by the faculty without oversight by an external board of trustees. The second tier consists of permanent private halls, identical to the colleges except they have an external relationship to an ecclesiastical body. Oxford has three permanent, private Protestant halls from different traditions: Regent's Park College is associated with the Baptists, Wycliffe Hall relates to the evangelical wing of the Church of England, and Mansfield College has a relationship with the United Reformed Church. Oxford has three permanent, private Catholic halls: St. Benet's Hall established for the education of Benedictine monks, Greyfriars for the Franciscans, and Campion Hall for the Jesuits. Although students of these permanent, private halls matriculate in the university and take university degrees, and fellows of these halls serve on university committees, everyone knows that the halls remain tied to religion. One might observe that the continued link between church and state in England has resulted in the continuation of religious instruction in state schools, though this formality has had little recognizable positive relationship on attendance in the Church of England.

Mandatory chapel services have disappeared from the weekly schedules of state universities in the United States since World War II, but religion still has a formal place within all well-balanced schools as a discipline of academic inquiry. Scholars now study religion as a legitimate field of knowledge apart from faith. Indeed, the practices and belief systems of religion provide insight into the human story.

Apart from the formal structures of institutional life, however, religion still flourishes as an aspect of faith among the students of the great universities. Church-sponsored ministries and parachurch organizations carry out an active effort to engage the students of the universities in a vital and involved expression of faith outside the classroom. In many communities around a major school we find the phenomenon of the "university church," a body of believers who might represent one of many different denominations. It may be University Presbyterian Church, University Methodist Church, or University Baptist Church. Such a church draws its name from the presence of the major school and has at some time in the past, if not in the present, drawn a significant portion of its membership from faculty, staff, and students associated with the school. Perhaps the church does not wear the label of the university church, and yet it has the clear identity of the university church.

Religion also flourishes as one of many extracurricular activities that students pursue outside of class and apart from formal institutionally sponsored activities. Some religious activities even enjoy a quasi-sanctioned status at secular and state institutions. Most denominational groups sponsor some sort of formal ministry to the major universities. These church-related campus ministries often have their own facility adjacent to the campus. In some cases the religious facility actually stands on the university campus alongside classroom buildings, the library, and dorms. Catholics have their Newman Centers as part of the Newman Apostolate and the Catholic Campus Ministry Association, which involves 1,700 campus ministers nationally.[1] Methodists have their United Methodist Student Movement with 700 ministries nationally.[2] The Presbyterian Church (USA) sponsors local campus ministries through various governing bodies of the PCUSA or conducts them in cooperation with Ecumenical Partners.[3] The Presbyterian Church in America (PCA) sponsors the Reformed University Fellowship on forty-five campuses,[4] and Southern Baptists have their Baptist Student Union. How denominations provide a ministry presence on the major college and university campuses in the United States varies. Denominational campus ministers often enjoy privileges as adjunct chaplains to the university.

Parachurch ministries also flourish on campuses, officially as student-led groups with staff support from the parachurch organization. This type of religious presence on campuses includes groups like Campus Crusade for Christ, InterVarsity Christian Fellowship, and the Navigators. While each of these ministries affirms many of the same things in different degrees, each has gained a reputation for its own characteristic methodology and emphasis. InterVarsity, for example, focuses on the intellectual engagement of the academy as it aims to establish "witnessing communities of students and faculty."[5] Of these ministries, InterVarsity has the longest pedigree, dating back to a student group at Cambridge University founded in 1877. By 1928 it had established a ministry in Canada that later expanded into the United States between 1938 and 1941, when it was incorporated.[6] InterVarsity has a ministry presence at more than 560 colleges and universities in the United States and involves more than 34,000 students and faculty in its programs.[7]

The Navigators, with its emphasis on "reaching, discipling, and equipping," focuses on discipleship. The Navigators was originally established in 1933 as a ministry to sailors in the United States Navy. Since then the ministry has expanded in several areas, including campus ministry. The Navigators has a ministry presence on seventy-one campuses in the United States.[8]

Campus Crusade for Christ focuses on evangelism with its purpose "to turn lost students into Christ-centered laborers." Established at UCLA in 1951, it now has full-time staff on 140 campuses while working with churches and student leaders on another 700 campuses.[9]

In recent years a new generation of academic community ministries has developed. While Campus Crusade, InterVarsity, and the Navigators have focused their attention on college and university students, the new generation of higher education ministries focuses on the faculty. The C. S. Lewis Foundation, established in 1986, fosters a renaissance of Christian scholarship and artistic expression within higher education. The Veritas Forum began at Harvard in the early 1990s and has since expanded through conferences at universities across the country. The Wilberforce Forum began in the late 1990s as an instrument to bring a Christian influence to all major areas of culture, including the academy. In addition to these nationwide initiatives, many local and regional groups have formed, often revolving around an annual conference designed for faculty who are Christians.

Educational Institutions and Formal Ties to Religion

In recent years, a great deal has been written about how religion has lost its place in American higher education. The list of schools that originally had a religious purpose for their existence reads like a who's who of the American higher educational establishment.[10] Years ago William F. Buckley Jr. gained prominence for writing a book that charged that God no longer had a significant place at Yale.[11] While many staunch Yale defenders were outraged at the time, few today would be surprised that Yale does not regard itself as a religious institution. The appeal to tradition, however, has little standing within the academy except, perhaps, as a reason for wearing funny clothes at graduation ceremonies. Within the present context, a fairly wide spectrum of relationships and ties between educational institutions and religious bodies or religious purposes still continues.

Religiously Affiliated Institutions

In 1998 the United States was home to 3,913 institutions of higher education. Of these, 1,644 were public institutions and 2,269 were private (see fig. 2.1). Of the private institutions, 919 had some religious affiliation,[12] the nature of which varies widely. A wide spectrum within the approaches of the formally religious schools suggests that *religion* has no monolithic meaning or form among religious schools. A school may have a denominational affiliation without necessarily being regarded as religious. A school might acknowledge a historic tie with a religious body through the maintenance of a symbolic practice, such as a chapel service or a required course on the Bible. Duke University in North Carolina, a school historically identified as a Methodist institution, might be compared with Bob Jones University in South Carolina, a school founded by a Methodist evangelist and without formal ties to any religious body. Both schools are outstanding in academic rigor, although they have wildly different reputations. William Willimon has written about the declining spiritual climate at Duke, and Bob Jones, regarding Billy Graham as not conservative enough, became famous for threatening to expel any student who attended one of his crusades.[13]

The approach to religion among religiously affiliated schools offers yet a further expansion of the religious spectrum in higher education today. Different analysts have offered different ways of understanding the diversity of formal, institutional approaches to religion. David S. Dockery offers an analysis that distinguishes colleges in four ways: private, Bible, church related, and Christian liberal arts.[14]

1,644 Private (919 of which are Religiously Affiliated)
2,269 Public

3,913 Total Institutions of Higher Education

This graph illustrates the proportion of public institutions to private in the United States, with religiously affiliated institutions representing a subgroup of private institutions (based on a graph developed by David S. Dockery).

Figure 2.1. Higher Education in the United States

The Private College. Private colleges operate independently of any external body. Although founded to advance a religious purpose, they have few, if any, remaining Christian commitments. Oberlin College of Ohio stands in this tradition. Most faculty and students are unrelated to the

Christian heritage of a private college, although some board members may acknowledge its historic tradition and recognize ways in which this tradition continues in a secular fashion. The approach to education is generally as diverse and pluralistic as most public institutions.

The Bible College. Bible colleges have a narrowly defined mission and purpose: to prepare students for church-related vocations. While the establishment of accreditation standards in recent years has moved Bible colleges toward the inclusion of some liberal arts courses in the core curriculum, for the most part students study only Christian material. The Bible college functions like an undergraduate seminary or an alternative to seminary. One of the most prominent Bible colleges in the United States is the Moody Bible Institute of Chicago, with a heritage stretching back more than a hundred years. Some Bible colleges have changed their mission, over time becoming Christian liberal arts colleges. Among the more prominent of these is the Bible Institute of Los Angeles (Biola).

The Church-Related College. Church-related colleges normally acknowledge their Christian heritage openly, closely linking their identity to, and viewing themselves as partners with, the sponsoring denomination. The church-related college derives financial support, faculty, board members, and students from its denomination. It typically distinguishes religious and academic programs as two distinct and separate aspects of college life. The religious program includes chapel and campus ministry; the academic program is the curriculum. The church-related college typically provides a caring, nurturing educational context that gives priority to relationships and community. An example of a church-related college is the University of the South (Sewanee), which is of the Episcopal tradition and has a strong national academic reputation.

The Christian Liberal Arts College. Christian liberal arts colleges have strong cultural ties with the sponsoring denominations or constituencies. Furthermore, the faculty and the students are conscious of these ties. The board of such a college also has strong ties to the denomination/constituency and in many cases is elected directly by the denomination's governing body. Christian liberal arts colleges regard the religious and academic programs as parts of a whole that should not be separated. Their approach to education is grounded in a Christian worldview and provides an opportunity to examine subject matter from a faith perspective. The educational enterprise is seen as a single learning community characterized by the integration of faith and learning, and faith and living. In terms of polity, the Christian liberal arts college may be private (e.g., Wheaton) or related to a church (e.g., Union University).

Religious Dimension within Institutions

For many years Harold Heie, director of the Center for Christian Studies at Gordon College and former vice president of academic affairs at Northwestern College (Iowa) and Messiah College (Pennsylvania), has used a slightly different model for understanding some of the different approaches to religion in higher education. Heie's model defines the distinctions in terms of the way in which an institution actually relates to the religious dimension, as opposed to how the institution might be defined in terms of formal polity or denominational affiliation. But while Heie is concerned with a variety of educational dimensions, his model is intended to address only the cognitive dimension of religious knowledge. According to Heie, "The issue at hand is the role that such religious knowledge should or should not play in the education offered by the institution and the relationship, if any, between this sphere of religious knowledge and the sphere of *academic disciplinary knowledge*."[15] Heie proposes three positions: truncation, coexistence, and integration (see fig. 2.2).

Truncation. Heie's truncation position either denies the existence of one of the two spheres of knowledge or relegates one sphere to relative unimportance when compared with the other. So a private college that has become secularized (the first category in Dockery's typology) may concentrate exclusively on academic disciplinary knowledge, relegating religious knowledge to the private lives of teachers and students, at best, or, in some extreme cases, denying that religious sensibilities even qualify as claims to knowledge.

At the other end of the truncation spectrum is the Bible college (Dockery's second category). Such colleges focus primarily on religious knowledge, giving the knowledge claims of the academic disciplines secondary status, if any status at all, unless such claims are viewed as supporting the primary religious knowledge.

Two schools may illustrate the truncated approach to religion in higher education: Dartmouth and Moody Bible Institute. Both are private colleges, but Dartmouth is a liberal arts college and Moody is a Bible college. Truncation involves an all-or-nothing approach on the part of the institution: Moody does only religion and Dartmouth does not require religion. In a sense, truncation flows out of the identity and mission of an institution. Moody exists to prepare people for ministry and, thus, does not deal with academic subjects perceived as unrelated to ministry. Dartmouth has intentionally or gradually rejected its early religious roots. Schools that take the truncated approach have either a secular or a religious orientation that avoids contamination by the other.

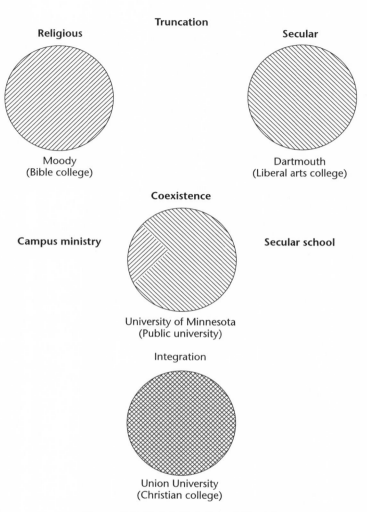

Figure 2.2. Heie's Relational Model

Coexistence. Heie proposes that coexistence represents a second discernible position relative to the relationship between these two supposed spheres of knowledge. Both spheres are considered viable and legitimate, but they merely coexist at the institution. No attempt is made to explore the possibility of connections between religious knowledge and academic disciplinary knowledge.

Though Heie developed his model primarily to discuss approaches to cognitive knowledge in colleges with some religious affiliation, coexistence could apply equally well to secular education. The difference is primarily one of attitude. The school that practices coexistence is warmly disposed toward religion but does not believe that it has anything to say or add to the other academic disciplines. Since World War II, coexistence has been one of the most popular approaches to religion in the public sphere. The term recalls the "peaceful coexistence" between the Soviet Union and the United States during the Cold War, when the two nations fought each other not openly on the battlefield but through subterfuge. Private religious exploration exists alongside public formal education in many of the great public universities in the United States, but neither dimension of human life has a connection with the other. On the contrary, the two dimensions of life often create internal conflict and cognitive dissonance for the person who attempts to compartmentalize life.

Integration. Heie's third discernible position, which he embraces as an educational ideal, is integration. He argues that these two spheres of knowledge should generally be viewed as two sides of one coin. Heie adds that the exception would be those cases where religious perspectives make no difference for disciplinary scholarship. For example, there may be no particular religious or secularist view of the mechanisms of photosynthesis, but in numerous other areas religious perspective has a profound influence on disciplinary scholarship. Further, how one understands human nature has a profound influence on how a social scientist deals with evil behavior, and human nature has profoundly religious implications.

Distinction by Institutional Ethos

David Guthrie has suggested that even among schools with a religious identity, a great variety occurs in how that identity finds expression. He has identified four varieties of institutional ethos that characterize approaches to Christian education: rationalist, credentialist, maturationist, and moralist.[16]

Rationalist. The rationalist approach concerns itself primarily with content or information. In this model, education consists primarily of acquiring knowledge or information. With a strong orientation toward the individual disciplines of the academy, this approach passes on to the next generation the past body of knowledge identified and preserved. Those who have mastered this body of knowledge are educated. Understandably, faculty tend to favor an educational approach that regards mastery of the discipline as the highest priority. In the ongoing academic battle for budgets and resources, faculty tend to favor mastery of their discipline over mastery of other disciplines.

Credentialist. The credentialist approach has a pragmatic bent that regards education as the means to acquiring a job. This model is vocationally driven and tends to cater to the market. In this model the educational process provides the means to an end, with its value determined by the kind of job and income one acquires at the end of the process. It is not unusual for students, their parents, and their future employers to hold this view of education. It is also not unusual for government to espouse this utilitarian view, which fosters the concepts of students as consumers, education as a commodity, and parents and employers as customers. Along with this approach come the calls for colleges and universities to be run like businesses. In an institution that adopts this model, decisions about the curriculum and the shape of the faculty may depend on current trends in the job market.

Maturationist. The maturationist approach places emphasis on personal and holistic development of students. It sees the growth of the person in emotional well-being and character as critical dimensions of education. This view receives strong support from the student services offices at colleges and universities. Life outside the classroom represents the major laboratory of the educational experience. While full-time students may attend classes 15 hours per week, they have a life outside of class for 153 hours per week—ten times as much time! In this context, student organizations and extracurricular activities form the focus of growth; students attend classes to earn a degree.

Moralist. The moralist approach has concern for the behavior of students and tends to establish standards of behavior consistent with an understanding of Christian life. Such matters as chapel attendance, dorm hours, dating practices, dress codes, and other dictates of behavior establish the norms of Christian behavior. The college sets these norms of behavior to encourage holiness and spiritual growth. School presidents, chaplains, and trustees take the lead in setting behavioral standards as they respond to the external constituencies of the institution. Depending on the expectations of the external constituency (whether donors, loyal alumni who send their children to the school, or an ecclesiastical body that elects the trustees and provides money for the operation of the school), standards may vary from strict to lax or nonexistent.

Each of these approaches has profound implications. They constitute the major issues facing higher education today—for any institution, whether Christian or not. These issues are discussed in the next chapter.

The Evolutionary Model

Larry Lyon and Michael Beaty, professors of sociology and philosophy respectively at Baylor University, offer an evolutionary model for understanding the attitude toward religion in religious and secular schools. Their model describes a series of steps from the old-time Christian college to full secularization (see fig. 2.3). The term *evolution* does not explain the existence of the secular school. Rather, it describes how a Christian school moves from its faith commitments to secular commitments.[17]

Old-Time Christian College →	Two-Spheres Approach →	Full Secularization
Faith and learning are integrated and equally important	Faith and learning are separate; faith is less important	Only learning has academic value; faith is irrelevant to learning

Figure 2.3. The Evolutionary Model of Lyon and Beaty

Old-Time Christian College. The old-time Christian college was founded as a religious school with a curriculum intentionally designed to integrate faith and learning. Lyon and Beaty do not elaborate on the characteristics of this approach to teaching, but they allow that the classical disciplines were not necessarily "made religious or taught from an explicitly Christian perspective."[18] What apparently made the old-time Christian college explicitly Christian was the capstone moral philosophy course that attempted to speak to virtually all human experience.

Two-Spheres Approach. When confronted with the modern secular research university and its dominance in the realm of higher education, most Christian schools adopt a "two spheres" approach to education. In this approach, the truths of both religious knowledge and scientific knowledge, which came to dominate the academy's understanding of legitimate knowledge, are regarded as "qualitatively different and intellectually insulated from" each other.[19] By adopting the two-spheres approach, an institution may remain loyal to its religious heritage in matters of doctrine while belonging to the academic guild in matters of knowledge deemed legitimate by the academy.

Full Secularization. Full secularization began with the educational experiment of the land-grant colleges in the nineteenth century. Cornell (1868) and Johns Hopkins (1876) established a paradigm of research, teaching, and application in which religion had no place. The modern university strove for "value neutrality" as it embraced an early theory of knowledge inspired by positivism. In their evolutionary model, Lyon and Beaty follow David Sloan as well as Christopher Jencks and David Riesman in arguing that the two-spheres approach is merely a way station on the road to full secularization.[20]

Building their study on this three-step evolutionary process, Lyon and Beaty conclude that Baylor University will not likely move from the two-spheres approach to full secularization.[21] Their data suggest a different conclusion, however, one more in keeping with the evolutionary model they examine. The evolutionary model involves change over time. To test its validity, one would expect a comparative study of attitudes and behaviors over time, but Beaty and Lyon focus on a survey of opinions by faculty, regents, and students in the present. The idea of change may be discovered in the responses of faculty new and old. According to the survey, faculty who are Baptist, are in the School of Business or Education, have a Baylor degree, have been at Baylor more than twenty years, are full or associate professors, have only a master's degree, or are male are more likely to be receptive of integrating faith and learning and more likely to choose religion over academics when conflicts arise. This pattern is also found at Notre Dame, with only minor variations.[22]

In other words, the "old guard" insiders supported the religious dimension of the university in a way that the younger, marginalized outsiders did not. Furthermore, Lyon and Beaty discovered that the liberal arts faculty as a whole, regardless of longevity and relationship to Baylor and Baptists, felt animosity "toward including religious dimensions in a Baylor education."[23] In their analysis of this animosity, Lyon and Beaty point out that liberal arts have been the targets of religious attacks over the years; the liberal arts faculty has the strongest support for pure academics, as opposed to pragmatic or professional education; and faculty in the social sciences and humanities are less religious than other faculty.[24]

What is the nature of the objection that faculty of a Christian school have toward religious dimensions in education? Faculty were asked to respond to this statement: "If I wished to do so, I could create a syllabus for a course I currently teach that includes a clear, academically legitimate, Christian perspective on the subject." More than half of the respondents (56 percent) disagreed.[25] Open-ended comments that some faculty added to their responses help to illuminate the heart of the issue:

"It would be absurd."

"Preposterous. Will ruin academic credibility of the course."

"I have no idea what this would look like. The Christian perspective I endorse is that 'actions speak louder than words.'"

"There is no such thing as a Christian perspective of quadratic equations."

"A physical science does not lend itself to a Christian perspective."

"Not in science, unless it was an ethics course."

"In my discipline [modern foreign languages], Christianity comes up only as a rare cultural aside."[26]

Even so, in responding to a separate statement on the integration of faith and learning, a slightly larger majority (58 percent) disagreed that faith and learning are separate tasks and ought not to be integrated.[27] The study indicates that faculty tend to favor the general idea of integrating faith and learning, but they oppose specific suggestions for how that might occur. In their open-ended responses, faculty suggested three basic concerns about an attempt to add a Christian perspective to the curriculum:

1. Religious perspectives are either nonexistent or irrelevant to the discipline.
2. No singular and clear Christian perspective exists.
3. Teaching from a Christian perspective would be unfair to other religious perspectives.[28]

Lyon and Beaty argue that in order to consider faith as having anything to do with their disciplines, faculty would need a paradigm that addressed these concerns. They conclude: "Since most academics assume that such a paradigm does not exist, they also suppose that a 'Bible college' in which religion dominates over academics is the only current option to the current secular or two-spheres paradigms."[29]

Of course, faculty have to deal with a paradigm on a daily basis. The models presented here, collected from the ongoing discussion, all deal with the macro level. Faculty teach at the micro level. Baylor illustrates the problem of these paradigms. The faculty may support the idea of being a Christian school in general, but they have no way of thinking about what that means for their individual classes, apart from an approach they consider anti-intellectual and contrary to their discipline's knowledge. The terms *Christian perspective, integration of faith and learning,* and *Christian worldview* all conjure up images of fundamentalism, Creation Science, Bible colleges, indoctrination, and ignorance draped in piety.

The Denominational Approach

Several important, recent studies have taken a denominational approach to understanding the place of faith in higher education. Richard T. Hughes and William B. Adrian compiled a collection of essays to illustrate that different denominational traditions have their own ways of dealing with faith in higher education. Their book, *Models for Christian Higher Education: Strategies for Success in the Twenty-First Century*, appeared in 1997. The next year James Tunstead Burtchaell published *The Dying of the Light: The Disengagement of Colleges and Universities from Their Christian Churches*, a work five years in the making. Though the two books take similar approaches, they arrive at quite different conclusions.

Models for Christian Higher Education. For their study, Hughes and Adrian selected seven faith traditions: Roman Catholic, Lutheran, Reformed, Mennonite, Evangelical/Interdenominational, Wesleyan/Holiness, and Baptist and Restorationist. For each of these traditions they selected two representative colleges on the basis of their academic reputation and continuing relationship with their historic faith tradition. They then invited a scholar from within each of the colleges to write a historical narrative "describing how his or her institution has sought to address the relation between faith and learning from the founding of the institution to the present."[30] In addition to the two narratives for each faith tradition, the editors also invited a scholar from each tradition to write a theological essay that introduces the reader to the distinctive elements of their tradition. This approach is valuable, not so much for its findings, but for the questions it asks and the assumptions its many authors make.[31]

The Reformed tradition stresses the sovereignty of God over all creation. As such, scholarship and learning are subject to God. Secularization results when a dimension of life escapes God's sovereignty. This approach emphasizes the cerebral.

The Mennonite tradition stresses radical discipleship to Christ. This emphasis includes service to the poor and needy. The transformation of the mind comes as a result of a lifestyle radically committed to Christ. This approach has an activist emphasis.

The Lutheran tradition involves Martin Luther's concept of the two kingdoms: the world (nature) and the kingdom of God (grace). These two kingdoms exist in dialectical tension. As such, a Christian worldview should not be imposed on any subject of study.

The Roman Catholic tradition is rooted in incarnational and sacramental theology. It is concerned with the presence of Christ in the midst of suffering, poverty, and injustice. The Roman Catholic tradition, however, has great diversity of expression because the sponsoring religious orders (e.g., the Benedictines and the Order of the Holy Cross, which founded Catholic colleges and universities) have varied emphases.

The evangelical/interdenominational tradition places major emphasis on biblicism, conversionism, and an evangelistic orientation.[32] While other groups, such as the Baptists and Churches of Christ, might share these same concerns, the emphasis on the interdenominational character would set these schools apart.

The Wesleyan/Holiness tradition refers not to Methodism but to the attempt to reclaim the old Wesleyan/Methodist vitality in the late-nineteenth and early-twentieth centuries by such groups as the Salvation Army, Church of the Nazarene, Church of God (Anderson), Free Methodists, and Wesleyan Church. These groups are characterized by their emphasis on the Wesleyan Quadrilateral (i.e., Scripture, tradition, reason, and experience), sanctification, and social holiness.

The Baptist tradition in this volume actually focuses on the Southern Baptist experience, though Baptist origins are considered. The Baptist tradition involves many elements that at times may come into conflict. Baptists historically have been concerned with biblical authority and freedom of conscience. They have promoted centralized missions and autonomy of the local church. They foster personal heart religion and tend toward separatism.[33] Baptists have started many colleges and universities, yet the generally lower social status of Baptists has also produced a suspicion of education.

To speak of the Churches of Christ tradition immediately prompts the need for a disclaimer because one of its primary distinctives is the rejection of tradition and even the idea that the Churches of Christ have a tradition. This group places principal emphasis on the recovery of the primitive pattern of the church found in the Bible. The Bible itself is viewed as a document that can be studied and understood with scientific precision. The Churches of Christ view themselves as the true church and insist they are not a denomination, since denominations represent departures from the true church.

The faith-tradition method of regarding the way religion and academics meet in higher education seems to focus on the extent to which a school remains true to its founding elements or the ecclesiastical body that nurtured its founding. This historical narrative approach tends to focus on institutional structures, sociology, campus politics, money, and the percentage of trustees, faculty, and students holding a denominational commitment. Rather than providing strategies for success in the twenty-first century, these narratives tend to recite how Christian faith can be conceived as almost anything other than part of the intellectual dimension of learning. This approach tends to equate continued institutional involvement in a faith tradition with successful Christian higher education. By defining Christian higher education in terms of parochialism and sectarianism, this approach may succeed in isolating the very things that have the least to do with what might be regarded as most Christian. Distinct elements separate these many

groups, yet what is decidedly Christian would be precisely what they
have in common.

In his conclusion Adrian states that the schools under investigation have broadened their scope and vision, both academically and theologically. Denominational identities have become less noticeable. Religious observances are required in fewer schools. Emphasis on doctrine or even student behavior has diminished. The curriculums have been broadened to include professional studies. Religion courses have been broadened to include other topics of currency, such as peace, justice, and ecology. Many schools have broadened their image to position themselves in a market beyond their faith tradition. Others have broadened their definition of themselves using terminology of more general cultural acceptance, such as community, values, and service.

This faith tradition approach may be merely a variation of the evolutionary approach without actually recognizing it. These chapters represent snapshots of schools at the moment, but the institutions are not stagnant. Successful schools like these have a momentum, but this study helps us understand neither what that momentum represents nor how it relates to faith in Christ and the academic disciplines.

The Dying of the Light. Burtchaell also takes a denominational or faith tradition approach to Christian higher education in his book. While the narratives in *Models for Christian Higher Education* are written by faith tradition insiders, Burtchaell wrote his historical narratives himself. For that reason, *The Dying of the Light* has a degree of objectivity lacking in the other book. It also succeeds in presenting a consistent pattern of assessment for each school.

Burtchaell also selected seven faith traditions: Congregationalists, Presbyterians, Methodists, Baptists, Lutherans, Catholics, and evangelicals. In each case he examines at least two schools (for Catholics, Lutherans, and Baptists he examines three schools each because of the diversity within these broad groups) and chooses a school that had a strong denominational tie at one time but has disengaged from that relationship fairly recently. In his concluding chapter Burtchaell identifies several trends that cut across denominational lines.

In most cases the turn away from Christian accountability came as the result of a clear initiative by a president who did not necessarily intend to be leading his or her school away from its mission as a Christian institution. In these situations the president and faculty continued strong personal religious involvement, though their role in education lacked a religious motivation. Only in later times, when a new president and faculty lacked the earlier religious observance, was it evident that "the purge of Christian purpose" had occurred.[34] When the change occurred, it typically resulted from the initiatives of trusted, religiously active presidents who

> felt that their institutions were somehow confined, stifled, or trivialized by their church or denomination or order, and at a critical moment they greatly enhanced the professionalism, resources and clientele of their colleges.[35]

The rhetoric rarely involved rejection of faith and usually involved a strong reaffirmation of denominational identity that proved meaningless.

In many cases, a change in the Christian purpose of an institution involved a formal break in governance between college and denomination. In most cases, governance was not direct but through the power to elect trustees. The power to change the charter and the method of electing trustees, however, normally rested with the board of trustees themselves. In some cases the colleges feared or actually experienced harassment from the churches. More often "the church representatives offended more by ineptitude than by intrusion."[36] Then there is the matter of money. As long as affiliation brought financial support, the relationship could be tolerated. When the dollars ceased to flow and better sources of income lay elsewhere, colleges had an incentive to break the ties that bind.[37]

While official action by presidents and boards may formalize changes, Burtchaell argues that the reason behind these changes came about because the faculties lost interest in a religious identity. With the growth of specialization of disciplines,

> the self-understanding of the teacher was slowly detaching itself from the colleagueship where he or she taught and fastening itself to the colleagueship of the discipline, and also of the teaching profession as that became more tangibly organized. The teacher thereby came to love his or her career more than his or her college.[38]

The shift came not so much from rebellion as from indifference. In terms of the rhetoric of identity, Burtchaell observes that it slid from a specific denominational label "to evangelical, to Christian, to religious, to wholesome, to 'the goals of the college' which by then were stated in intangible terms."[39] In the name of "liberating learning from an authoritative master-perspective, . . . they were usually just transferring their credence to those old divine surrogates: civilization, rational inquiry, communism, science, fatherland."[40]

Burtchaell's analysis of the schools he studied led him to write that vision statements and other documents typically gave assurances that the schools would continue their tradition of Christian values, albeit without any plan to guarantee the promise nor with any commitment to hire people who could achieve it. He observes: "While working on the menu they declined to hire a cook."[41] Submission to the church and a religious understanding grounded in Christian doctrine were exchanged for submission to governmental regulations, accrediting associations, and professional associations that often even prescribe curricular requirements.

Ultimately Burtchaell seems to consider the failure of the denominational schools as a failure of intellectual and theological dimensions. Lacking a vital theological foundation, the colleges also lacked the requisite critical framework to understand what they were going through. Burtchaell argues:

> They usually lacked a critical philosophical tradition as well, even an interest in philosophy or history, so those colleges were innocent of the important languages whereby the discourses of faith and worship and theology could be made conversant with those of the other academic disciplines. One result of the narrowing definition of each faculty member's academic interests was an education that might include very little of the history, philosophy, and theology required to give them a disciplined perspective on their own scholarly pursuits.[42]

Thus, Christian education became a matter more of formalities than of substantive intellectual discussion, so much so that Burtchaell laments, "If the faith of the Christian sponsors was really 'permeating' these colleges, it was more like mildew than grace."[43]

Contributing to this climate was what Burtchaell refers to as "the subversive influence of Pietism."[44] He finds no fault with first-generation Pietism, which had a prophetic role in challenging the moribund state of religious life in the seventeenth and early eighteenth centuries. Although Pietism sought to call people back to the simplicity of faith when the church had grown cold through a dry scholasticism that made the deep matters of doctrine stale, it also had a reductionist tendency. This tendency lent itself to misuse by any preacher prone to move from a simple message to a simplistic message to mere sloganism. The value of making the complex understandable, however, does not become an issue for people who remain ignorant of the doctrines of faith. In addition, Pietism's emphasis on spiritual experience and the individual believer leaves little place for the church beyond one's own personal associations. Thus, under the pietistic influence, religious life on campuses focused on "the individual life of faith, as distinct from the shared labor of learning."[45] In this context, worship, devotional acts of piety, and moral behavior defined Christian education rather than anything that took place in the classroom.

In conclusion, Burtchaell describes an evolutionary model based on his denominational study. Having found that colleges affiliated with a variety of denominations tend to go through the same situations on their journey of disengagement from their denomination and Christian identity, Burtchaell proposes a three-step process of disengagement (see fig. 2.4): pietism, liberal indifferentism, and rationalism.[46]

Pietism →	Liberal Indifferentism →	Rationalism
Observance of personal piety and moral behavior	Retention of formal acts of piety without faith conviction	Abandonment of the forms of piety and religion in general

Figure 2.4. The Disengagement Model of Burtchaell

From the research at Baylor as well as the research of Burtchaell, one quantitative and one narrative, we see that the role of the faculty is the critical factor in the Christian identity of an institution. More than the formal ties to a denomination, the policies of the board, or the initiatives of the president, the extent to which students ever see any relationship between God and what they study depends upon the faculty.

Faculty cannot convey to students a relationship between God and their discipline if they themselves do not grasp the relationship. Some attempt at forcing a connection between God and an academic discipline seems contrived to many. Such perceptions arise precisely because a forced connection really has been contrived. There is real danger that a contrived connection between God and a discipline may be imposed, a connection not inherent to the discipline.

The Fly in the Ointment

The various ways of describing the relationship between religious thought and higher education reflect a spectrum, or continuum, of approaches. They deal with different dynamics of this relationship, but they tend to agree with one another. Yet all of these approaches grant an option, claimed by many in the academy, that may not actually exist. The pure secularist position needs to be a purely objective approach that makes no comments on matters pertaining to the religious domain. Such a position would present no threat to the faith of any religious orientation, be it Buddhist, Hindu, or Christian. The texts of virtually every discipline, however, contain assumptions and presuppositions that have profound religious sentiments.

The absence of a religious perspective in education would not hinder the practice of religion, the development of faith, the moral underpinnings of society, or self-understanding. Truly objective education that does not comment on the transcendent or the spiritual would leave people free to examine these dimensions on their own. Yet truly objective education does not exist. On this point, the postmodern deconstructionists are quite correct. Christianity may not have a voice or a place in the classroom, but religious opinion flourishes, and it often travels under false colors. It takes place, not under the banner of religion, but under the banner of the discipline being considered. Without being noticed, views about, and attitudes toward, religion filter through the normal conversation about a discipline. How often does a Christian teach a religious idea that stands opposed to Christianity and never realize it? The first step toward understanding how faith informs learning and scholarship begins with truly understanding how to adopt the two-spheres approach. By this I do not mean to advocate withdrawing a Christian perspective from teaching. Rather, I advocate withdrawing all of the non-Christian perspectives from teaching as well. In other words, we must begin to recognize religious ideas in nonreligious clothing. Unless all the other religious ideas are withdrawn from education, it would be derelict to withdraw the Christian perspective alone.

One of the best models for Christian thought in the academy in the twentieth century was C. S. Lewis. Although known to the Christian reading public for his popular theology, apologetics, and children's stories, Lewis established a reputation as a critical scholar for his studies of medieval literature: *The Allegory of Love* (1936), *A Preface to Paradise Lost* (1943), *English Literature in the Sixteenth Century, excluding Drama* (1954), and *The Discarded Image: An Introduction to Medieval and Renaissance Literature* (1964). To these might be added his shorter, and more polemical, monographs on the philosophy of literary criticism: *The Abolition of Man* (1944) and *An Experiment in Criticism* (1961). Lewis had little interest in the efforts to develop an integration of faith and learning, which had begun in several U.S. Christian schools in the 1950s. He thought that the effort suggested that faith had no intrinsic relationship to learning and had to be artificially imported. Lewis believed that all knowledge had latent religious thought at its foundation.

In a famous essay he wrote for a group of Anglican clergy who wanted to know how to do apologetics, Lewis argued:

What we want is not more little books about Christianity, but more little books by Christians on other subjects—with their Christianity *latent*. You can see this most easily if you look at it the other way round. Our Faith is not very likely to be shaken by any book on Hinduism. But if whenever we read an elementary book on Geology, Botany, Politics, or Astronomy, we found that its implications were Hindu, that would shake us. It is not the books written in direct defence of Materialism that make the modern man a materialist; it is the materialistic assumptions in all the other books. In the same way, it is not books on Christianity that will really trouble him. But he would be troubled if, whenever he wanted a cheap popular introduction to some science, the best work on the market was always by a Christian. The first step to the re-conversion of this country is a series, produced by Christians, which can beat the *Penguin* and the *Thinkers Library* on their own ground. Its Christianity would have to be latent, not explicit: and *of course* its science perfectly honest. Science *twisted* in the interests of apologetics would be sin and folly.[47]

In his own discipline Lewis recognized that the religious ideas often went unchallenged because they lay embedded in literary criticism as latent assumptions.

Personal Exercise

Draw a line. At the left end of the line write "secular." At the right end of the line write "fundamentalist." At each end of the line record the names of schools with some religious identity that would embody the most extreme case of each polarity. Think of the line as a graded continuum. Now think of schools that would fit between these extremes. What labels would you place on these schools? Is there a relationship between their religious orientation and their academic reputations? On what basis have you arranged the schools? What do you really know about what goes on in each school's classrooms and dorms? Is there a difference between a school's "image" and what would have once passed for its reputation?

Further Reading

Several books have explored the history of higher education in relation to Christian faith in the United States. This selection offers some variety of perspective:

Burtchaell, James Tunstead. *The Dying of the Light: The Disengagement of Colleges and Universities from Their Christian Churches.* Grand Rapids: Eerdmans, 1998.

Carpenter, Joel A., and Kenneth W. Shipps. *Making Higher Education Christian: The History of Evangelical Colleges in America.* Grand Rapids: Eerdmans, 1987.

Hughes, Richard T., and William B. Adrian, eds. *Models for Christian Higher Education: Strategies for Success in the Twenty-First Century.* Grand Rapids: Eerdmans, 1997.

Marsden, George M. *The Soul of the American University: From Protestant Establishment to Established Nonbelief.* New York: Oxford University Press, 1994.

Sloan, David. *Faith and Knowledge: Mainline Protestantism and American Higher Education.* Louisville: Westminster/John Knox, 1994.

3

The Challenges
of Higher Education

[handwritten: fragmentation]

[handwritten: vision]

Almost three thousand years ago a Semitic writer said that without vision, people perish. Higher education in the United States today faces a major dilemma, one that has several dimensions and whose symptoms crop up in a variety of ways. In general, higher education no longer has a purpose governed by a vision. Over the last hundred years, the increased specialization of disciplines has bred fragmentation, rather than integration, of knowledge. Fields of knowledge increasingly pull apart and fail to deal with the relationship between different spheres of knowledge.

At the same time, professional education has been given up by the professions that once controlled membership in the guild through the apprenticeship process. The academy has now assumed the function of training, replacing the earlier apprenticeship model. As a result, higher education has become torn between liberal arts and professional departments. The former see as their mission the development of critical thinking; the latter see as their mission the development of "competent" practitioners or professionals. These parties are embattled in educational institutions over the purpose of higher education.

Sections of this chapter are adapted from material that originally appeared in "When Survival Becomes the Highest Purpose," *The Campus Minister* 19.2 (fall 1997): 14–20, and in "More than Survival," in *The Future of Christian Higher Education*, ed. David S. Dockery and David P. Gushee (Nashville: Broadman & Holman, 1999), 205–13.

Institutions are also embattled over institutional priorities between teaching faculties and administrative staff who tend to keep score by counting how much money is spent by whom. In this climate, decisions about curricula and basic academic directions often become politically, economically, and ego based. Such a dynamic appears in a wide range of institutions today, including state universities, private liberal arts colleges, state technical schools, private religious colleges, and well-endowed private universities. A wide range of agendas, from conservative to liberal, come into play when deciding what ought to be taught, how it ought to be taught, what emphasis ought to be given, and what kind of values, if any, should permeate the academy.

Society as a whole now demands a greater stake in the "product" produced through higher education. Increasingly, this business or economics model of education has grown to dominate. What product does a university or college produce? Who is the customer? Am I getting value for my dollar? Education has come to be regarded as an investment or commodity by different interests: the state, private enterprise, philanthropists, religious groups, parents, and students.

The way out of this growing indolence of the academy has become clouded because the academy no longer has a clear purpose, no overarching ideal of what it should be doing. It has no clear reason to be.

The Collapse of Christendom

Higher education in the West came about as an invention of the church, and its purpose was intrinsically related to its form and function. The church created higher education to deepen one's faith, knowledge of God, and knowledge of God's creation. Education existed as a part of the church. God provided a basis for understanding the relationship of all knowledge. Because all things came from God, all things could be legitimately studied and understood as a gift from God. This basic view of education's purpose created a stack pole,[1] or the *universitas*, the basis for universal knowledge.

Different religious orders during the Middle Ages created their own collegium, or college, which was a religious community. The members of each community who completed their initial period of instruction advanced to the rank of novice, or bachelor. Thus, the first degree of progress was a bachelor of the arts, a bachelor of knowledge. (*Bachelor* became synonymous with an unmarried man because only a man could enter the male religious orders charged with preserving the knowledge of God and civilization.) A member of the community who advanced in his instruction might become a master of the order. The different houses of learning each had a master as their head, just as many of the different religious orders had a master as their head. The head of the Knights Templars was the Grand Master. Thus, those pursuing knowledge advanced in their degrees. (The Masons and the academy have preserved this terminology to measure one's advancement in knowledge and status within the community.) The very few who became doctor were those authorized to teach the religious doctrine of the church. All ways of knowing came under the umbrella of theology and doctrine, but those who studied were all monks. To this day, the official uniform of the academy is the monk's simple gown and hood.

The Collapse of Value and Vision

The academy holds on to the traditions and terminology of the church, but it has separated itself from its ecclesiastical foundations. The form and tradition remain, but without the purpose. Without purpose, the academy (or any other institution, from a business to a government agency) drifts along through the inertia of tradition. Without vision, however, functionality no longer has a relationship to value. In the absence of true values, the academy constructs pseudovalues, such as the amorphous and ubiquitous terms espoused by all up-to-date schools, *quality* and *excellence*.

The academy now speaks of itself as offering "quality" education. What does that mean? We do it the way we have always done it, of course. We define ourselves as the standard. The way we do it is the best way to do it, because we are the standard. To depart from the way we do it would diminish our quality. For instance, a student must be in class fifteen hours per semester for every hour of credit they receive. Why? Because that formula makes for quality education. Why? Because that is how it has been done for as long as anyone can remember. Of course, the real reason the academy started requiring fifteen hours of class time per semester for every hour of credit was because the Carnegie Foundation wanted "a day's work for a day's pay" from faculty. Institutions that did not follow its formula did not receive money from the Carnegie Foundation. As a result, U.S. schools adopted a formula driven by the economic pressures of external stakeholders.

The academy also regards the method of instruction as a sign of quality. The faculty lectures because education has come to be regarded as the dispensation of a body of knowledge that comes best by hearing. The lecture actually represents a veiled imitation of the sermon, wherein "faith comes by hearing." The lecture hall of the academy duplicates the ecclesiastical model of dispensing knowledge to the congregation. Why does the academy still do it that way, so long after its divorce from the

church? Because lectures are a sign of quality. Why? Because we have
always done it that way. Professors replicate the method of instruction
they experienced, not because it is the best way to learn, but because it
is the only way they know to do it. Like Pavlov's dog, we associate education with the sound of our voices. Without a clear vision and purpose,
higher education has nowhere else to turn but to tradition, even during
the exposition of the most radical social ideas.

The problem of higher education relates to its retaining the forms of
the medieval church but without a purpose to give it unity and meaning.
Professors do the same old things, but without any overarching reason
to do them. This situation manifests itself in the fragmentation of disciplines of learning within the institutions, fragmentation of personal
life, and also fragmentation of society in a country where this model of
education prepares people to live fragmented, meaningless lives.

Without vision, schools will pull themselves apart and lapse into ha-
bitual, internecine turf warfare spawned by budget battles. Nevertheless,
they will survive as institutions. Institutions have an amazing capacity
for continuing to exist, regardless of how far they have moved from their
founding purpose. Existence becomes the reason for existing. Institutions
take on a life of their own devoid of any purpose. Jesus referred to this
institutional phenomenon two thousand years ago when he said that
a person does not put new wine in old wineskins because the old skins
cannot tolerate the dynamic ferment of the new. Higher education in the
West finds itself in the same position today. The university has divorced
itself from the old purpose, which revolved around a universal concept
of knowledge. With the emergence of postmodernity, however, the university no longer holds to the ideas of universal knowledge, universal
values, and universal norms. In their place the university champions
relativism and fragmentation.

Growing Dissimilarities

As fragmentation grows, institutions become increasingly dissimilar
in their appearance as they pursue particular visions for themselves.
The failure in consensus about the purpose of the university occurs at
the same time an explosion in educational experimentation has begun.
This experimentation began in the late 1960s and early 1970s with ideas
like the "open university." Driven largely by students' lack of interest
in following the prescribed curriculum after the spring riots of 1970, a
number of loosely structured programs emerged that allowed students
to earn academic credit toward graduation for a variety of life experiences they deemed valuable.

By the mid-1980s, private colleges and public universities struggled to balance budgets while sources of revenue shrank in the face of skyrocketing costs. This climate turned these experiments in education into innovative approaches to nontraditional education. Educational institutions discovered a huge market of people who had never finished college but found their careers stalled until they could earn a college degree—any college degree. The nontraditional pool of students has grown in proportion to the total number of students. Through the use of adjunct faculty and accelerated courses that dramatically reduce the amount of faculty-student interaction, allowing students to complete a degree in as few as eighteen months, colleges have found the goose that lays the golden egg.

The revolution in technology that began with the introduction of the personal computer in the early 1980s led also to a transformation of college culture by the late 1990s. Schools that do not have sophisticated campus networks and do not provide Internet access stand at a decided disadvantage in recruiting students. Technology has bred another revolution in teaching methodology, not only as faculty begin to incorporate technology in the traditional lecture class but also as technology becomes an alternative, and in some cases a replacement, to the traditional book. The Internet has also opened the possibility of distance education in which students have a virtual class experience with peers around the country or the globe. Traditional student-faculty interaction occurs, not in real time and space in a classroom, office, or commons area, but over the Internet, through compressed video, and through immediate audio exchange.

Private colleges, publicly funded universities, well-endowed universities, successful grant-writing research universities, publicly funded technical schools and community colleges, and religious schools—all grow increasingly dissimilar as they pursue different educational visions. The kind of institution that once characterized itself as in loco parentis, today often takes little or no interest in the personal life, character development, and moral habits of those who pay tuition. Alma mater has taken a laissez-faire attitude toward the raising of her children since the boomers of the late 1960s and early 1970s rebelled so successfully against any attempts to restrict or control college lifestyle. Religious institutions have come to experience this reorientation of mission as much as secular schools. Schools with historic ties to denominations have to rethink what it means to be a "Christian" school in this era. In most cases it means little more than that a denomination started the school in the last century. Sometimes it means that a course on Bible or religion is part of the core curriculum. One looks hard to see much difference between the college experience at the denominational school and a state school, except in terms of the size of the school.

The pragmatic, hard-nosed businesspeople who raised the baby boomers and sat on the boards of trustees of religious schools saw nothing particularly Christian about an English course or a history course. Decisions at such schools tended to be driven by economic considerations. Yet, religious worldviews filter through every discipline of knowledge. One cannot simply dismiss a discipline as not being religious. All knowledge is religious. I once participated in a meeting between several trustees and several administrators at a Christian school in which someone posed the possibility of eliminating the school's faith requirements for admission. One of the trustees argued that it was not a theological issue but a business issue, since the school would still be a Christian school. An administrator argued that it would be even more Christian because the Christians would have an opportunity to evangelize the non-Christians.

Today's Student

At a time when the average college and university has draped itself in the self-authenticating trappings of scholarly tradition while pursuing a policy of marketing a product and surviving at any cost, a different kind of student enrolls in the traditional undergraduate program today than did so twenty years ago. College students today are the children of baby boomers. They were raised by arguably the most self-centered generation the country has yet seen. In that regard, these young people were not raised so much as they were allowed to raise themselves. While their parents reveled in the higher standard of living that a two-income family can enjoy, these children took up the slack at home. These are the children who a few years ago were referred to as *latchkey kids*. They cared for themselves after school, and the television set was their baby-sitter and nanny. This generation became the first emotional beneficiaries of quick, no-fault divorce as the divorce rate climbed to the 50 percent range during their formative years.

In terms of values development and worldview, this generation grew up without any significant exposure to religion. In their study of marginal church members, Penny Marler and Kirk Hadaway point out that 75 percent of baby boomers had a significant baseline experience of at least two years in church while growing up. The baby busters reversed this statistic, with only 25 percent having a significant baseline experience in church. No one was left to take these "echo boomers" to church. While the baby boomers rebelled against their parents' religious conventions, the echo boomers have no such emotional involvement, pro or con, with religion. Baby boomers, having been forced to go to church when they were little, opt to let their children decide about religion for themselves.

The sentiment has a certain egalitarian flare, but in practice it means that echo boomers have been denied a basis for deciding about faith, because they were never exposed to the option.

Implications for Campus Ministry

Campus ministers undertake their responsibilities in a different world from that of twenty years ago. The academy represents the intellectual, moral, social, and religious direction of culture, and the academy is adrift. Oddly clinging to the last trappings of Christendom or cultural Christianity, the academy represents the maelstrom of religious ideas percolating in society as a whole. The academy also represents the breakdown between belief system and behavior. Belief and behavior, always a difficult marriage to maintain and often leading to the charge of hypocrisy, have a necessary relationship without which individuals and society as a whole become dysfunctional. The value slogans of universities take on the air of television commercials that exist only as a hook to the buyer, a feature the sophisticated echo boomer recognizes immediately. A university cannot speak of the importance of community if it does not also have a value basis for community that all community members embrace in covenant together. Without a basis for value, the university cannot supply the fundamental element of education it was created to supply.

Bishop Lesslie Newbigin has argued that Christians in the West no longer enjoy a dominant cultural position but once again live as missionaries in an alien culture.[2] The greatest outpost of this mission occurs on the college campus, and the campus minister represents the fresh voice that provides a new generation with an option to make sense of their world and to give them some direction in life. A generation of emotionally disengaged people has never had the option of faith because they have never been in a context to even know what it meant. The university offers a smorgasbord of religious ideas, but Jesus Christ will not be one of those options explored during the formal education process. Campus ministers have the advantage, however, of being able to put the gospel in a relational framework rather than in a formal educational setting. In the past the faculty had credibility because they were the faculty. Students offered them respect because they stood in authority over them. With the coming of postmodernity, the university's conventional marks of status, which created degrees of authority and credibility, have begun to crumble. The person who relates to students creates his or her own credibility.

In the past, campus ministers have had the luxury of functioning as chaplains to the Christian students on campus. That role will shift as the pressures of postdenominationalism continue to erode the sense of denominational loyalty that might have once connected a student to a campus ministry. The effectiveness of campus ministers in the future will correspond to their willingness to shift their own approach to ministry as they move from chaplain to missionary.

The Path to the Future

Christians build institutions. Usually the result of a movement that emerges from a period of spiritual vitality or awakening, institutions are well intended as a means of carrying on the work or contribution of the genius of that period. This effort at bottling spiritual vitality has never worked. It did not work with the monks of Cluny in the early Middle Ages, and it did not work with the YMCA. Spirituality cannot be institutionalized. This observation is central to the problem of maintaining a Christian college or university. If an organization with such a clearly defined purpose as the YMCA can go from being the leading organization for evangelizing young people in America to the largest franchised health club, then one should not expect that a college with such diverse interests can remain Christian for long. Institutions assume the character and agenda of the financial interests that support them.

Christians often complain about how our great institutions have been "stolen" by the liberals or the secular world. The litany usually begins with Harvard and Yale, then proceeds to some of the great regional universities with denominational backgrounds, such as the University of Chicago (Baptist) and Vanderbilt University (Methodist). Rarely do Christians complain about the loss of the great hospitals and children's homes. Therein lies the problem. At present, few people have a concern for the caring ministries. Great Christian institutions have never been "stolen." They have always been thrown away by Christians who had no particular interest in them. So much attention has been given to the litany of great colleges and universities lost to the Christian faith that little attention has been given to why some institutions continue to remain Christian beyond the generation that founded them.

Carl Lundquist, for many years the president of Bethel College and Seminary, often explained why he had no plans for raising an endowment for Bethel: "The churches are our endowment!" This statement may seem rather cavalier and irresponsible at a time when the economic picture of U.S. colleges and universities looks so gloomy to the ones who must balance the budget. It does, however, reflect a commitment—of accountability to the churches that founded the school to serve the mission of Christ. A healthy endowment has the potential to free a school from any accountability to its founding purpose and mission. Few Christian institutions have survived prosperity. The institutions flourish, but somehow Christ gets left behind.

Poverty by itself, however, is no particular virtue. Even more important than the economic issues are the relational issues at work. Bethel was kept Christian by the care of the churches of the Baptist General Conference. Apart from the official lines of governance, the churches "owned" Bethel. They did not govern it; they felt responsible for it. They cared what kind of experience young people had at Bethel. They held the school accountable. The school, in turn, took the churches seriously. Bethel was part of a family that went beyond formal denominational structures.

Nevertheless, denominational structures and formal lines of funding, reporting, and trustee selection do not guarantee the continuation of a distinctive Christian mission for a college or university. Denominational politics is easily reduced to a game of avoiding accountability. The informal relationship serves a more important function than the formal relationship in keeping a college connected with its purpose and mission. As long as the churches care about Bethel, and as long as Bethel cares what the churches think, Bethel will continue to have a distinctively Christian mission.

A vision for the future of Christian education can only emerge from a clear grasp of an institution's founding purpose to serve Christ in relationship with churches. Christian colleges and universities that successfully deal with the dramatic challenges of higher education in the United States at the turn of the new century will focus on the strategic issue of how to fulfill the mission for which they were founded. Christian colleges and universities that drift away from their purpose will tend to focus on the tactical issues that confront every institution in the education industry today. Preoccupation with the unending stream of trend shifts without a governing universal basis for knowledge and integration will leave such schools devoid of identity and powerless to form the character of students. In such situations the only universal value is the dollar. Operating from this perspective, trustees are in danger of making "wise decisions" for the survival of the institution. Unfortunately, survival is not a very lofty purpose.

Curiously, Christian colleges and universities must risk death to fulfill their mission. This phenomenon will only accelerate with the increasing influence of a post-Christian, postdenominational, postmodern world. The National Commission on the Cost of Higher Education has recommended that governments develop new approaches to academic regulation that emphasize performance and differentiation, and that academic communities develop accrediting processes that emphasize effectiveness. With the collapse of the old academic tradition and the emergence of radically different educational models, the right to grant degrees may no longer be available to institutions in the future, at least not the way it has been in the past. In most countries the government controls the granting of degrees. In the past, many Christian colleges have not accepted government aid in any form so that they might avoid entanglement with governmental restrictions. How would Christian schools respond if they could no longer grant degrees? The answer to this question quickly identifies where an institution stands with respect to its foundational purpose and mission. Does the school exist to grant degrees or to do something else?

Common Issues

Despite the distinctive elements of public and private education, particularly those of Christian institutions, all institutions face some common issues that will not go away. If anything, they seem to grow worse. One need look no further than the index of *The Chronicle of Higher Education* for a catalog of recurring themes: faculty and research issues, government and politics, money and management, information technology, student issues, athletics, and international issues—some of which are addressed in the following sections.

Faculty and Research Issues

Often news related to faculty and research involves an ethical issue. The poet laureate of California, who teaches at the University of California at San Diego, lied on his résumé about graduating from college.[3] Michael A. Bellesiles was forced to resign from Emory's faculty when an investigation found that his research methodology for a book on America's gun culture brought into question his "scholarly integrity."[4] Ansley Hamid, an anthropologist teaching at John Jay College of Criminal Justice, lost his position as a result of his personal experimentation with heroin while conducting a $3.1 million research program on the heroin drug culture.[5] These three episodes were reported within a month of one another. They made the news because they seem a bit out of the ordinary. Faculty members who engage in sexual relations with students rarely even warrant mentioning, supposedly because the practice has grown so common that it has ceased to be newsworthy.

Episodes of this kind raise ethical and moral questions about both the personal behavior and the research of faculty members. Does character affect research? Does character affect the educational experience of students? Do personal experience and involvement with a research project enhance or invalidate it? If morality and ethics matter to the success of scholarship and the educational enterprise, what can form the basis for ethical and moral standards?

Money and Management

Money has always mattered to higher education. The grand old colleges of Oxford and Cambridge had grand old benefactors who endowed them as religious institutions. The money gave out long ago. For many years the British treasury acted as the endowment for the two old universities until Margaret Thatcher became prime minister. In the 1980s, for the first time in the colleges' ancient histories, the Oxbridge establishment began to take fund-raising seriously and went about raising hundreds of millions of dollars to support Oxbridge education. The new benefactors, in turn, set the agenda for the future direction of education by virtue of what they funded.

For lesser-funded schools, which have no prospects of raising hundreds of millions of dollars in support, tuition drives everything. In 2002–3 the average percentage increase of tuition for public four-year colleges was 9.6 percent. For private schools the increase was 5.8 percent. Many state schools, hit hard by climbing state budget problems, had to increase tuition dramatically to make up for shortfalls in public funding. Governors State University increased tuition by 55.2 percent, Purdue by 34 percent, and Clemson by 29.9 percent.[6]

At the same time that state funding has declined, enrollment has begun to rise as the echo boomers reach college age. Echo boomers have the potential to stress college resources just as much as baby boomers did thirty-five years earlier. This trend has led to a call for stiffer admission standards, enrollment caps, and even higher tuition. Suggested "market methods" for solving the problem all suggest enormous social implications, one of which is the question of whether higher education is a privilege for the economic elite.

Where does the money go? Clara M. Lovett, president emerita of Northern Arizona University, has suggested that the average public school spends 80 percent of its budget on salaries, and 80 percent of the salary budget goes to faculty. When budget cuts come, they come in areas other than faculty salaries. When personnel are cut for financial reasons, the cuts tend to affect staff other than faculty. All the while, maintenance is deferred and needed instructional resources go wanting, all in the name of maintaining "academic excellence."[7] Of course, faculty know that it is difficult to maintain academic excellence if the necessary resources are not available.

The roots of financial troubles in lean times can probably be traced to poor management decisions during prosperous times. A certain mentality prevailed in the 1990s that believed prosperity would never come to an end. In the new economics, recessions would never again occur. The greatest problem Congress faced was how to spend the budget excess. The combination of the peace dividend and the dot.com phenomenon produced a euphoria of economic optimism that bled over into personal financial decisions for many Americans, not to mention financial decisions by major corporations such as Enron and WorldCom. In this mentality companies no longer had to show a profit to be considered a sound investment. A spirit of delusion prevailed. Unfortunately, many colleges became wrapped up in the cultural climate of the age.

In some cases this mentality has led to terrible consequences. The president of the University of Mobile was forced to resign following the accumulation of a $3.9 million debt associated with a branch campus he started in Nicaragua. He later pleaded guilty to tax evasion related to the incident. The president of Mississippi College was fired and later prosecuted for embezzlement of millions of dollars. His successor was forced to resign following what appeared to be a period of great success that included expansion of programs and facilities when the board finally realized that the "growth" had driven the college deeply into debt.

Many academic administrators probably do not understand how and why their budgets got out of control. The projections looked good. Unfortunately, many business administrators do not understand the academic side of things well enough to know where the budget is out of control. It is easy to point to the escalating costs of health care and insatiable technology requests as the chief culprits. In most cases, however, the fault lies in the proliferation of courses, majors, and degrees that legally obligate the college to deliver courses regardless of enrollment. This pattern has a domino effect. It frequently requires the addition of faculty and facilities to accommodate the expanding program. The problem is exacerbated when combined with poorly designed delivery systems or administrative systems that involve the duplication or multiplication of administrative services.

What does any of this have to do with Christian faith and its correlation to learning? Learning takes place in various environments, some of which are more conducive to learning than others. Some environments stimulate and encourage the creativity and faith of teachers, while other environments lead to cynicism and strife. Some of the models for Christian higher education seem to focus on piety to the neglect of the intellect, but it would be a catastrophic mistake to neglect piety simply to pursue an intellectual faith. Faith involves character as well as intellect.

Character affects the learning environment. Many of the financial woes of colleges can be laid at the feet of character. It is easy for the faculty to complain about the president's pet building project, claiming that it is merely to gratify the presidential ego. We are less skilled at recognizing when the course we want added or the new major that will focus on our particular interest might somehow involve our egos as well. Petty jealousies that require an extra secretary because the unit in the next building got an extra secretary are numerous. Of the promulgation of "centers," there will be no end as long as one dean has more than the other dean. Name the campus. We all recognize the trait . . . in others.

We should all want our work to prosper, our department to grow, the reputation of the college to grow. Expansion and development are legitimate aspects of college life, just as they are for business. A healthy pride in doing good work is but a mere breath away from a destructive arrogance that has abandoned all critical self-awareness in its malicious view of others. Character matters in academic life. Henry Kissinger is quoted as saying that academic politics are so vicious because the stakes are so low. The quote always gets a laugh from professors because they have experienced the reality.

Information Technology

Night school and correspondence courses were beneath the contempt of most faculty until the mid-1980s, when degree completion programs began to appear, largely at smaller private colleges. These smaller private colleges soon became larger private colleges as the degree-completion programs swelled with adult learners whose employers paid for them to earn their degrees within two years on accelerated schedules. Offering their classes in "cohort groups" in lockstep, one course at a time, these new programs offered something that the old night school never offered: the opportunity to actually graduate. By the mid-1990s the Internet had made it possible to offer courses and degrees at a distance, with a degree of interaction between and among students and faculty, in a way that the old correspondence courses could never have done. Now the new technology appears to be changing the nature of teaching and learning even on campus.

The Massachusetts Institute of Technology (MIT) is now putting materials for more than two thousand campus courses on-line. Everything from the professors' lecture notes to learning exercises will be accessible without charge, for noncommercial use, to anyone who visits the Web site.[8] Students like the ease of Web-based research, although they have also found that the Web can deliver complete term papers on virtually any subject. Professors have begun to turn to the Internet as the first step in research. While the Web is full of information, a great deal of that information is unreliable. Anyone with modest computer skills can set up a Web site and post text and images on the site. A study conducted for the Digital Library Federation found that 96 percent of researchers seek some other source to verify the information if they consult an on-line source first.[9] In a postmodern environment of relativism, why would reliability still be important? In a subjective environment, why would scholars still be concerned with the truth or falsity of propositions found on the Web? How does information relate to knowledge and knowledge to truth? If truth is not objective and values are all relative, why should students be punished for plagiarism? On what basis can the secular academy answer these questions?

The Internet-based distance program of the University of Phoenix, a for-profit university with stockholders, has grown from 4,700 students in 1997 to 49,400 students in 2002, with 70 percent pursuing undergraduate degrees. Of that total, 40 percent are members of a minority group.[10] The success of programs like this relates to their ability to serve a population that traditional education cannot serve. Those who take advantage of these programs tend to be adults with full-time jobs, and possibly families, for whom going to school in the traditional format with eighteen- to twenty-two-year-olds is not realistic.

Many traditional schools do not accept transfer credit from on-line colleges that have national accreditation through the Distance Education and Training Council rather than through one of the regionally accrediting associations. This problem does not arise for larger on-line institutions like the University of Phoenix and University of Maryland University College because they have regional accreditation. The issue of transfer credit, however, raises the thorny issue of the idiosyncratic nature of higher education in the United States. Higher education lacks an "industry standard" for what constitutes a course or a major or a degree, unless a discipline-specific accrediting association mandates the content of a course and the elements of a curriculum. Usually, degree requirements depend on the personalities and preferences of those who compose a given department. When those persons retire or move, the requirements change. Such change occurs because the elements of the program have a subjective nature. Given this reality, on what basis does one weigh the quality of a program of study?

What does the revolution in technology mean for Christian education? *The Chronicle of Higher Education* explored this question in an article about Eastern University in Pennsylvania. Eastern has 360 students enrolled in distance-education programs mediated by a mix of media, including CD-ROM, email, and Web-based material. Students in Eastern's programs belong to cohort groups that facilitate community and enable discussion of faith issues. Students in the United States must visit the campus for orientation, while faculty members from Eastern travel to sites outside the United States to meet international students. Eastern has made the deliberate effort to develop its delivery system in accord with its mission of providing personal, Christian education. This mission distinguishes Eastern's program from a secular program. The added program features represent an attempt to make the distance program comparable to the traditional on-campus program.

For education to be Christian, however, which campus experiences must a school attempt to duplicate or replicate in a distance program or even an adult program? What does *comparability* mean in this context? What are the essentials of Christian education such that if these ingredients were missing the education could no longer be called *Christian*? The variety of new programs based on nontraditional students raises these questions of Christian education as well as the broader questions of education in general. What are the essential ingredients of education? Such a question assumes an enormous value system. What is the origin of this value system, and does the entire academy agree to it?

Athletics

At every lull in conversation in a faculty lounge, a reference to the scholarship money available to the athletic program will generally revive the energy of the exchange. Concern over exploitation of athletes usually veils jealousy over precious scholarship dollars. The controversy has been around for years, but it has grown in intensity as college sports have become big business for even small schools. For some small schools that cannot compete, however, collegiate athletic programs are a black hole. One aspect of the problem involves the graduation rate of athletes. Of football players who entered athletic powerhouse Ohio State between 1992 and 1996, only 36 percent graduated within six years. This figure is considerably less than the Division I-A average of 50 percent.[11] The scandal of college athletics reaches from major schools like Ohio State to little schools like Gardner-Webb in North Carolina, whose president was forced to resign following a vote of no confidence by the faculty when it was discovered that he had altered a student's grades so that the student could maintain athletic eligibility.[12] However, such scandals serve as an easy diversion from an important question: What is the place of sports in higher education? We should be careful how we answer; for any answer will be based on some set of values. What is the origin of these values, and how valid are they? In England, the rowing of a long, narrow boat by eight people meets with all the passion and enthusiasm of a bowl game in the United States. Why is there such a cost differential?

This section has done little more than summarize how *The Chronicle of Higher Education* has recently covered the recurring themes in higher education. Student issues and the trend toward globalization require greater treatment and will be addressed in chapter 4. These issues frame the environment in which higher education takes place, and when students and faculty are not in class, these issues play a large role in defining the context of higher education.

Toward a Christian Educational Vision

In what sense can anything be called *Christian*? Can we speak of a Christian pencil or a Christian piano? We speak of institutions as Christian. Do we mean the institution as an institution, the people of the institution, or the reason for the institution? What is Christian higher education? Is more meant by the term than is meant by the idea of integrating faith and learning or teaching informed by faith? Must one be employed by a Christian college to be a Christian teacher?

It may be useful to consider these questions in relation to another approach to education. What is Montessori education? Must one be employed by a Montessori school to be a Montessori teacher? Does one use Montessori pencils and Montessori pianos in a Montessori school? Does a Montessori education mean more than the content of what is taught?

A Montessori education involves an educational vision that includes basic ideas or presuppositions about people and how they learn. It includes a goal for the total person who experiences a Montessori education. Integral to the vision of Montessori education is the set of values that creates its context. These values include attitudes about people, processes, and the purpose of education. A Montessori school can be identified by its adherence to the vision and values of the Montessori approach to education. Some who espouse the Montessori vision and values may teach in a non-Montessori school. They may believe in Montessori education, yet not teach in a Montessori school. They may believe much of the Montessori educational vision and values, yet not believe that Montessori approaches should be applied in a non-Montessori context. Other Montessori believers, however, may attempt to apply some of the Montessori approach in their own classroom. The teacher at a Montessori school is involved in Montessori education, and the teacher at a non-Montessori school may teach from the perspective of Montessori vision and values. The Montessori vision for education goes beyond what one person can accomplish in the classroom.

Christian education comes where a college has an educational vision that is based on Christian values. A Christian who holds the Christian understanding of reality may not believe that this understanding should be applied in a non-Christian context. Some Christian believers, however, may attempt to apply some of a Christian approach in their own classroom. The teacher at the Christian school is involved in Christian education, but the teacher at the non-Christian school teaches from the perspective of Christian vision and values. The Christian vision for education goes beyond what one person can accomplish in the classroom.

The issues facing higher education today call for a comprehensive understanding of education in all of its complexity. *The Chronicle of Higher Education* devotes itself to reporting on many features of education that go beyond the curriculum. The problems of higher education from the perspective of professors, presidents, deans, and trustees rarely involve the content of lectures. The greatest challenge for Christians serving in secular institutions is that they find themselves on the crew of a ship without a rudder. Higher education in the West has lost a unifying vision that is not likely to be regained, short of a dramatic spiritual awakening. Such things have happened before, but they have come as a surprise rather than a strategy.

The challenge for Christian institutions, or institutions that represent themselves to be Christian, is actually to be guided by Christian vision and values. This challenge is greater than it seems. A school may have a confessional document, yet neither attend to a Christian vision of education nor operate from a perspective of Christian values. The man who for many years served as president of one of the largest seminaries in the world, in defense of his corporate model of administration, was quoted as saying that a Christian institution cannot be governed by Christian principles. If he is right, there are no Christian colleges any more than there are Christian pencils. For this reason, faculty members who believe in a Christian vision of education, and who espouse Christian values to guide that education, find themselves in the same situation as the Christian who teaches at a secular institution. They may not be involved in Christian education at all. Rather than bring the perspective of faith to the problems of higher education, their colleges have adopted the approach of the secular academy that lies adrift.

Conclusion

A Christian vision for education still involves those unique contributions of the gospel of Jesus Christ that fostered higher education and the scientific method in the West. The gospel offered a unifying principle for knowledge and education that the West seized. God created a good physical world and made people in his image, with the capacity to know and acquire knowledge. This purposeful creation has a consistency that allows people to learn about it. God not only made the world, but also entered into it through Jesus Christ, thus affirming the physical as well as the spiritual. Christians in the academy have the potential advantage of a unifying theory of knowledge, although they may not understand its implications after years of neglect. Chapters 5, 6, 7, and 8 will explore how these faith implications may be recovered.

Christian values in education are a more difficult problem. Unlike the intellectual issues of faith and learning, we know the Christian values. They are not difficult to know; they are difficult to practice. We may not know how our discipline relates to our faith, but do we know how our behavior relates to our faith? Is it possible to distinguish Christians by their behavior if not by their teaching? The problems of higher education, as reported in *The Chronicle of Higher Education*, appear to come back to a question of character. In a series of lectures given in 1943 and later published as *The Abolition of Man*, C. S. Lewis suggested that the academy was planting the seeds of its own ruin by abolishing a basis for character.[13] Character issues in the academy rest largely on one aspect of human nature: pride. Unfortunately, in the English language the word *pride* refers to two quite opposite situations. We speak of pride in relation to the self-respect that comes from doing a good job. It also refers, however, to a destructive tendency to find our identity in comparison with, and in opposition to, other people. Pride rather than larceny lies behind ineffective college administration. Pride rather than hatred lies behind the byzantine politics of the academy. Pride rather than deceit leads a person to steal the intellectual ideas of another. Deceit is the means, but pride is the cause. C. S. Lewis referred to pride as the "great sin."[14] Christianity provides a basis not only for understanding reality but also for understanding the problems of humanity.

A theory of ethics that ignores the reality of sin may make a constructive contribution to human society, but it operates from the same disadvantage as a theory of medicine that ignores the reality of germs. It will inevitably tend toward legal and penal solutions to society's problems rather than address the root cause. An understanding of sin that does not also provide a basis for redemption leaves the human race trapped in a hopeless fatalism. The academy is ornamented with pride, vanity, jealousy, and envy. These are not the sorts of things that in themselves cause a person to spend time in jail. They are the respectable sins. In themselves they account for almost all the problems of higher education. While the academy lacks a unifying theory of knowledge, it also lacks a basis for character. Nothing makes the case for Christianity quite so strongly as a life that seems to work based on Christian values. On the other hand, nothing repudiates the intellectual arguments for Christianity quite so much as a life that affirms Christ and yet looks no different from that of the most worldly don.

Only presidents and trustees can address the issue of whether a college will offer Christian education. But any Christian who teaches in higher education can determine whether his or her teaching reflects a Christian vision for education guided by Christian values.

Personal Exercise

This chapter has examined only a few of the major issues that face higher education today; there are many others. Make a list of the five greatest issues you face in your own school. Now identify the nonnegotiable factors related to these issues for which you are willing to fight. As you examine your nonnegotiables, consider the origin of the value system on which you have based your selection. Are your nonnegotiables based on eternal truths, tradition, personal preference, or something else? Why do you value them so highly?

Further Reading

The most helpful habit in staying abreast of the major issues that face higher education is skimming *The Chronicle of Higher Education* every week.

4

From Modernity
to Postmodernity

How does the cultural shift from modernity to postmodernity affect the educational enterprise? Postmodernity focuses on the freedom of thought and action of the individual, unrestrained by custom, religion, culture, community, or consequence to the whole. Postmodernity often comes under assault from conservative thinkers because it denies absolute values, but this denial of absolutes comprises a subsidiary rather than a primary dimension. For conservative thinkers, the irony of postmodernity is that it grows from the seedbed that conservatives cherish: individual liberty and freedom.

It would be much simpler to deal with the contradictions inherent in postmodernity if the matter simply involved a debate over ideas.[1] The great Western tradition of debating ideas to arrive at the truth is rooted in a basic confidence in rationalism. Within the postmodern mind-set, however, one cannot arrive at truth because truth falls within that group of absolutes that do not exist. Not only that, but the reliance on rationalism as a means to truth no longer enjoys the confidence it once did because rationalism forces people to choose between conflicting ideas. Conservative thinkers like to think according to standards of logic practiced by Western civilization for thousands of years. In the past, it was only necessary to point out the logical fallacy of a line of argument to defeat an idea, at least in theory. Now we live in a new world. The old standards no longer apply, and many people no longer accept the old standards.

Rejection of the Past

The old standards involved the basic rules of logic. Rejection of the old standards goes in many more directions than simply educational or political philosophy. Rejection of the old standards involves a general rejection of authority, seen during the antiwar demonstrations and campus riots of the late 1960s and early 1970s. Rejection of authority involves much more than the resistance to governmental authority, however. It involves more dimensions of life than disagreement over foreign policy. Rejection of authority extends to other institutions besides government and includes religion and the press.

Behind the public institutions that represent authority, a vast array of particular individuals and groups stand as authorities that no longer command the attention of the postmodern generation. Civic groups that once spoke on issues and swayed public opinion no longer have the kind of standing they once had. The Daughters of the American Revolution once played a major role in fostering patriotism and love of country, but this organization now languishes from neglect. The current rejection of authority has not occurred like the cultural revolution in China, a concerted militant effort to destroy all of the institutions of traditional Chinese culture, an effort that failed. Rather, cultural institutions of the West have been ignored to death. The triumph of the counterculture in the United States came not with fire and sword but with drugs and sex. The cry to "turn on and drop out" met with enthusiastic support.

Throughout the period of campus unrest, ideological conservatives met the threat of communist ideology, idea for idea. While the bombs fell on Hanoi and while American troops clashed with communist guerillas in the jungles of Vietnam and Cambodia, conservatives and radicals squared off in a debate of ideas on the campuses. The amazing success of Richard Nixon in capturing a decisive percentage of the college vote signaled the final victory of the counterculture, though it appeared at the time as a victory for conservative ideals. Nixon's win in the 1972 presidential election was due not to the passion of his supporters but to the apathy of American voters. The following year the Supreme Court issued its landmark ruling in the case of *Roe v. Wade*.

Conservatives won the election but lost the battle of ideas. Nevertheless, from a broader perspective or vantage point, which we do not yet have, the conservatives may have lost the war of ideas. At the time, it seemed to be a simple debate over two sets of ideas or ideologies.

In fact, it may well have been a debate between those who advocated, and those who denied, that ideas matter. Nixon's success on the college campuses resulted from the decision of the liberals, radicals, disaffected, and otherwise nonconforming young that it really did not matter who won the election. In the great debate of ideas in the past, none of the adversaries would have taken the position that it does not really matter who wins. In the past, people of radically different opinions agreed that ideas matter.

In *Ideas Have Consequences,* one of the classic works of social thought in America, Richard M. Weaver discusses the danger of ignoring tradition. Writing in the aftermath of World War II, Weaver began to recognize the danger that would result if his generation did not pass tradition on to their children. He observed:

> It has been well said that the chief trouble with the contemporary generation is that it has not read the minutes of the last meeting. Most modern people appear to resent the past and seek to deny its substance for either of two reasons: (1) it confuses them, or (2) it inhibits them. If it confuses them, they have not thought enough about it; if it inhibits them, we should look with a curious eye upon whatever schemes they have afoot.[2]

For the most part, the children of those who fought for freedom and kept the home fires burning did not receive tradition gladly. It has been said that Christianity is always just one generation away from extinction; its survival depends on the next generation accepting its teachings. The same can be said of culture. Culture must be taught and learned. It must be passed on by one generation and received by the next. If a single theme runs through the writings of Weaver, who died in 1963, it is the importance of each generation learning from the wisdom of the past and taking on the mantle of the culture. When people do not take the mantle, it is either because they do not understand the issues at stake or because they understand the issues all too well. Rather than view the past as a mantle to be worn proudly, they view it as a straitjacket that will constrain them.

During the same period in which Weaver taught and wrote, adults who grew up during the Great Depression and who bore the onerous responsibility of defeating the Axis powers began to raise their own children, the children known as the baby boom generation. Every individual goes through a period of struggle or rebellion in reaching adulthood, but never had so many individuals gone through adolescence together. Nor had they gone through adolescence in such numbers without parental guidance.

Normally we think of adolescence as the high school years, but institutional life tends to prolong adolescence or create adolescent regression. World War II veterans were the first generation of Americans to go to college in large numbers, although they were adults when they went to college on the GI Bill (many were married and had children). This generation dramatically increased the middle class that could afford to send their children to college. Working hard to wipe out the memory of deprivations suffered during the depression, they gave their children every advantage.

The 1950s and 1960s were generally not a time for middle-class Americans to "do without." While Weaver stressed the need to remember the past, many Americans preferred to forget, specifically, the poverty and hunger and death of the past. In an upwardly mobile society, the key to success involved status and image. The opinion of others mattered. It was important to keep up with the Joneses. In such an atmosphere, morality is not based on a higher universal principle; it is based on popular opinion. However, when morality is based on what the neighbors might think, what happens to morality when the neighbors stop thinking or caring?

The Abandonment of Moral Education

Masses of baby boomers arrived on college and university campuses in a great flood, overwhelming the physical capacity of the dorms as well as the personnel resources charged with enforcing long-standing rules of behavior. Baby boomers were not the first generation to have overactive sex hormones; they were just the first generation to overwhelm the system to the point that they could not be socialized. By the mid-1960s boomers found themselves in college environments intended for smaller populations. Colleges no longer had the infrastructures in place to enforce moral behavior, and the historical peer pressure from neighbors to conform to a standard of behavior did not exist. Rather than regroup and face the challenge of education, in one swelling tide colleges succumbed to students' demands and abandoned the ancient tradition of alma mater as in loco parentis. Many colleges ceased to have any concern about the moral beliefs and moral behavior of students. Everything happened too fast; surrendering the moral aspect of education was the easiest thing to do. Character development disappeared from the perceived purpose of most institutions.[3]

During the baby boomers' influx into American colleges and universities, higher education in the United States abandoned one of its essential cultural functions. Education became little more than the mastering of facts in the sciences, opinions in the humanities, and skills in the vocations. By abandoning the moral dimension of education, it became much easier to develop the industrial model of education as an assembly-line process. Typical of the fragmentation of modern society, higher education separated an essential dimension of life from the educational process. Values ceased to have a place in education.

A classic definition of *culture* is

> an integrated system of beliefs (about God or reality or ultimate meaning), of values (about what is true, good, beautiful, and normative), of customs (how to behave, relate to others, talk, pray, dress, work, play, trade, farm, eat, etc.), and of institutions which express these beliefs, values and customs (government, law courts, temples or churches, family, schools, hospitals, factories, shops, unions, clubs, etc.), which binds a society together and gives it a sense of identity, dignity, security, and continuity.[4]

While religious institutions have the primary public responsibility for expressing and teaching beliefs, the educational institutions have the primary public responsibility for expressing and teaching the values of a culture. Other institutions of a culture play a role in beliefs and values, but their primary public responsibility is for the maintenance of the customs of a culture. The family crosses all of these boundaries, serving as the private and ultimate institution of responsibility for culture. In a less technological society, the process of socialization occurs without the benefit of formal education. The family and local institutions oversee the completion of a young person's transition from youth to adulthood and marriage. In technological Western society, however, young people are turned over to colleges and universities for the "completion" of their education. After the 1960s, this primary function of higher education ceased to take place. As a result, the identity, dignity, security, and continuity of the culture began a steep decline.

Judicial Collapse

The law courts' retreat from their role as conservators of the culture's values followed the retreat of colleges and universities from their role as teachers of cultural values. In *Roe v. Wade* (1973) the Supreme Court announced the abandonment of ultimate values in culture to make way for embracing individual preference as a standard of law. The Supreme Court merely recognized and made part of constitutional law the countercultural revolution that had taken place on the American campuses during the previous decade. The Supreme Court had issued a number of landmark decisions related to civil rights between 1954 and 1973, but in *Roe v. Wade* its decision to legalize abortion represents a radical departure from the tradition of the law.

In framing the U.S. Constitution, designers of the republic adopted the tradition of English common law. Thus, a new nation had a legal tradition that went back for centuries. The English legal tradition depends on the application of the law to particular situations and relies heavily on precedents established by earlier courts. Lawyers and judges look for similar situations to draw analogies and apply the law to situations that may never have occurred before. This system has worked remarkably well for centuries. Hundreds of cases work their way through the system each year with little notice, except to the parties involved.

From time to time, however, the Supreme Court reaches a decision that dramatically alters society. In *Brown v. Board of Education* (1954) the Warren Court ended legal segregation of the races in public schools. The Court reasoned that segregation violated the equal protection clause of the Fourteenth Amendment. Unfortunately, many communities resisted integration, and later court rulings had the effect of replacing the community school with the government school. This decision signaled the rejection of a particular "custom" within the culture, but it did not challenge the idea of customs within the culture. The case centered on "civil" rights.

By the 1960s, however, the Supreme Court began to enter the area of privacy rights. In *Griswold v. Connecticut* (1965) the Court overturned the 1879 Connecticut birth-control law. In this decision the Court inferred a right of privacy not specifically mentioned in the Constitution and with little precedence in case law. In great measure, the court responded to what it viewed as a shift in popular opinion on the part of the American public and, lacking any clear precedent, "engaged in a piece of activist judicial 'legislation.'"[5]

While advancing the new privacy doctrine, the Supreme Court also handed down two socially transforming decisions that would tend to relegate religion to the domain of privacy. In *Engel v. Vitale* (1962) the Court held that a school board could not require the recitation of prayer in public schools. Since prayer is a religious activity, the court cited the "establishment clause" of the First Amendment as grounds for prohibiting government-mandated prayer in schools. Even a nonsectarian prayer would represent "the establishment of religion" from the perspective of someone who had no belief in God. Although the prayer banned by the Court did not represent an organized religious institution or church, the Court left the impression that religious activity mandated by a school board constituted an establishment of religion, even if it only meant the establishment of a religious concept. Public religious sentiment had always been a feature of the republic, but the 1962 ruling began to change the cultural attitude toward the appropriateness of religious ideas in public. In his great work on the philosophy of history, Arnold Toynbee concluded that religion bears civilization along. Rather than being a private matter within a public society, religion is the point of that society. This decision, however, led to a new way of thinking about religion (see chap. 5, below).

Prohibiting state-mandated prayer served to protect the minority of people who did not believe in prayer from the tyranny of an established religion. In short, though its reasoning dealt with public religion, the Court's ruling protected the privacy of individuals. The strong division between state and religion that the Court sought to establish had the effect of making religion, or the absence of religion, a matter of privacy.

A year after its decision on prayer, the Court handed down another decision related to religion in the public sphere. This time the issue related more clearly to respecting one religion or religious tradition over others. In *School District of Abington Township v. Schempp* (1963) the Court declared unconstitutional a Pennsylvania statute that required the reading of the Bible each day in public schools. The Court reasoned that the state should avoid not only any law that favors one religion over another but also any law that favors religion over nonreligion. While this interpretation took great latitude with the meaning of making "no law respecting an establishment of religion," it also had within it the precedent for "prohibiting the free exercise" of religion.

More than forty years have passed since these two rulings that dealt so particularly with religion within the cultural mainstream. At the time of these rulings, public schools represented the primary training ground in basic cultural values. This training included a general introduction to many of the central stories of the Christian faith as interpreted from a Protestant perspective. While the Court banned neither prayer nor Bible reading, the public at large and school officials in particular developed a mind-set that religion had no place in public education, in any form. During the last four decades other forces have worked to shape American culture in ways that seemed unimaginable when the Supreme Court issued its rulings. At that time, the American public still had a general consensus on the basic values of society. Within ten years, however, that consensus would lie shattered as the result of the cultural revolution.

A Society Uninhibited by Moral Values

The American public has heard news reports about biological warfare. Anthrax, it seems, resembles the common cold in its early phase. Imagine deciding to treat something as a cold and then waiting to see how it works. Take two aspirin, drink plenty of liquids, and get plenty of rest. If the patient dies, then we know it was actually anthrax. In many ways American culture has suffered from a severe malaise for decades, and the patient continues to get worse. Weaver warned of the symptom, the rejection of the past, and suggested two possible diseases. One had to do with understanding. Conservatives have addressed this disease head-on. The other disease, however, represents the deadly malaise. We now have a culture that rejects anything that inhibits them. Among the inhibitors are reasoned arguments used by conservatives. The postmodern generation rejects these reasoned arguments not because they are flawed but because to accept them would be inhibiting. *Roe v. Wade* served to relieve women of inhibitions toward abortion. Perhaps the driving force in the disintegration of public values lies not with the intellect but with passion.

The judicial revolution seems difficult to understand when analyzed solely on the basis of the intellectual interpretation of the Constitution based on case law. If people were merely intellect, such an analysis would be so much more satisfying. As it is, however, people are not merely intellect. In fact, even the justices of the Supreme Court are subject to the same impulses that other people face. The framers of the Constitution believed that judges appointed for life, well paid, and independent of either the executive or the legislative branch would not be swayed by popular opinion or the swelling tide of the moment. In *The Federalist Papers,* Alexander Hamilton argued that such a court would never use their power to construe the laws of the land "according to the *spirit* of the Constitution" and thus "mould them into whatever shape" it thought proper.[6] Hamilton assumed that a judiciary free from the uncertainties of the popular vote would be free of "a disposition to consult popularity."[7] While recognizing "the ordinary depravity of human nature," Hamilton apparently allowed himself to believe that judges appointed under the Constitution would be of a superior sort, not liable to "arbitrary discretion."[8] No doubt Hamilton would have been surprised to see the Supreme Court swept up in the tide of popular sentiment that prevailed on American college campuses in the late 1960s and early 1970s.

The Court did not foster the collapse of sexual morality among young people so much as it accepted it as the new "community standard." Though the new morality began with a concern for ideas of peace in the midst of the Vietnam War, it descended to a preoccupation with sex and pleasure, passion and gratification, uninhibited behavior and irresponsibility in relationships of all kinds.

In a 1989 study, anthropologist Michael Moffatt found that the most influential factor in college students' attitudes toward sex was the media. Although peers, parents, and religion were mentioned as factors by two-thirds of his sample, the most significant determining influence was the media. Moffatt comments:

> The direct sources of the students' sexual ideas were located almost entirely in mass consumer culture: the late-adolescent/young-adult exemplars displayed in movies, popular music, advertising, and on TV; Dr. Ruth and sex manuals; *Playboy, Penthouse, Cosmopolitan, Playgirl*, etc.; Harlequins and other pulp romances (females only); the occasional piece of real literature; sex education and popular psychology as it had filtered through these sources, as well as public schools, and as it continued to filter through the student-life infrastructure of the college; classic soft-core and hard-core pornographic movies, books, and (recently) home videocassettes.[9]

The cultural role once filled by the pulpit and the school is now filled by the entertainment industry. Within any culture the role of forming values falls to some institution. In the United States that role has now shifted largely from the church and the academy to the entertainment industry.

This shift in values represents a deference to indulgence that exalts the immediate desires of individuals without consideration of the long-term consequences. The media have given attention to the AIDS epidemic, although popular perceptions still tend to regard AIDS as a disease that affects only gay men. While the disease has swept across sub-Saharan Africa, to the devastation of the heterosexual population in such prominent nations as Kenya and South Africa, it is also growing most rapidly in the United States among the heterosexual community. By 1996 more than half a million people had contracted or died of AIDS. Less well known are the alarming figures that 12 to 13 million Americans annually contract a sexually transmitted disease (STD).[10] In the United States, the STD epidemic has followed the dramatic change in attitude toward sexual behavior outside of marriage. By 1999 sex had become such an acceptable part of adolescent dating that almost half of all high school students had experienced intercourse.[11]

Besides the change in attitude fueled by popular culture, another set of factors contributes to the actual change in behavior. These factors point to other areas of instability in the culture. Teenagers are more likely to engage in sexual intercourse if they have moved frequently (thus lacking a stable community with established values), have divorced parents (lack adult models of loving relationship), belong to a single-parent family or remarried family (lack the supervision needed during adolescence), begin dating before the age of sixteen and "go steady" (have more opportunity for sex), use alcohol and other drugs, engage in delinquent behavior or associate with delinquents, have poor academic performance, and have permissive parents or parents who model extramarital sexual activity.[12]

Both family prosperity and family tragedy can foster sexual activity in adolescents. Parents who relocate for job promotions and enjoy the financial rewards of two incomes raise their children without the benefit of a community that upholds values and without the time to provide close supervision. Parents who divorce place their children at financial risk, and single parents who must work to provide for the family often provide little supervision. Nearly 50 percent of all divorced men neither see nor support their children after divorce.[13]

The collapse of traditional values related to sex has followed the divorce curve. At the beginning of the twentieth century less than 10 percent of marriages ended in divorce, but by the end of the century, that rate had grown to 50 percent. In California two divorces occur for every three marriages.[14] Today it is not uncommon to hear certain sociologists and other professionals who study marriage say that marriage is an outmoded institution and that the family is no longer a necessity. To some, marriage has become as meaningless as sex. This is the context in which the contemporary exercise of law, government, and higher education occurs.

Considerations

During the last twenty years of the twentieth century, many conservative Christians became politically active for the first time in an effort to bring about a political solution to the issues of abortion and prayer in public schools. They met with great success in electing their candidates to public office. The presidents they helped to elect appointed Supreme Court justices who were sympathetic to their views on abortion. Though some initiatives now prohibit the use of federal funds for abortions, open access to abortion has become as American as apple pie. The government (executive, legislative, and judicial branches) represents just one aspect of culture and probably the least important aspect in the development of values. Conservative Christians who opposed desegregation insisted that "you can't legislate morality." Nonetheless, it is possible to modify behavior by law. Few governments, however, have the moral will to legislate against popular opinion.

Christians play a declining role in the formulation of popular opinion. Denominations have been in steady decline against a growing population since the 1960s. Even evangelistic churches that experience some growth, like the Southern Baptists, have experienced a steady decline in the rate of growth relative to the general population.

The *Roe v. Wade* decision may represent one of the first major signals that the old social consensus of modernity had come to an end. The decision is symptomatic of the broader collapse of the primary institutions of culture in America. Though they continue to exist, they have ceased to exercise their function within a vital, healthy culture. Any solution to the problem must address the breadth of American culture as well as the intricate interrelation of life's different dimensions. A political or legal initiative by itself will fail. Politics follows the culture. It does not lead!

Past cultures in danger have experienced revitalization. Some historians credit the Wesley-Whitefield revival in England with rescuing that land from the same fate that overtook France in the French Revolution. The revitalization of churches set in motion a catalytic experience that rippled through all of society for over a century, resulting in legal reform, educational reform, penal reform, the abolition of slavery, a transformation of literature, and reform of the political system itself.

The great challenge facing those concerned with the state of American society involves bringing revitalization to every institution of the culture. Before the laws of the land will once again reflect a regard for ultimate values, the institutions of culture must once again reflect this reality and play their part in preparing the next generation.

The Opportunities of Postmodernity

Postmodernity may be one of the most overrated trends of recent times. Its name suggests that it is a full-blown epoch like the medieval or ancient periods. Its champions describe it as the epoch that follows modernity. If it is, it certainly is an unusual epoch in the world of remarkable epochs. The transition from antiquity to the Middle Ages took centuries. The transition from the Middle Ages to modernity took more centuries, but postmodernity was born and matured all within the life of the baby boom generation. The same decade that defined the characteristics of the next epoch also witnessed the debate over how to spend (1) the "peace dividend" that was supposed to result from the permanent state of peace in the world, and (2) the government budget surplus that was supposed to result from the new economy, in which there would never again be a recession. Rather than view postmodernity as the worldview of a great global culture, the pattern of things to come, it may be more helpful to view the characteristics of postmodernity as evidence of the continuing decay of the old culture.[15]

As a term, *postmodernity* is a helpful way of saying that the present culture is in a state of change. It is an egocentric term those in the West use to suggest that they still define the world. At a conference of some ten thousand delegates from around the world, held in Amsterdam in 2000, I discovered that most of the world regards with detached amusement or indignant anger the Western urge to think of postmodernity as a global issue when most of the world is struggling to enter the modern age. The rise of Islamic fundamentalism, nationalism, and ethnic conflict suggests that the pluralism of postmodernity has not yet filtered out to the rest of the world. The prevalence of racism within American and western European society also suggests that postmodern pluralism may not be as common as is often assumed.

Nonetheless, the dynamics of postmodernity do have a powerful role to play in Western culture in general and in higher education in particular. Even if postmodernity does not characterize the broader culture, it has certainly become the ethos of academic subculture. It provides an intellectual rationale for a valueless value system and an agnostic theory of knowledge. Professorial distrust and cynicism over the structures of institutional life have become dogma in postmodern thought. The rivalry and pettiness of academic politics have blossomed into the autonomous individual of postmodern society. All of these trends, however, represent reaction against aspects of modern society. Postmodernity has no positive agenda. As such, it is not a worldview so much as the expression of longing made manifest in the rejection of what has failed.

The longings of postmodernity create the opportunity to provide alternative answers and solutions. Contrary to popular opinion, postmodern persons have not rejected Christ or his claims; generally they are unaware of Christ. Postmodernity rejects modernity, not Christ. The rejection of modernity involves a great deal of uncritical rejection of earlier cultural features that modernity employed, such as rational thought. Nonetheless, postmodern people do not reject rationality so much as they reject much of the absurdity that had become rationalism by the twentieth century. Most of all, postmodernity rejects the dehumanizing tendencies of modernity expressed by such clichés as "a cog in a wheel." Earl Palmer argues that this experience is one of intense loneliness.[16] Modernity had no place for the spiritual dimension of life, but the postmodern person realizes that people are more than physical beings. As such, postmodernity creates the opportunity for Christians to bring fresh answers to the new questions people ask. The danger is that Christians will want to offer only answers to questions people asked during the transition from the Middle Ages to modernity. Answers from the Reformation fit the questions people asked then. These answers may continue to be valuable answers to those questions, but people are now asking different questions.

The popular media provide a means of gauging the pressing questions that people ask. The top television shows from the 1970s to the early twenty-first century—*M*A*S*H, Cheers, Seinfeld,* and *Friends*—remained popular for many years and continue to be broadcast in syndication. All of them have the same subject: the conflict between the need for autonomy and the need for friendship.

Personally Centered

The postmodern generation is personally centered. This self-centeredness expresses itself in a number of ways, including socially, politically, intellectually, and spiritually. Socially, self-centeredness affects the nature and quality of interpersonal relationships. Politically, it tends to isolate people from involvement in institutions. Intellectually, it tends to promote an extreme subjectivism. Spiritually, it encourages a self-tailored approach to religion.

Existential isolation has come to full flower in the postmodern generation. The latchkey children who raised themselves with the television as their baby-sitter have learned to protect themselves in relationships. A generation that grew up moving about every three years and leaving their friends behind, postmodern people have been conditioned to view personal relationships as temporary. Raised in an environment in which one out of every two marriages ends in divorce, the postmodern generation experiences families as a game of Russian roulette.

The avoidance of conflict is a major aspect of the personally centered lives of the postmodern generation. For the baby boom generation, conflict meant the Vietnamese War. For their children, however, conflict often means the interpersonal relations that led to their parents' divorce. Argument is the most familiar face of conflict. This generation has a deep-seated desire to avoid personal conflict and the possible pain that may result. Oddly, the males of the postmodern generation, who distance themselves from commitment to personal relationships and the possibilities for conflict, have from their childhood immersed themselves in a culture of vicarious or virtual violence. Teenage Mutant Ninja Turtles and Transformers have led easily into the extreme violence of video games, while a new form of movie has appeared in which people become the props, and attention has focused on the bigger and more elaborate high-tech explosions. These technological innovations allow people to experience a surge of adrenaline without emotional risk. The implications for higher education are enormous. Faculty members often complain that students today do not seem as engaged with the class as were previous generations of students. They seem apathetic.

Historically, the academy has been a place where different positions were argued. A primary dynamic of teaching has been the effort to help students understand the nuances of argument, develop the skill to critique an argument, and gain experience in constructing arguments of their own. One of the dynamics of postmodernity's self-centeredness is the tendency to disengage from argument and debate. This generation of students may adopt a philosophical position, not because of its logic or conformity to truth, but because it fits their emotional state.

The affirmation of radical pluralism as an aspect of the postmodern milieu should not be regarded as merely philosophical or political. In many ways it has more to do with sociology and psychology than with philosophy and political science. Radical pluralism enables people to avoid dealing with conflicting points of view. Radical pluralism does not really protect the person who holds divergent views any more than it protects the person who does not hold such views and does not want to have to deal with them. Radical pluralism allows a person to avoid not only conflict with others but also internal personal conflict. Having to choose between alternative views creates tension and stress, especially for people who have never been taught to make critical judgments.

This dimension of the postmodern milieu may very well pass from the scene to be replaced by some other passing fad, or it may characterize the culture for generations to come. Whatever the situation in a constantly changing cultural environment, those who teach in higher education have the responsibility to ask continually what role they should play in such a context.

Institutionally Alienated

The World War II generation founded great institutions, and the baby boom generation attacked great institutions. The postmodern generation has taken a radically different approach to institutional life: they ignore the great institutions. They tend to be disinterested in political parties, civic clubs, and religious denominations, as well as government, corporate America, the military, and the institutions of higher learning. For the most part, they have opted out of American institutional life. The institutional alienation of the postmodern generation grows out of their personally centered lives.

Much of American institutional life was shaped by the great global ideological conflicts of the twentieth century. Fascism, communism, and democracy fought dreadful wars for the mastery of the globe. After communism and democracy combined forces to defeat their mutual enemy in World War II, they turned on each other for the forty-five year Cold War. Despite the Cold War's impact on American society, to the postmodern generation that sits in the classrooms of American colleges and universities today, the ideological struggles of the Cold War are little more than a vague idea, like prohibition. Compared to the fascism of Germany or the communism of the Soviet Union, U.S. capitalism looks quite admirable. Taken by itself, however, corporate America can look rather sleazy. Older generations have the benefit of memory to fill in the gaps and keep the scandals in perspective. The postmodern generation, however, has no historical perspective. It has no memory. It is as though the great struggles of the twentieth century never occurred. If postmodernity were a global phenomenon, this cultural amnesia would suggest some wonderful possibilities for world peace. Unfortunately, most of the world not only remembers the past but also nurtures the grudges of the past and passes them on to the next generation.

The postmodern generation has seen the seaminess of American institutions through a series of scandals made all the more sensational by the late-twentieth-century approach to journalism, a scandal in its own right. This attitude toward institutions relates to a rejection of both ideology and authority. Are students still interested in the unending ideologies spawned by professors? Postmodern philosophers will often speak of ideology as the *metanarrative,* the grand story that makes sense of life. The postmodern generation has no story. It has no way to belong. In a sense it did not reject its story so much as it never heard its story. Raised as they were, these people were isolated from hearing the story that could invite them to belong to something bigger than themselves.

Rejection of the metanarrative also relates to the personally centered nature of postmodern thought. For me to accept a metanarrative would be to acknowledge that something bigger than me has a claim upon me. It would inhibit me. Can a society exist without cement to hold it together? Can people survive individually if nothing binds them to others? The philosophy of postmodernity is not simply a philosophical issue. It is also a sociological and a psychological issue, and it has implications for anthropology, economics, marketing, language study, political science, and education. The rejection of ideology and authority is not a characteristic of a culture so much as it is a symptom of a vacuum. Something will arise to fill the void. People will find something to believe in that will bind them together. It happened in the cultural chaos of Germany in the 1920s and 1930s. In that case, a dark and sinister force arose that bound the people together. Something will always arise to fill the void, but it need not be dark and sinister. In this context of confusion and searching for an idea to make sense of the world, what is the responsibility of a Christian in higher education? In the marketplace of ideas, is it ethical to withhold an idea that has had such a profound impact on the world for two thousand years?

Epistemologically Confused

For the postmodern person, rationalism (the acquisition of knowledge through mental deduction) and empiricism (the acquisition of knowledge through sensory perception) are both ideologies. Rationalism and empiricism no longer have privileged status in a postmodern context, any more than Christianity has privileged status in the modern state. Much of the West's great success in the last five hundred years, at least in its acquisition of knowledge, has depended on the recognition of certain norms of thought. We speak of these norms as the *rules of logic*. Francis Bacon proposed that a method of inquiry using careful observation guided by the norms of thought would lead to more fruitful discoveries and advances in knowledge. We refer to his approach as the *scientific method,* and it has been highly successful.

What would happen to advances in knowledge if the rules of logic were ignored? Essentially, postmodern thinkers have put this situation in place with varying degrees of emphasis. Some people successfully compartmentalize their lives into areas where logical consistency is followed and other areas where it is not. Others simply follow the old maxim that "consistency is the hobgoblin of little minds."[17] In conferences I have attended over the last few years, I have heard a growing concern among older scientists that research by younger scientists is beginning to show a disregard for method. Other issues, whether political or social, have also begun to influence the findings. If true, this would bode ill for the quality of research being undertaken in a postmodern context.

What might we expect of higher education when professors in one department teach their students that there are no binding rules of logic while teachers in other departments teach their students that knowledge depends on logic? Who decides? Which department owns the field of epistemology? Shall the philosophy department inform the others? Who has a stake in the discussion, and where does the discussion take place?

When these two ways of knowing have been treated as ideologies rather than methodologies, the postmodern rejection of empiricism and rationalism as ideologies has a legitimate basis. Taken together, they have often been embraced as a semireligious cult that excluded any other way of knowing. In their ideological manifestation, empiricism and rationalism view the universe as purely physical or natural. The ideology of empiricism and rationalism has no place for a god or even for a human spiritual dimension. In rejecting this ideological aspect of empiricism and rationalism, the postmodern generation has opened the door to something else. They have not named that something else, but they have embraced the intuitive way of knowing that tells them that there is something else.

The question of what can be known and how it can be known is a question that every discipline has a stake in answering. It is a profoundly religious question without ever posing the question of the existence of God.

Spiritually Impoverished

The rejection of absolute values is the aspect of postmodern thought that has attracted the attention of most conservative Christian commentators. More disturbing for the conservatives, perhaps, is that evangelical Christians have embraced the same relativism as have their secular neighbors. Born-again college students are just as likely to jump into bed for sex without marriage as their pagan dorm mates, although some recent studies suggest that the young have grown weary of indifferent sex. It is difficult to go against cultural norms when almost every institution that has accepted the responsibility for shaping the culture (cable television, rap music, comic books, the daily funny paper, Hollywood) teaches children and grownups alike that normal people have casual sex all the time. It is also easy to lose sight of the fact that the question of absolute values involves more than sex, alcohol, and drugs.

Legalism ignores the reality that many cultural values actually are relative, but relativism ignores the reality that some values apply to all cultures. These transcendent values are what C. S. Lewis referred to as the *Tao*. The recognition of these transcultural values leads some people to conclude that all religions are the same. Is the rejection of universal absolutes a permanent feature of culture for the next epoch, or is it a sign that people have merely rejected the superficial dimensions of their consumer culture? For years social commentators lamented the absence of heroes for children. Then, quite unexpectedly in the last five years of the twentieth century, children found a hero. He was a hero who was only accessible to children who read. Because of him, millions upon millions of children began to read.

Harry Potter truly proved to be a powerful wizard to draw children away from their technological baby-sitters. This character goes against the grain. He is not postmodern. Harry Potter is actually quite old-fashioned. He is complex to the extent that he is self-aware; he knows his own failings. Good and evil have real meaning in the Harry Potter books, but one need not look at a monster like Lord Voldemort to understand evil. Harry Potter experiences it every day from an abusive aunt and uncle, from a selfish schoolmate, from an unjust teacher. Harry Potter offers children a glimpse of a world in which old people are respected, even though not all old people can be trusted. His world is one in which some rules are meant to be broken, but the truth is worth dying for. The absolutes stand. Why would young people into their twenties (and older) embrace such a series of books?

If the postmodern generation has rejected anything, it is the reductionist materialism of the modern world. In such a world, people were merely cogs within the great machine. It was easy to get lost. The values that served the state or the company did not ultimately nurture the individual. Postmodern people discovered that they still had a spiritual dimension after all. They discovered that they are religious beings, but they do not know what that means. Some pursue it while others do not. Whether or not they want to pursue their own spirituality, postmodern people have grown quite curious about the question. They have settled the question that something bigger is out there somewhere, or perhaps in there somewhere; they are not quite sure which. They do not know what kind of god exists, or even if one should use the word *god*, but they know that the modernists were wrong. The postmodern world has proved Freud wrong in his idea of religion as the projection of a father figure on the universe. When postmodern people perceive the spiritual behind the universe, they do not project an authority figure on it. They want something beyond their lives, but they want no authority figure to whom they might be accountable.

Whereas the modern world managed to segment and fragment all of life into carefully distinguishable piles, the postmodern generation yearns to have their lives pulled back together. A modern Christian was content to be Christian on Sunday and just before eating the evening meal, unless it was at a public restaurant. Postmodern people, however, realize that all of life involves the spiritual and that the material and the spiritual cannot be so easily separated. The Book of Hebrews suggests that only the eternal Logos himself can separate the spirit from the total soul (Heb. 4:12). The postmodern generation yearns to recover a part of what it means to be human. They will find something to fill the void, but will Jesus Christ be one of the options open to them?

Because the spiritual cannot be separated from the material, every discipline of the academy deals with spiritual issues. What does a Christian do about it? When spiritual issues arise in the course of study, does the Christian examine every option available except the Christian position? Does the Christian continue to ignore the spiritual dimension of his or her discipline while the professor with another worldview engages the subject two doors down the hall? It is foolish to suggest that religion will not be discussed in the classrooms of higher education in America. It only remains to determine who will discuss it and how it will be discussed.

Conclusion

The postmodern mind-set of students presents many challenges for teachers in American colleges and universities today, without ever bringing up the issue of faith. It is impossible, however, to understand the postmodern phenomenon apart from its spiritual dynamics. Such thinkers as Derrida and Foucault have presented an intellectual framework for postmodern thought, but it would be a mistake to confuse the philosophy of postmodernism with the cultural phenomenon of postmodernity. Postmodern philosophy lends an air of respectability to what would otherwise be merely a great and plaintive plea.

We have entered a period of great soul-searching for the academic community, where preoccupations may have tended dangerously toward the mundane in the past. Professors may have the greatest opportunity of the last five hundred years to shape the future. Modernity's answers to life's persistent questions have begun to fail. The person who can engage the new generation creatively with alternative answers that fit may help to shape whatever culture does finally emerge from modernity. Though the West has dominated the globe these last five hundred years, we would be ill advised to presume that this monopoly will continue.

The Islamic world has made its dissent known. As I write these words, China has announced its new initiatives in space travel. These two great cultures are moving in opposite directions as Christians encounter new persecutions in the Islamic world. Yet China has been quietly relaxing its old Maoist attempt to eradicate religion and by some accounts has as many as 100 million Christian converts since 1980. Neither of these situations allows much room for the self-indulgent brand of postmodernism enjoyed in the suburbs of North America. But children from these homes are the ones going to college. It is important for them to understand why 100 million Chinese would convert to Christianity when it offers no obvious social or financial advantage. It is also important for them to understand why Islam so vigorously opposes Christianity within the countries it controls. These are the factors that will be of greatest significance in shaping the new age that follows modernity. If American students have not been exposed to the spiritual and religious dynamics at play, they will be totally unprepared for life in the emerging global community.

Further Reading

A great deal has been written on this subject in recent years. These three books, however, deal with postmodernity in a way that relates to a Christian understanding of culture and higher education:

Dockery, David S., ed. *The Challenge of Postmodernism: An Evangelical Engagement.* 2d ed. Grand Rapids: Baker, 2001.

Poe, Harry Lee. *Christian Witness in a Postmodern World.* Nashville: Abingdon, 2001.

Willimon, William, and Thomas H. Naylor. *The Abandoned Generation: Rethinking Higher Education.* Grand Rapids: Eerdmans, 1995.

5

A Christian Worldview

When someone speaks of the integration of faith and learning, or teaching from a faith perspective, or teaching and scholarship that are informed by faith, what is the faith we intend to integrate? What is it that we bring to the table when we talk about faith in the academy? What was it about the work of Copernicus, Descartes, Galileo, Kepler, or Pascal that made it "Christian"? And, how can we speak of Galileo and Pascal as Christian scholars when they were opposed by powerful forces within the religious establishment?

Arnold Toynbee began his massive study of history and civilization while thinking that religion was an ornament of culture. Somewhat like Marx, although not a Marxist, Toynbee had the idea that religion is something the culture uses to keep people in line. It served as a "mere" ritual to celebrate the culture. He concluded his study many years later, deciding that religion is in fact the essence of culture, that it carries culture, that it is the most important feature of culture, and that it survives culture after culture has collapsed.[1] People are religious.

When we talk about faith from a Christian perspective, we do not simply mean the idea of spirituality or religion, or even of faith in general, but a very specific faith. We mean faith in Jesus Christ. We sometimes call the content of this faith in Christ *the gospel*. During the modern period, the gospel has suffered from fragmentation, just as the rest of society suffered from fragmentation. We can see this tendency in how the church has fragmented denominationally. In simplistic terms, people have taken the aspect of the gospel that most appealed

93

to them and then elevated it above other aspects of the gospel, to the point that different aspects of the gospel seemed to conflict. This tendency made the articles of a common faith a reason to separate from other Christians. This tendency to isolate, distinguish, and separate, which became so critical to modern thinking, led to the rise of denominationalism.

We can also observe this tendency of fragmentation in theology and practice. For instance, in the twentieth century evangelism and piety became fragmented from social action and involvement. It appeared as though these different dimensions of faith represented antithetical ideas, somehow at war with one another. True Christians would be expected to do one and not the other, depending on which camp they had joined.

In modern times, we have also seen the theological fragmentation of groups oriented around a particular systematic theological position. For example, we can think of the camps in terms of theological systems: the Calvinists, the Arminians, the dispensationalists, or the neo-orthodox. We may also divide the camps along broad party lines, such as Protestant, Catholic, and Orthodox. We could even consider the camps within each broader alliance, such as the divisions within Protestantism that would include mainline, evangelical, fundamentalist, charismatic, and pentecostal. There are so many different ways to carve up the family of Christ. And we do the carving.

Within the academy, any successful dialogue that involves the Christian faith needs to be carried out from the perspective of what C. S. Lewis called "mere Christianity." By successful, I do not mean instantaneous conversion, but simply the idea that other people are interested enough in what we have to say to carry on a normal conversation. By mere Christianity, Lewis meant the essential faith that all these different fragmented groups would agree upon, and in fact *do* agree upon when we allow ourselves.[2] It may be helpful to think of how we approach children when we talk about faith. I remember the great conversations I had as a child: for example, "Mama, who made the sky?" "God made the sky." It was the simplest of theological statements and expressed an essential aspect of Christian faith. It tells us something about God and something about the universe. If true, it has implications for every realm of knowledge.

In thinking about how faith informs the work of scholarship, however, we sometimes have complicated it within our own Christian communities. Through a series of overlays of culture, tradition, philosophy, and systematic theology, we bring more to the table than is appropriate in a basic conversation with believers or unbelievers. Even when engaged in written or spoken dialogue with highly educated scholars within the academy, we contribute to misunderstanding by making the faith dimension overly technical. When we bring faith into the conversation, we make the conversation interdisciplinary. Each discipline has its own technical language that depends on specialization; hence, when interdisciplinary conversation occurs, each participant becomes a pedestrian with respect to the "other" discipline. When a discipline utilizes a philosophical assumption within its field of study or methodology, it has become interdisciplinary to the extent that it has relied upon a discipline outside of itself. In other words, when a discipline borrows from the methodology or knowledge base of another discipline, it has become interdisciplinary. To a certain extent, examining the relationship between faith and scholarship will provide insight into how scholars already go about assimilating perspectives they have never hitherto recognized or acknowledged.

Think of how the Christian faith arose. Originally an event took place. It may have been the creation of the universe, it may have been the birth of a baby in Bethlehem, or it may have been a trial and an execution in Jerusalem. People repeated the story of the events. Eventually people recorded the oral account for others to read after them. In Scripture we find the story of what happened. The Gospels relate the story of Christ, but not just the event; we also find the meaning of the event. The meaning sets the Gospels apart from ordinary biography. They represent a theological interpretation of the meaning of the event: not simply that Jesus Christ died on a cross, but also that Jesus Christ died on a cross for our sins.

Understanding the meaning of the events represents a key feature of the Gospels. Jesus taught about the significance of who he was and what he did in terms of fulfilling God's dealings with the people of Israel up to that point. When Jesus came to the disciples that first Easter evening, he said to them, "This is what I told you while I was still with you: Everything must be fulfilled that is written about me in the Law of Moses, the Prophets, and the Psalms" (Luke 24:44 NIV). Throughout the Gospels Jesus spoke about the idea of fulfillment. He did not represent himself as starting a new religion. Instead, he insisted upon the continuity between his activity and all that God had done from the creation of the world:

> Then he opened their minds so that they could understand the Scriptures. He told them, "This is what is written: The Christ will suffer and rise from the dead on the third day, and repentance and forgiveness of sins will be preached in his name to all nations, beginning at Jerusalem. You are witnesses of these things. I am going to send you what my Father has promised; but stay in the city until you have been clothed with power from on high." (Luke 24:45–49 NIV)

Here Jesus expounds the fulfillment of all that God had foretold: the crucifixion, the resurrection, and the promise of the Holy Spirit. What Luke makes clear is that during the resurrection appearances, Jesus devoted himself to explaining to the disciples the meaning of the events surrounding him. This teaching came to be the gospel, the good news.

The New Testament contains numerous passages that refer to the gospel and its implications. A familiar passage found in Paul's writings discusses these basic events and what they mean: "For what I received I passed on to you as of first importance: that Christ died for our sins according to the Scriptures, that he was buried, that he was raised on the third day according to the Scriptures" (1 Cor. 15:3–4 NIV). In this passage, however, Paul does not exhaust what he means by "the gospel." In other places he would insist that the gospel includes the return of Christ (Rom. 2:16). In fact, in the New Testament we do not find a systematic statement of the essential gospel. We find the apostles talking about it in a number of places, but it is not presented comprehensively as a list.[3]

From Gospel to Creeds

Over time, Christians began to formulate a list of beliefs. This Western tendency toward systematizing, categorizing, and cataloging entered Christian theology at an early stage. In the generation after the apostles had died, the early church began to write these things down. Ignatius, in his *Letter to the Trallians* 9.1–2, said:

> Be deaf, then, whenever anyone speaks to you apart from Jesus Christ, who was of the family of David, who was the son of Mary; who really was born, who both ate and drank; who really was persecuted under Pontius Pilate, who really was crucified and died while those in heaven and on earth and under the earth looked on [cf. Phil. 2:10]; . . . who, moreover, really was raised from the dead when his Father raised him up, who—his Father, that is—in the same way will likewise also raise us up in Christ Jesus who believe in him, apart from whom we have no true life [cf. 1 Cor. 13:12–20; Rom. 8:11].[4]

Gnostic

In this passage, Ignatius refers to elements of the gospel that were in conflict with the growing heresies of Gnosticism and Docetism, which denied a true incarnation—Christ only seemed to be human. These heresies held that Christ did not really die because he was not really of the flesh, and thus he was not raised from the dead because he did not die. Each aspect of the gospel, therefore, had importance for every other aspect in explaining who Christ is and what he means to the human race.

As heresies began to grow, the Christian leaders increasingly systematized statements about the gospel. From early on, Christians were concerned with having a clear understanding of the gospel in order to withstand heresy (cf. Gal. 1:6–9; 1 John 4:1–3; Jude 3–4; 2 Peter 2:1–3). Irenaeus took up this theme in his treatise *Against Heresies* (circa 185). Speaking of the faith of the church, he said:

> [She believes] in one God, the Father Almighty, Maker of heaven, and earth, and the sea, and all things that are in them; and in one Christ Jesus, the Son of God, who became incarnate for our salvation; and in the Holy Spirit, who proclaimed through the prophets the dispensations of God, and the advents, and the birth from a virgin, and the passion, and the resurrection from the dead, and the ascension into heaven in the flesh of the beloved Christ Jesus, our Lord, and His [future] manifestation from heaven in the glory of the Father "to gather all things in one," and to raise up anew all flesh of the whole human race, in order that to Christ Jesus, our Lord, and God, and Saviour, and King, according to the will of the invisible Father, "every knee should bow, of things in heaven, and things in earth, and things under the earth, and that every tongue should confess" to Him, and that He should execute just judgment towards all.[5]

Later in the second century, Tertullian wrote similar words in his *Prescription against Heretics* (circa 200):

> Now, with regard to this rule of faith—that we may from this point acknowledge what it is which we defend—it is, you must know, that which prescribes the belief that there is one only God, and that He is none other than the Creator of the world, who produced all things out of nothing through His own Word, first of all sent forth; that this Word is called His Son, *and*, under the name of God, was seen "in diverse manners" by the patriarchs, heard at all times in the prophets, at last brought down by the Spirit and Power of the Father into the Virgin Mary, was made flesh in her womb, and, being born of her, went forth as Jesus Christ; thenceforth He preached the new law and the new promise of the kingdom of heaven, worked miracles; having been crucified, He rose again the third day; (then) having ascended into the heavens, He sat at the right hand of the Father; sent instead of Himself the Power of the Holy Ghost to lead such as believe; will come with glory to take the saints to the enjoyment of everlasting life and of the heavenly promises, and to condemn the wicked to everlasting fire, after the resurrection of both these classes shall have happened, together with the restoration of their flesh. This rule, as it will be proved, was taught by Christ, and raises amongst ourselves no other questions than those which heresies introduce, and which make men heretics.[6]

We see in the writings of the early Christian leaders that, largely in response to heresies, the church increasingly systematized the gospel to preserve the meaning of Christ's life and death and resurrection. This process eventually resulted in what came to be called the *creeds*, from the Latin verb *credo* (I believe). The creeds were simple statements of essential faith that Christians recited together in worship. In their simplest and earliest forms as aspects of worship, the creeds were spoken as baptismal confessions by those who embraced Christ. The Apostles' Creed, though not adopted in its final form by the church in the West until the eighth century, has its origins in the kinds of statements made by Irenaeus and Tertullian.

The Apostles' Creed

I believe in God the Father Almighty, Maker of heaven and earth;
and in Jesus Christ his only Son, our Lord,
>   who was conceived by the Holy Ghost,
>   born of the virgin Mary,
>   suffered under Pontius Pilate,
>   was crucified, dead, and buried.
>   He descended into hell.
>   The third day he rose again from the dead.
>   He ascended into heaven and sitteth on the right hand of God the
>   Father Almighty.
>   From thence he shall come to judge the quick and the dead.
I believe in the Holy Ghost,
>   the holy catholic church,
>   the communion of saints,
>   the forgiveness of sins,
>   the resurrection of the body,
>   and the life everlasting. Amen.

The Nicene Creed, though adopted by the Council of Nicaea in 325, did not reach its final form until after 858.[7]

The Nicene Creed

I believe in one God, the Father Almighty, Maker of heaven and earth,
>   and of all things visible and invisible;
and in one Lord Jesus Christ, the only-begotten Son of God,
>   begotten of his Father before all worlds,
>   God of God, Light of Light,
>   very God of very God,
>   begotten, not made, being of one substance with the Father,
>   by whom all things were made;
>   who for us men and for our salvation came down from heaven,
>   and was incarnate by the Holy Ghost of the Virgin Mary,

and was made man,
and was crucified also for us under Pontus Pilate;
he suffered and was buried;
and the third day he rose again according to the Scriptures,
and ascended into heaven, and is seated on the right hand of the
    Father;
and he shall come again, with glory, to judge both the quick and the
    dead;
whose kingdom shall have no end.
And I believe in the Holy Ghost, the Lord and Giver of life,
who proceedeth from the Father and the Son,
who with the Father and the Son together is worshiped and
    glorified,
who spake by the prophets.
And I believe in one holy catholic and apostolic church. I acknowledge
    one baptism for the remission of sins,
and I look for the resurrection of the dead,
and the life of the world to come. Amen.

As is evident from the statement by Irenaeus, the composition of the Apostles' Creed precedes that of the Nicene Creed. Comparing the creeds, we notice that the later creed has doubled in length while retaining the same basic affirmations.

In the formulation of the creeds, the early Christians began with a simple statement and increasingly qualified, explained, and interpreted it as different heresies arose. The simple Apostles' Creed is a fairly straightforward account of the event and what it means, without any elaboration or explanation of the implications of the events. The simplest creed contains no theories of the atonement or of the incarnation. It takes no stand on the nature or timing of the return of Christ. It has no opinion about a young earth or an old earth. It is silent on the matter of speaking in tongues.

From the creeds and their expansion, it is a short step to systematic theology. Over the centuries Christian theologians have increasingly elaborated, qualified, modified, explained, and speculated on these simple statements and affirmations of the gospel. The meaning of the events, however, goes far beyond the events themselves. The elaboration of the meaning and implications of the gospel have led to long, systematic treatises on the various affirmations of the gospel until we have such massive works as Karl Barth's multivolume systematic theology, *Church Dogmatics*. It is both exhaustive and exhausting. Unfortunately, our tendency has been to proclaim our systematic theology rather than to go back to the simple statements of the gospel to see what implications those statements might have for us and for other people.

The very reason theologians have developed different systems over the last two thousand years is because they are addressing new questions that new generations ask. Augustine, informed by the philosophy of Plato, developed one kind of system. A thousand years later Thomas Aquinas, informed by the philosophy of Aristotle, developed an entirely different kind of system. Though their systems move in two entirely different directions, both of them proceeded from the simple affirmation that they "believe in one God, the Father Almighty, maker of heaven and earth." Creeds are a mechanical means of enforcing orthodoxy, but they tend to ignore spirituality and practice. Mere recitation of the creed cannot keep the church orthodox. The creeds are always open to new interpretations or distortions.

From Creeds to Doctrines

What does the gospel have to do with academic disciplines? As I suggested, systematic theology grows out of the simple gospel. Each element of the gospel has formed the basis for the development of full-blown doctrines, the teachings of the church. Oddly enough, people with different systematic theologies will agree that there is a doctrine of creation. A process theologian and a Reformed theologian will have radically different understandings of the content of the doctrine of creation, but they will both agree that there is a doctrine of creation. The concern expressed by Christ for the fulfillment of the Law and the Prophets has grown into the doctrine of revelation and the doctrine of inspiration. Likewise, a full-blown Augustinian and a full-blown neo-orthodox theologian will have radically different understandings of how revelation occurs, as well as the meaning of the doctrine of revelation, yet they will both agree that there is a doctrine of revelation. They agree that an essential aspect of Christianity involves a teaching about revelation. This teaching involves the consideration of what it means for God to communicate with people. It asks if God is capable of communicating with people, and it asks if people have the capacity to receive communication from God. This issue of revelation relates to the issue of what kind of God exists: Is God a self-conscious personality who can communicate with people? The doctrine of incarnation and the doctrine of Christology relate to the idea that we believe in Jesus Christ, God's only Son, our Lord, who was conceived by the Holy Ghost and born of the Virgin Mary. All of the doctrines are based on simple statements.

We might also observe how these doctrines enter the worshiping church. The hymnals of most churches (where hymnals are still used) have an index that builds around these basic ideas. The same basic statements that might be found in the creeds also appear in the hymnals as a basis for organizing the topics of Christian hymns. Typically, a hymnal will arrange hymns as they relate to God the Father, God the Son, and God the Holy Spirit, followed by hymns related to the benefits of salvation, the individual's relationship to God, and the corporate relationship of the church to God. Within these broad categories, the aspects of the creeds become more evident. In the 1916 revision of *The Hymnal* of the Protestant Episcopal Church in the United States (pub. 1920), hymns are arranged according to the Christian year, which in turn gives a chronological order to the affirmations of the creeds.[8] Even within a denominational group like Southern Baptists, which does not use creeds in worship or follow the Christian year, the hymnal reflects common matters of faith. Under the heading "Jesus Christ the Son," the *Baptist Hymnal* (1956) lists hymns related to Jesus' birth, life, suffering and death, resurrection and exaltation, and return. And so the worshiping church orders its worship around these basic ideas.[9]

Jesus' death for our sins is the basis for the doctrine of the atonement, although there are many different understandings of how the atonement works. Some say that the atonement has to do with redemption. Some say that it has to do with purification, or cleansing. Some say it has to do with forgiveness. Some say it has to do with the expression of God's love. Different Christian theologians have arrived at various understandings of what the atonement means. Most have found the basis for their view in Scripture. In our modern approach to systematic theology, we have been quite reductionistic. That is, we tend to reduce the atonement to one thing rather than accept the possibility that it may mean a number of different things all at the same time. In explaining his understanding of the atonement, or what it means that Christ died for our sins, C. S. Lewis observed, "Such is my own way of looking at what Christians call the Atonement. But remember this is only one more picture. Do not mistake it for the thing itself: and if it does not help you, drop it."[10] In fact, each doctrine has many "pictures," or implications, none of which can completely express what it means.

With the exaltation of Christ to the right hand of the Father we find the doctrine of ecclesiology. That is, the church itself is based on the fact that there is an exalted Lord at the right hand of God the Father who is the head of the church and who, through the Holy Spirit (and thus the doctrine of pneumatology), indwells the church, guides the church, teaches the church, and empowers the church. The exalted Lord Jesus Christ and his Father have a dynamic relationship with each other and with the Holy Spirit, through whom they are active in the world today.

Thus, the doctrine of the Trinity exists as an implication of the other affirmations of the creeds.

The return for judgment, or the second coming, forms the basis for the doctrine of eschatology (from the Greek *eschaton,* meaning "last things"). The *eschaton* is the point toward which everything is moving. There are many different eschatologies. There is realized eschatology, the idea that all the fullness of God and Christ and the Holy Spirit is present now. It is through the church that Christ is realizing the kingdom. The kingdom will grow as leaven filters through dough. There is also dispensational eschatology, which claims that there will be a "rapture" (ascension) of the church and a period of tribulation before a final coming of the Lord in power. Eschatology may also be understood in terms of whether Christ returns before (premillennialism) or after (postmillennialism) the establishment of the kingdom. Another view argues that Christ will return, but there will be no literal kingdom (amillennialism). In other words, there are many different approaches to eschatology, but all agree that there is a doctrine of eschatology.

From Doctrines to Divisions

If we move beyond doctrines, we find a more complicated situation. Each of the basic elements of the gospel forms the basis for doctrines. Over the last two thousand years different theologians, groups of people, and movements have oriented themselves around one doctrine or another. They may all affirm every doctrine, but the stack pole around which they order themselves, organize themselves, and which becomes the driving issue for them, will vary from group to group.[11] From time to time, Christians have divided over issues of interpretation related to different doctrines. The Roman Church and the Eastern Orthodox Church separated over whether the Holy Spirit proceeds from the Father or from the Father and the Son. The Protestant Church separated from the Roman Church largely over differences about the final authority (the role of Scripture, Christ, the Holy Spirit, human leaders, and tradition) for determining right doctrine.

Even in ancient times the creeds were not developed until some great controversy had arisen that required the churches to speak authoritatively about the content of their faith. Only when Christians believe that some departure from right doctrine has occurred do they feel compelled to establish a formal statement to correct the error. During the first three hundred years of Christianity, a period of frequent persecutions, the church had little leisure for the kind of speculative theology that breeds heresy. The churches dealt with Montanists and

Donatists as well as with Gnostics and Docetists, but the creeds affirmed by all churches did not begin to arise until after Constantine granted Christianity his protection. The Council of Nicaea (325) dealt with the deity of Christ and resulted in the Nicene Creed. The Council of Chalcedon (451) dealt with the human and divine nature of Christ and resulted in the Chalcedonian formulation. During times of theological dispute, Christians have met to define once again what they believe. In so doing, they have drawn the lines that separate people who have believed different things about the gospel. The Lutherans who separated from Rome drew up the Augsburg Confession. When the Church of England separated from the Church of Rome after the death of Queen Mary, they drew up the Thirty-nine Articles. The Puritans who opposed the Church of England drew up the Westminster Confession. The Baptists who separated from the Church of England drew up the London Confession.

As new issues arose, the process of theological engagement continued into the twentieth century, and it is safe to assume that this process will not cease. At the beginning of the twentieth century a broad coalition of orthodox Protestants issued a collection of essays entitled *The Fundamentals*. As theologians grew entranced with naturalistic interpretations of Scripture, *The Fundamentals* drew attention again to the "fundamentals" of the faith, which the authors identified as the infallibility of Scripture, the virgin birth, the substitutionary atonement, the bodily resurrection, and the imminent return of Christ. Notice that these five fundamentals correspond to articles of the Apostles' Creed, but they do not duplicate all of them. They elaborate only on articles in dispute in the early twentieth century. At that time, not even the more radical element within mainstream Protestantism denied that God the Father Almighty had created heaven and earth. In the present climate, however, even this article finds disputants.

A brief survey will illustrate how during the last two thousand years different questions have arisen over articles of faith, questions that have resulted in major controversies or redirections for Christianity in times of cultural change. During periods of great change, new questions arise in relation to the gospel. We now live in such a period of change. Questions now appear that have never been faced before, merely because of the dramatic growth in knowledge and the proliferation of ideas. The questions may be new, but the gospel itself does not change. Old theological formulations may not address the questions people now ask, but the gospel can be applied, just as it was applied to questions that arose in the past.

The gospel does not answer all of life's questions: for example, Where do I catch the bus? or What is the square root of pi? Neither does the gospel answer all of the questions that arise in the academy. It is important to recognize, however, when the gospel does address a current issue. Faith's most appropriate place in a discipline is where it already is. In other words, questions of faith often arise in the context of an academic discipline. When faith questions arise, it is appropriate to consider the question in light of the gospel. The essential articles of mere Christianity have implications that run the gamut of human experience and relate to many critical issues in the modern academy.

Creator God

The big issue in the conversion of Augustine (circa 386), and then in all of his theology, was the question What kind of God exists? In his *Confessions* Augustine describes the struggle he went through when trying to understand what kind of God exists. The theological system that he developed grows out of his final conversion, in which he understood God to be One, the Creator, the Sovereign over all things. Augustine came to believe that God was always active in his life, leading him along, although he had not known when God was working in the events of his life.

A thousand years later, Thomas Aquinas would also orient his theology around a creator God, but his theology looks entirely different because he was dealing with different questions. He was not concerned with what kind of God exists; he already knew. In the medieval period everyone knew that God was sovereign, that he was the Creator of the heavens and the earth, ordering everything. Aquinas wanted to know what it is possible for us to know because that kind of God exists. He developed an approach to theology that was highly informed by Aristotle's philosophy and essentially became the intellectual basis for the modern period and for the development of modern science. Because a creator God exists, we can know about the world around us and explore it. In fact, in exploring it we are glorifying God and celebrating his creation all the more.

So we find that two different theological systems may have a particular element of the gospel as their stack pole and yet be dealing with quite different questions. In such a case, the resulting systematic theologies will look quite different.

Not all religions believe in a creator God. Not all religions believe in a self-conscious, personal God. The existence of such a God defines what kind of universe exists. If such a God does not exist, then the universe is a vastly different place. A Hindu universe is a vastly different place than a Shinto universe, and both of these are vastly different places than an Islamic universe. None of these are like a Christian universe. In terms of the ultimate questions of life, what kind of God exists is as important as whether or not any God exists.

Does the universe have a purpose? If a creator God exists, then the universe has purpose. If we believe that the Creator exists and refuse to take this information into consideration in our intellectual work, however, in what sense can we say that our work has integrity? Is disbelief more credible and respectable than belief? A discipline of the academy need not address the issue of purpose, but if it does, it has made the conversation a religious conversation. Whether history, physics, biology, or literature, any discipline that raises the issue of purpose has invited faith to take part in the conversation. When a spokesperson from one of these disciplines speaks to the issue, he or she does so not on the basis of a discipline but on the basis of some philosophical or religious belief brought to that discipline.

Questions of absolute values have raged in recent years within the humanities. Different religious and philosophical systems account for values in different ways. Some religious traditions espouse ethical values; others do not. In the Platonic philosophical system, values exist as things in themselves in the ultimate world of ideals. In the Christian system the only absolute values are the opinions of God. People, made in the image of God, have the ability to form opinions for themselves. Their opinions are relative values. Many other views abound, including the perspective that no absolute values exist. It is important to understand, however, that when the question of value has been raised, faith has been invited into the conversation. Those who raise the question of value may intend to exclude faith from the conversation. Whether they will succeed entirely depends on the faithful.

Fulfillment of Scripture

The fulfillment of Scripture represented a major feature of the Christian understanding of reality during the first few centuries after the resurrection. In the second century, Justin Martyr converted to Christianity because he came to realize that the prophets of the Old Testament were greater philosophers than the philosophers of Greece. The philosophers of Greece tried to think their way up to God; the prophets of Israel received illumination and knowledge directly from God. Proof of their philosophy's superiority came in the fulfillment of the word they brought, God's word. The idea of fulfilled prophecy provided a powerful argument for Christianity in the days of the Roman Empire. In the Middle Ages John Wycliffe organized his theology around Scripture as well, but not in terms of the fulfillment of Scripture. Wycliffe focused his concern on scriptural authority. If we know that Scripture comes from God because it was fulfilled, then we know that every word of God must be obeyed, that the church must submit itself to the Scripture, and that the pope is subject to the authority of Scripture. This theme of scriptural authority carries into the Reformation.

For several centuries, philosophers attempted to make a case for the validity of general revelation, or the idea of obtaining knowledge of God through creation. They succeeded so well that confidence in specific revelation began to erode. If the Bible is specific revelation from God, it needs to be taken very seriously. A wide range of views about the Bible may now be found within the church and outside it. Believers and nonbelievers have opinions about it. If God spoke through the prophets and their word came to pass, however, the implications for the knowledge of God and the authority of the Bible are significant.

How one views the Bible depends largely on one's concept of God. All of the major world religions have sacred texts, but not all have specific revelation from their deity. Such religions speak of inspiration or illumination rather than revelation. The attitude toward specific revelation cannot simply be settled by an appeal to a naturalistic epistemology. As soon as one raises the question of the validity of specific revelation, the problem of knowledge has been raised. As soon as a naturalistic epistemology is asserted, the possibility of knowledge through means other than empiricism and rationalism is raised.

Any question of the possibilities of knowledge is an invitation for faith to join the conversation. Those who deny the possibility of religious knowledge do so on the basis of enormous philosophical or religious assumptions. Once the issue is raised, then faith has the responsibility of identifying and distinguishing those assumptions from the discipline of study. The sciences depend on empiricism and rationalism, two ways of knowing that the Christian faith asserts would be highly unlikely except in a created universe. Some religions and philosophies deny the validity of empiricism and rationalism. While Christian faith defends both as gifts of God, any discipline that puts these two forward as the only valid way of knowing has exceeded what these two ways of knowing can confirm or deny. It is not necessary for most disciplines ever to raise the issue of knowledge, but once the issue is raised the conversation has become religious.

Son of God/Son of David

The theme of Jesus as the Son of God and the son of David (the idea of being both truly God and truly human) formed the central issue for Christians following the legalization of Christianity by Constantine.

Athanasius defended the view that God truly came into the world and truly experienced full humanity—and thus fully identifies with us, is sympathetic with us—and on our behalf was crucified. These issues of incarnation (in what sense God came in the flesh) and Christology (in what sense Jesus as Christ is related to God) formed the primary reason for calling the first great church council in Nicaea and the development of the Nicene Creed.

In an entirely different way, the theology of the black church in North America centers on the incarnation. The black church stresses that it is not enough to think a certain way, or to have a correct doctrine; it is important to put the doctrine into practice. That is, the black church seeks to live out or to incarnate the teachings of Christ, particularly with respect to care for others. Because God took concrete, physical action to deal with the plight of humanity, Christians need to do something as well. This attitude has driven the theology of the black church in North America.

Several of the disciplines, especially among the caring professions, the humanities, and the social sciences, operate based on values that affirm the worth and dignity of all people, or at least significant numbers of their guild entertain such ideas. The problem of alienation and the need for reconciliation also filter through many of these disciplines, as do concern for social justice and care for the poor and oppressed. On what foundation can these ideas rest? In a naturalistic world they make no sense. This mass of ideas, so rarely embraced, did not spring full grown like Venus from the sea; they entered the West through the lips of Christ. Whenever these ideas are raised, their foundation is brought into the question.

Christ may be dismissed as merely a great teacher, thus avoiding the supernatural view of faith. This approach, however, only opens the door to question on what grounds his deity is denied. The denial comes not from the discipline but from some religious or philosophical view through which a person views the discipline. I view my discipline through the eyes of faith, but I am aware of it. I have the obligation as a scholar and as a disciple of Christ to recognize the difference between my faith and my discipline. Everyone views his or her discipline through some organizing (or disorganizing) principle. Those who view their discipline through some other lens need to recognize that they hold their organizing principle by faith. Those who hold to naturalism do so by faith. They delude themselves if they think their naturalistic view of Christ is more respectable than my supernaturalistic view of Christ. The question goes back to what kind of God exists and what kind of universe was created. If God can take on human form, what is the underlying rationality of the universe?

Death of Christ

Christ's death for our sins was the central issue for the Celtic church. The Celtic peoples of Ireland, Britain, the Lowlands, and Germany, as well as their Norse kinsmen, practiced cannibalism. They worshiped their gods through sacrificial meals at which they sacrificed their eldest child. (Religious piety also allowed the custom of using a captive from battle as a substitute for the eldest child.) Originally they sacrificed their eldest child and then ate the child during a ceremonial meal with the gods. They believed that the gods inhabited the trees, because the trees were the oldest things around. Hence, they nailed each sacrifice to a tree, slit the sacrifice open, and caught his or her blood in a skull. Celts believed that the gods sought human sacrifice in order to draw the life force from the victim's blood. They believed that the gods entered the dying victim's blood and that participants would gain the power and life force of the gods by drinking the blood and eating the body of the sacrifice.

When monks such as Patrick went to the Celtic lands—not just to Ireland but also to Scotland, England, Belgium, Holland, and Germany—they brought a simple message that the great God who created all things had entered the world and become our sacrifice, and in so doing put sacrifice to an end. Through his sacrifice we received divine power. In a single generation, the Celts of Ireland embraced the new faith. According to the old conversion stories of the Celtic and Norse peoples, the queen typically converted before the king. One can only imagine the power of the motherly impulse upon hearing that the gods who held the Celts in dread had been defeated through Christ's sacrificial death. Celtic mothers no longer had to eat their children. Christ had freed them from that spiritual bondage. Not surprisingly, the death of Christ became the central motif of the Celtic church, and it was from the Celtic church that the Roman Catholic doctrine of transubstantiation developed.

Raised from the Dead

The idea of Christ's resurrection is the primary motif of the Eastern Orthodox Church. Whereas the Western Church places greater emphasis on the death of Christ, the Eastern Church emphasizes the victory of Christ through the resurrection. Likewise, the visual image of the Catholic Church is the crucifix on the altar, with Christ on the cross; the Orthodox Church focuses on the ceiling painting above the altar, depicting the exalted Christ, who now lives and reigns.

The resurrection of Christ calls into question all of the naturalistic presuppositions a person might have about the nature of the physical

is resurrection

world, the cause/effect continuum, and the way that God may relate to the physical world and to human history. It is the most massive intrusion by God into the laws of nature that is imaginable, and the Christian faith stands or falls with it (1 Cor. 15). Yet, it is the least controversial of all the faith affirmations since the first Easter.

The Exaltation

The exaltation of Christ after the resurrection to the throne of God has not had a significant place in modern Western theology, although the idea that Jesus Christ is Lord appears throughout the New Testament as perhaps the most significant theme. Present-tense references to Christ in the New Testament imply the exaltation, and it was the exaltation that was the focus of interest for the martyrs. For those who died for their faith in Christ, the present experience of the exalted Christ was more real than the sufferings of this world. According to their accounts, the martyrs had an awareness of Christ's presence even as they were dying. Heaven had already opened, and they inhabited two places: physically they were still on earth, but spiritually they were already entering the heavenly realm. This experience is first described in the confession of Stephen as he faced death: "'Look,' he said, 'I see heaven open and the Son of Man standing at the right hand of God'" (Acts 7:56 NIV). Present experience of the reality of the exalted Lord Jesus Christ marks the witness of the martyrs as they faced death. This kind of terminology is also in the writings of Dietrich Bonhoeffer in the twentieth century. Compare the writings of the second- and third-century martyrs with Bonhoeffer's *The Cost of Discipleship*. The ancient documents could have been written in the twentieth century, and the twentieth-century document could have been written in the second century.[12]

Gift of the Holy Spirit

The gift of the Holy Spirit marked the fulfillment of God's promise of a new covenant. Jesus made it the topic of conversation with Nicodemus and the woman at the well (John 3:1–21; 4:1–26). Peter made it the focus of his sermon on the day of Pentecost (Acts 2:14–41). The Holy Spirit has also been the subject of great controversy in the church, beginning in Corinth. The split between the Eastern Church and the Western Church occurred in great part because the Western Church altered the creed to add that the Holy Spirit proceeds from the Father *and the Son*. The addition was the insertion of a single Latin word, *filioque* (and the Son). The change was made with the noblest of motives: to combat the Arian heresy that Christ was not divine. The Western Church emphasized the deity of Christ by signifying that the Holy Spirit proceeds from the Son as well as from the Father. The Eastern Church was upset that a council was not called to vote on the alteration. The two churches have been separated ever since. Although the Holy Spirit has been the subject of controversy, the Holy Spirit has also been the source of spiritual awakening and vitality within the church.

Return of Christ

The return of Christ was the focal point of the Montanist movement in the second century. Montanus taught that Christ would return soon, and he encouraged wives to leave their husbands and husbands to leave their wives. The Montanist movement was a major force within the church for four hundred years. Tertullian, one of the most significant and influential theologians of the first thousand years of the church, became a Montanist. From time to time over the last two thousand years, this expectation of the immediate return of Christ has formed the central concern of various groups within the church. Whether it is the dispensational theology of late-nineteenth-century American Protestantism or the effort by the crusaders to restore Palestine to the church in preparation for the return of Christ, people have responded to the simple promise of return in a variety of ways.

Several sciences question whether the universe or life itself has a goal. The question involves determinacy and indeterminacy, uncertainty and predictability, and human freedom. When the questions of the fate of the universe and human destiny are raised, faith has been invited into the conversation. Does anything lie beyond death? For the physicist, the fate of the universe is linked to the problem of the origin of the universe. Calculations about its endless expansion or its ultimate collapse relate to its initial expansion from a finite singularity, the theological implications of which have caused major physicists to reject the big bang theory. A large measure of Albert Einstein's greatness lay in his willingness to admit that his greatest mistake came in imposing Aristotelian philosophy, with its view of an eternal universe without beginning, on his physics. Not many scholars can admit that they have rigged their data to fit their philosophical presuppositions.

Conclusion

The gospel may be simply stated, with much of it tacitly implied among those who believe it, yet its implications go in many complex directions. It is possible to view life from the perspective of any of the gospel's simple affirmations and arrive at quite different life perspectives. It is possible to view life in light of the same aspect of the gospel as someone else yet, because of the issues one might address, develop an entirely different expression of faith. It is possible to develop different teachings about the implications of a single aspect of the gospel. Theologians refer to these teachings as "doctrines."

The simple affirmations of faith have implications for the major issues of life. Theological doctrines arise in the interchange between the gospel of Jesus Christ and the issues of everyday life. The gospel itself never changes. It centers in the person and work of Jesus Christ. Theological doctrine changes because the questions brought to the gospel change. Not all theological doctrine changes, of course, but doctrinal views change as they attempt to answer new questions in light of the gospel.

One narrow slice of doctrine illustrates how this change takes place. Augustine formulated his theology around the central issue involved in his conversion: What kind of God exists? The simple affirmation of the gospel's creator God answered this question for him. Augustine's theology, however, explored the implications of what it means that God has made all things. A thousand years later, Thomas Aquinas formulated an argument for the existence of God based on the order of the universe. The order of the universe was viewed as a self-evident truth. This order must have some origin; therefore, God must exist as the source of order. The problem with this argument is that it assumes a degree of order, meaning, and purpose in the universe that the people of Augustine's day would not have assumed. Society had dramatically changed under the thousand-year influence of Augustine's theology. In the medieval world in which Thomas Aquinas wrote, the average person knew that the universe had order, meaning, and purpose because the Creator exercised sovereignty over all creation. Under the sovereign God, the pope exercised spiritual authority and the emperor exercised political authority. Everyone knew there was order in society, and everyone knew their place within that order. The truth of the doctrine has not changed, but the context in which it is explained has changed radically.

The assumption of order in the universe no longer holds in the twenty-first century, especially in the area of physics with its chaos theory and analysis of the quantum world. As the assumptions of society change, doctrine addresses new questions. In a sense, the current theological scene resembles the era of Augustine fifteen hundred years ago more than it resembles the West in 1900. Once again people are asking what kind of God exists, just as Augustine did. The argument of Thomas Aquinas might be turned on its head. Rather than argue that a Creator must exist because the universe has order and meaning, one might argue that the universe has order and meaning because a Creator exists. As it is, science cannot answer the question of whether the universe has meaning. Several philosophies of science, such as Darwinian naturalism, would argue that the universe and life have no meaning; they just are. It is important to recognize that this view comes not as a result of scientific discovery but as an interdisciplinary conversation with philosophy. As soon as the question of order arises, the conversation has entered the realm of faith. Philosophy has no more legitimate or exclusive claim to the conversation than does theology. Yet the philosophical assumptions through which we view the world often determine what our religious or theological perspective will be.

To the extent that an academic discipline has relied on the prevailing philosophical assumptions of culture or borrowed a philosophical perspective from another discipline, it has moved outside the boundaries of that discipline and into another sphere. Virtually all disciplines involve some kind of philosophical grounding. Within this realm, faith in Christ has as much legitimacy as faith in a philosophical position. Disciplines inevitably raise questions that cannot be answered without engaging in an interdisciplinary conversation. The gospel has implications for these kinds of questions.

It is also important to note that Christians may attach themselves to an interpretation of the gospel or some part of Scripture that is not true. If this brief survey demonstrates anything, it is that Christians are just as susceptible to stubborn attachment to error as anyone else. If Christ had returned every time a theologian had calculated his return, he would have been operating a shuttle service to heaven these many centuries. Humility is the proper posture of one who hopes to live by faith. Arrogance is the vocational hazard of the academy and is no respecter of confessional creed. Christians in past centuries were likely to allow their philosophical perspective to influence their interpretation of Scripture, just as contemporary scholars may now be likely to allow a philosophical perspective to influence their understanding of their discipline. Christians who intend to take their faith seriously in the academy have the responsibility to ensure that they expound mere Christianity, not some old science or philosophy.

Further Reading

The following book explores how the gospel has spoken to the critical life issues of different cultures and generations over the last two thousand years:

Poe, Harry L. *The Gospel and Its Meaning.* Grand Rapids: Zondervan, 1996.

The following books explore how to understand the biblical worldview and its relationship to contemporary culture:

Colson, Charles, and Nancy Pearcey. *How Now Shall We Live?* Wheaton, Ill.: Tyndale, 1999.

Walsh, Brian J., and J. Richard Middleton. *The Transforming Vision: Shaping a Christian World View.* Downers Grove, Ill.: InterVarsity, 1984.

6

The Doctrines
and the Disciplines

T hose who spend too much time in the academy may develop a tendency toward the negative. Eventually, through practice, it becomes possible to see the dark cloud behind any silver lining. One develops the skill to see something wrong with every administrative decision made by the institution. One can easily imagine a modern version of the story Jesus told about the Pharisee and the tax collector who went up to pray. Does the professor ever raise the eyes toward heaven and cry, "Thank God I am not a sinner like this academic administrator"?

The ability to notice flaws, however, lies at the heart of critical thought, scholarship, and the quest for new knowledge. Sometimes the ability to recognize that the emperor has no clothes is the very skill needed before the emperor will take action to clothe himself. Some have the critical skill to recognize that a problem exists, and others have the creative skill to suggest answers that will, in turn, be put to the test. Some have the ability to recognize a work of fiction as a piece of tripe; others have the ability to write *The Sound and the Fury* or *The Grapes of Wrath*. Faulkner and Steinbeck did one kind of thing; members of the English department do another sort of thing. One creates and another critiques. Yet because they share a common subject, the two spheres of knowledge have a unique relationship. Though they approach the subject from two entirely different perspectives, they still have points of contact. In fact, many great writers also have the gift of great criticism. Edgar Allan Poe was as noted a literary critic in his day as he was a poet and short-story writer. In this day of academic turf and credentialing, however, many of the major contemporary writers who hold academic posts as writers in residence at major schools are looked down upon by those within the English department who hold a doctor of philosophy degree. Somewhere at the heart of academic life lies a massive sense of insecurity.

One perfectly reasonable objection to the idea of religion creeping into other subjects is that religion has its own department within the academy. It ought to stay put and not encroach on the turf of other departments. This legitimate objection safeguards the methodologies and content of the various disciplines. A justifiable fear exists that the interposition of religion into a curriculum would endanger the body of knowledge and skills of a discipline. What do we do, however, when two disciplines overlap? Do we ignore the common ground? In many cases within the academy, we do just that.

At this point it may be helpful to fall back on what academics do best: examine flaws. We can begin by expressing the matter as dogmatically as possible: Religion never has anything at all to do with my discipline, under any circumstances whatsoever. All at once my suspicion is aroused. Never? I see flaws in such a dogmatic statement. I can conceive of the possibility that religion has something to do with my discipline; therefore, I desire some qualifiers. I want a less strident statement. In the dialogue between science and religion, Stephen Jay Gould established a reputation for insisting that science and religion belonged to non-overlapping magisteria (NOMA).[1] His very insistence on the point actually advanced the science-religion dialogue because it appeared quite evident to many scientists, theologians, and philosophers that science and religion were concerned with many similar subjects, even though they approached the subjects with different questions and different methodologies. It is possible to conceive of some disciplines barely overlapping with religion, while others almost completely share an interest in the same material. In order to discuss the issue, however, we need to borrow the terminology and imagery of mathematics, yet another discipline. This phenomenon will be addressed at length in the next chapter.

If we acknowledge that a strident, dogmatic, absolutist statement about the strict demarcation between religion and other disciplines is too strong and reminiscent of a fundamentalist approach to knowledge, we are left with the academic's best friend: questions. If religion is not totally and completely isolated from other disciplines, in what circumstances and in what ways does it relate to other spheres of knowledge? Under what circumstances is it appropriate for the two realms of knowledge to be discussed together in the interest of understanding the discipline under examination? One would suspect that the answers to these questions would be different for almost all disciplines, though there may be similarities and patterns.

The Academic Disciplines' Relationship to Religion

A brief survey of many of the adademy's most common disciplines, which might have their own freestanding departments in a college or university, will illustrate how religion overlaps other realms of knowledge.

Art

Art involves the creative imagination of people, specifically their ability to express themselves through some physical medium. Painting and sculpture are two of the most common media for the artist, but the very creativity that demands expression also devises other intriguing forms of expression through everything from textiles to garbage. From the Christian perspective, art is a result of being made in the image of God (*imago dei*). If God is a creator and people are made in the image of God, people must create.

Current artists would probably object to a description of their work that centered solely on the creative expressiveness of art. In the twentieth century, art took on a more intentional prophetic role that involved a critique of society. In this sense the old paradigm of communicating beauty to the audience was replaced for some artists by a paradigm concerned with eliciting a response or making a statement. Art moved away from presenting the world realistically as it is and toward re-presenting the world as the artist sees it, or so the audience might see it in a new way. In other words, during the twentieth century something quite unusual happened with art in the West. This unusual thing applies to literature, dance, drama, and music as much as to visual art. One of the most ancient aspects of culture ceased to function as its preserver and instead began to challenge culture. Art ceased to be what it had always been. Despite its change, however, art continues to mirror its culture as that culture contorts. Todd Pickett, professor of literature at Biola University, has argued that art has as much to do with order and form as with creativity.[2] With its concern for visible patterns and forms, however, the arts still relate primarily to the doctrine of creation and the problem of why we should be able to perceive order and patterns at all. Creativity and order are two different implications of the doctrine of creation.

Biology

Biology involves the study of living organisms, although one could narrow the category to focus only on botany, which studies plant life. Many specializations exist, from microbiology to hybrids like biochemistry, but all share a concern for the phenomenon of life. The doctrine of creation also involves the study of life. As biology examines human life, it deals with the same subject as the *imago dei*. While theology describes how people relate to God, biology describes how people relate to living organisms, plants and animals.

Business Administration

Business administration in all of its subcategories deals with commerce and industry as developed in the modern West. In simplest form, however, it is concerned with livelihood or work. The concept of stewardship of life, time, skills, resources, and other factors that might contribute to livelihood derives from the doctrine of creation. People have certain obligations to the Creator in how they treat each other, nature, and themselves as they go about their business.

The world of business illustrates the tension involved in the relationship between faith and vocation. Walton Padelford, professor of economics at Union University, has observed:

> Human labor is a divinely imposed task. . . . However, the Fall is also reality and here begins the tension between the glory of God reflected in the products of our hands, and the vanity of much of what we do.[3]

Chemistry

Chemistry is concerned with the basic properties of the physical world, particularly the atomic description of the elements and how they relate to one another. Like biology, it deals with the same subject matter as the doctrine of creation.

Communication Arts

Communication arts deals with different dimensions of human communication, including oral and written communication as well as mass communication. As rhetoric it would have formed part of the classical education within Plato's academy in ancient times. Dealing with humans, communication arts shares the subject matter of the *imago dei* as it relates to the doctrine of creation. As creatures made in the image of God, humans share with God the capacity for communication. This capacity for communication also implies another major doctrine, that of revelation. The Bible is understood as revelation from God, God's communication with humans. Just as humans have the capacity to misunderstand communication from other humans, they have the capacity to misunderstand communication from God.

Computer Science

Computer science represents one of the most recent additions to the academy. As such, some members of the academic community struggle to understand it. Some think of it as applied mathematics. Others think of it as a language. Still others regard it as a form of logic. In a sense it can be regarded as all of these and more. Computer science depends on numbers and logic to reflect a reliable degree of order to the universe. This idea of order, which proceeds from the doctrine of creation, assumes that the universe is a rational place where reliable and logical calculations can be made.

Drama

An ancient art form but one that continues to be performed, drama involves the acting out of a story. It represents a highly creative advance in the primitive and universal practice of telling stories. People tell different kinds of stories, some of which will be examined in relation to other disciplines. For drama, however, the fictional story represents the classic art form. As a work of fiction, drama involves the creative imagination of the author who constructs the story. The very idea of human imagination and creativity involves what it means to be made in the image of the creative God. Thus, the doctrine of creation forms the background to this discipline.

Education

Education concerns the process of teaching and learning. Although we usually think of its role in intellectual development, it is concerned with the growth and development of people in many spheres of life. Education examines the roles of humans as teachers and as learners. People's capacity for both of these activities reflects the doctrine of creation. As creatures, we were made in such a way that we can learn. As creatures made in the image of God, we have the ability to teach. This whole enterprise also implies purpose, another quality derived from the concept of the Creator, who made the universe for a purpose. Education implies a goal or object of growth and suggests that human growth and development are part of God's plan for people. This idea relates to the doctrine of eschatology.

English

As a discipline or department within the modern academy, English is both old and new. Grammar and the study of literature date back to Plato's academy, but the study of contemporary literature is a modern phenomenon. Like drama, literature is concerned with storytelling. The telling and hearing of stories seem to be a universal human need. Storytelling involves creative imagination and the need to communicate. It involves the doctrines of creation and revelation played out in creatures made in the image of God who create and express themselves.

Don King, professor of English at Montreat College and editor of *Christian Scholar's Review,* reflects on the relationship between his discipline and his faith:

> Human language itself is a reflection of our divine connectedness, the *imago dei*; put another way, that we have language and use language and enjoy language intimately and irrevocably links us to God. On the one hand, God used language, or *logos,* to create the natural world, and on the other hand, he sent his *Logos,* his Word, his Son to us. One part of my task, then, is to explore and discover with my students how language, and by extension literature, participates in the revelation of God's natural creation as well as his revelation of his own character in the life of Christ.[4]

History

History represents another form of storytelling. Through history, humans tell the story of who they are through past events. It involves not only the narrative of the events but also an interpretation of the significance of those events. In history, people form the primary object of study. History examines what people have done and often seeks to understand why they have done it. History strives to make sense of triumphs and disasters. The Christian perspective of history relates to the doctrine of eschatology in that the Christian faith teaches that history has a direction. It is moving toward a grand conclusion according to the will, purpose, and knowledge of God. Although a broad range of theological descriptions of God's relationship to history have been offered by orthodox Christians, they all agree that the goal of history is the kingdom of God. With this understanding in mind, history also relates to the doctrine of God as it specifically involves the sovereignty of God.

Languages

Languages within the academy involve the study of discrete communication systems by different people groups. Both modern spoken languages and ancient "dead" languages form part of the modern academy. Language is the means by which people make their thoughts and emotions known to others in a rational, logical pattern of communication. Language study shares certain common elements with communication arts, drama, and English. The different languages of peoples illustrate the compounding problem of human communication. While language study relates to the doctrines of creation and revelation, it also dramatically illustrates the problem of human alienation embodied in the doctrine of sin.

Mathematics

Mathematics also formed part of the ancient curriculum of classical education. Like computer science, it is concerned with order. Whether the order actually exists in the universe, in the sense that numbers have independent existence, or merely exists in the human mind as a mental construct, does not alter the issue of order. In either case, order involves the doctrine of creation and the *imago dei*. Humans have the kind of minds that allow them to recognize the patterns and organize the data of the universe in such a way that they may be understood as orderly.

Music

Music formed another aspect of the ancient classical curriculum. It involves the same capacity for creative imagination found in art and storytelling, but music adds an abstract dimension not unlike the creativity involved in recognizing the numerical patterns of the universe. Like languages and communication arts, it also involves self-expression or revelation. Hence, music is related to the doctrine of creation and what it means to be made in the image of God.

Nursing

Like biology, nursing has a concern for living organisms. It focuses its concern, however, specifically on humans. Unlike biology, nursing does not maintain a detached indifference to its concern. Nursing actually cares about humans as something other than an object of study. Nursing exists to relieve suffering and aid the healing of sick people. It shares with other disciplines the doctrine of creation, but to this it adds the doctrine of the incarnation. Through the incarnation, God has demonstrated a loving concern for the welfare of people.

Philosophy

Philosophy explores how people think about the world. So many approaches to philosophy exist that it is difficult to name a single methodology or set of presuppositions that guides philosophy. Unlike a discipline such as chemistry, different approaches to philosophy conflict with one another. However, despite the apparent chaos of philosophy, the discipline shares certain common values. Paramount among these, philosophy values thought and the knowledge gained through the process of rational thought. Its chaos and confusion correspond to human fallenness described by the doctrine of humanity, but the rational thought so valued by philosophy reflects a remnant of the *imago dei*.

Physical Education

Physical education has a place in the life of human society that dates at least to classical antiquity and the Olympic Games. From antiquity the Bible describes the importance of physical training for the body and the need to nurture the body as well as the spirit. This academic discipline relates to the doctrine of humanity as a subcategory of the doctrine of creation. While the *imago dei* stresses our spiritual relationship to God, the doctrine of humanity also stresses that we are physical creatures and have a responsibility to care for our bodies.

Physics

Physics examines the properties, changes, and relations of matter and energy. The fundamental understanding of physics underwent a revolutionary change in the twentieth century as a result of the theories of general relativity, special relativity, and quantum mechanics. These theories have spawned metaphysical speculation on the part of physicists about whether the universe actually exists. The doctrine of creation explains the nature of the universe in terms of its relationship to its Creator and thus affirms the existence of the physical universe as a good thing.

Political Science

Political science deals with the study of government, leadership, and the processes of decision making in society. This discipline examines the acquisition and use of power as well as the values at play in the brokering of decisions. Political science examines an area of life that corresponds to the doctrine of humanity, a subcategory of the doctrine of creation. Made in the image of God, people have responsibilities for the stewardship of society and the earth, while at the same time they have the power to exercise whatever authority they choose. Thus, this discipline examines the practical ramifications of the doctrine of sin in political systems.

Psychology

Psychology is a recent discipline that explores mental processes. While it studies people in a particular context, one in which external relationships are important, it does so to arrive at an understanding of the internal dimension of people as self-conscious beings. The doctrine of humanity also relates to this discipline. As psychology examines how mental processes break down, it is exploring the domain of the doctrine of sin as it affects mental processes. Psychology also describes remnants of the *imago dei* in mental processes.

Religion

Religion explores how people have responded to their experience of the spiritual. As an academic discipline, religion has no more to do with faith than any other discipline. Religion can be explored as a purely social or psychological phenomenon. In fact, these have been some of the more popular approaches over the last hundred years. This study will have more to say later about the choice of methodology and the extent to which disciplines borrow methods from one another that are not inherent to a discipline. In the broad sphere, however, religion relates to the doctrine of God and the doctrine of humanity. In the broadest terms, it involves the interaction between God and people. By now the attentive reader will have already objected that religion must relate to more of the doctrines than these two. Indeed it does. The reader will also have begun to notice that each previously mentioned discipline may relate to multiple doctrines of the Christian faith. For now we will content ourselves with thinking about how the basic idea of a discipline relates to the central teachings of the Christian faith.

Social Work

Social work concerns itself with how to care for society's needy in their social context. This discipline proceeds from several enormous values, including the imperatives to care for others and to value all people as having dignity and worth. Social work relates to the doctrine of creation through the doctrine of humanity, which bases human value on the purposive creation of God. The activity of social work relates to the doctrine of the incarnation: through the ministry of Christ, God has demonstrated the responsibility to care for the needy. As such, social work is concerned with remedying the physical effects of sinfulness that people inflict on others and themselves.

Sociology

Sociology examines social processes. Whereas psychology focuses on the internal world of a person, sociology focuses on the external world of a person within a social context. As a subcategory of the doctrine of creation, the doctrine of humanity also deals with the corporate experience of people. Sociology describes the patterns of corporate sin as well as the remnants of the *imago dei* in society.

Some might object at this point that they do not believe in the doctrine of creation or the doctrine of sin. The *Millennium Falcon* and the starship *Enterprise* both involve space travel at warp and hyperwarp speed. Yet they differ from one another in that one existed in a distant galaxy long, long ago and the other exists in our own galaxy many years in the future. That both ships are imaginary does not alter the fact that they both relate to the same subject: space travel. It is not the purpose of this book to make the case for Christianity. Others have done that much more ably than I. For those who accept the truth of Jesus Christ, however, the issue of his relationship to education arises as a practical problem. The purpose of this particular exercise is to demonstrate that the basic teachings of Christianity deal with the same material as the academic disciplines in the modern university.

One might object that the modern disciplines have the accurate picture of the material while Christianity merely perpetuates a primitive myth. Bringing the same argument closer to the modern disciplines themselves, one might ask if sociology, psychology, political science, or history gives the more accurate explanation for the use of power. All of these disciplines explore the issue from a different perspective. No single discipline exhausts the discussion. Christianity merely provides another perspective that these disciplines lack. It cannot be stressed strongly enough that faith is not a substitute for these disciplines, but neither are these disciplines a substitute for faith.

One might object that Christianity deals with spiritual matters while the disciplines deal with physical matters. The exercise of power would be one such physical matter. Yet, the Bible regards power and its use as a spiritual matter. Because people in the modern world have tended to relegate the spiritual to the formal exercise of religion, they have lost the skill of recognizing a spiritual issue when confronted by it. Every spiritual issue can be described by an academic discipline because every spiritual issue expresses itself in the physical world. We mistakenly believe that we have explained a matter once we have described it phenomenologically.

Families of Disciplines

This brief survey of the way each discipline deals with an area of concern shared by a major Christian doctrine leads to a surprising observation. At least it surprised me. All of the disciplines identified share concerns in common with the doctrine of creation. They branch out in a variety of directions, but they all relate to the same broad doctrine. When I began thinking of this issue, I expected to find a broader base of doctrinal relationships. Should this situation be surprising? As secular as the modern academy may be in its orientation, its areas of concern arose from the medieval monastery and the desire to understand the works of God. The universe of knowledge, as the medieval scholars pursued it, all converged on the Creator, from whom all things come. Whether or not one believes in the Creator, the foundation for Western critical thought remains the same.

Beyond the broad relationship between the disciplines of knowledge and the doctrine of creation, several subgroups begin to emerge. The disciplines seem to be grouped by shared interests that, in turn, relate to a subcategory of the doctrine of creation. These families of disciplines, while composed of discrete areas of thought or method, share common themes that bind the families together in their overall concern. At one time the members of the family might have been considered a single discipline. Over time, however, specialization has led to separate identities for these disciplines. Nevertheless, the common concern remains.

The Arts

The arts come in a variety of forms, including visual arts, literature, music, and drama. A basic curriculum would be expected to have at least these. A more thorough curriculum would include modern art forms, such as film, and more ancient art forms, such as dance. These disciplines explore humans as creative, expressive beings. They explore the phenomenon of imagination and its communication. They explore the valuing of artistic expression by cultures. They explore issues of meaning related to artistic expression.

In the twentieth century the member disciplines of the arts engaged in momentous debate over fundamental concerns. The nature of beauty, the place of meaning, the need to communicate, and the place of the community in art appreciation formed a tempest that has not subsided.

These questions and many more have an intimate relationship to the doctrine of creation. That people have a need to create seems curious in a naturalistic universe, although a theory for how artistic expression might advance an organism would not be difficult to formulate. Still, the creativity of making a bowl for storage is different from that of making a beautiful bowl for display.

The doctrine of creation proceeds from the idea that God is the Creator. The doctrine of humanity explores what it means for humans to be created by God. Perhaps the most important aspect of what it means to be human is that, from a biblical point of view, people are made in the image of God (*imago dei*). Made in the image of the Creator, people must create just as they must think, live in community, and communicate. People have a need to know and be known. The ideas of value and meaning are rooted in the concept of intentional creation. In the Bible, absolute values do not exist as eternal entities in themselves, like the categories of Plato. Instead, absolute values are the opinions of God. God evaluated the creation and called it *good*. Created in the image of God, people have the capacity to form their own opinions and make evaluations of every aspect of life. Meaning comes from purposive creation. The presence of meaning and purpose in the universe does not prove the existence of God, as Aristotle and Thomas Aquinas argued. Rather, the existence of a personal Creator proves the existence of meaning and purpose.

As Dr. Pickett has suggested, however, the arts involve more than creativity. Because of the twentieth-century concern for the audience and the re-presentation of the world, Pickett suggests that the arts have as much to do with eschatology as with creation. Art has as much to do with how we should live as it has to do with aesthetic pleasure or entertainment. As a Christian involved in literature, Pickett goes on to say, "I see my efforts in literature not just repeating the movement of creation but in anticipating (cocreating?) the fulfillment of the kingdom."[5]

The Sciences

The sciences explore the nature and behavior of the physical world. A modern college or university would normally offer study in the fields of biology, chemistry, geology, physics, astronomy, math, and computer science. More comprehensive research universities will include the ever-growing specializations that have emerged from these disciplines in recent years, including biochemistry, astrophysics, genetics, microbiology, and many more. The term *science* as applied to this family is a relatively new invention. Until the nineteenth century these disciplines were known as *natural philosophy*. Until then, they did not exist as discrete disciplines. Natural philosophy, in turn, belonged to an earlier family that included moral philosophy and metaphysics.

Every culture has a form of science, discoveries it has made about the physical world. Ancient cultures tracked what appeared to be the motion of the stars. Primitive peoples utilized the medicinal properties of plants. Some of the most glorious cultures on earth that produced magnificent art and architecture flourished while the peoples of Europe were still cannibals who ate their children in cultic Druid meals. Though advanced cultures in Africa and Asia had the advantage of centuries, and in some cases millennia, in their lead over the primitive and barbaric peoples of Europe, science as we know it arose in Europe within a few centuries of the abandonment of cannibalism. Alfred North Whitehead, a great physicist and philosopher of science who was not a Christian, argued that science arose as it did and took the form that it has because of Christian faith in the West. Unlike the East, where religion tended to deny the physical world and regarded it as an illusion or as the embodiment of evil, Christianity brought to the West a view of the physical world as both real and good as the result of God's creative act. Unlike the Druids' old world of hostile spiritual forces and unreliable gods, the created world of a supreme God who had authority over all other spiritual powers was a stable and ordered world. Unlike cultures in which the physical world is regarded as a living, divine thing, too sacred to probe, the created world of the West invited people to examine nature as an act of awe and wonder or worship. Thus, modern science began as part of the discipline family known as theology.

Social Sciences

Social sciences study people in their variety of dimensions and relations. Sociology studies people in their social relationships. Psychology studies the internal, mental world of people. International relations studies the interactions between people as nations and members of nations. Political science studies the ways people govern themselves and make group decisions. Economics studies the production, distribution, and consumption of wealth. History studies how people have behaved over time. Philosophy studies how people order their worlds rationally.

Some of these disciplines, such as history and philosophy, are quite old and may be found in most cultures. Political science and international relations have been practiced since ancient times, but they are new members of the academy as scholarly disciplines. Psychology and sociology are new disciplines in terms of their names and methodologies, but their object of study has been a matter of concern since ancient times. These diverse disciplines share a concern for people.

Like the other sciences, the social sciences deal with a subject related to the doctrine of creation. Like the arts, the social sciences deal with the doctrine of humanity. Unlike the arts, the social sciences are as concerned with the implications of the fall as they are with the implications of being made in the image of God. The social sciences examine the best and the worst of people. In short, the social sciences explore the potential for which people were created alongside the reality of sin.

What makes this family intriguing is the extent to which its member disciplines have sought to adapt the methodology of the sciences to their pursuit of knowledge. The social sciences have not had the same success in prediction that the sciences have had, and this struggle can be summed up by the recent insights of chaos theory. According to chaos theory, some systems have too many variables to predict with any accuracy what behavior will be. The attempt of meteorology to predict the weather represents an elementary example of chaos theory. As a class, the social sciences deal with chaos systems; each person is a chaos system of its own. Collectively the chaos grows exponentially. For this reason, the social sciences are handicapped in their effort to employ scientific method in understanding past behavior and predicting future behavior of people, individually or corporately.

Rhetoric and Grammar

Although surviving under different names, this family of disciplines remains from the ancient academy of Athens and includes the study of foreign languages and the study of composition within one's own language. Also part of this family are grammar, which studies the mechanics of language, and communication arts, which focuses on the craft of articulate and persuasive oral and written communication (the ancients called this *rhetoric*).

The disciplines that make up rhetoric and grammar have a place in the core curriculum of most colleges and universities. Some schools require demonstrated proficiency prior to admission. Many schools stress the need to practice these skills as a part of the broader curriculum and hence emphasize "writing across the curriculum" as well as cross-cultural, international experience. Skill at communicating within one's own language is regarded by the academy as absolutely essential, and knowledge of another language is preferred in an increasingly global society. The presence of these disciplines within the academy underscores the fundamental difficulty people have in understanding and being understood. The simple task of communication is monumental. As social creatures, however, people need to communicate.

The need to communicate, the ability to communicate, and the failure to communicate relate to the doctrine of creation as an aspect of the doctrine of humanity. Grammar and rhetoric, the fields of communication, reflect the same theological dynamics as the social sciences. They deal with the best and the worst dimensions of what it means to be human. Made in the image of God, we have the amazing capacity to make our thoughts and feelings known. As fallen creatures, however, we bungle the job. Though we are social creatures with a need to communicate, we often live in isolation, alienated from one another.

The Humanities

The arts, the social sciences, and grammar and rhetoric have an unusual relationship to one another. We may view them as quite different in terms of methodologies and mechanics of study, yet they all deal with an exploration of what it means to be human. These families of disciplines explore what it means to be simultaneously made in the image of God and yet fallen from that state of being. They do not use the theological categories of Christian doctrine to understand or define what they do. Nonetheless, what they study and explore about humans involves the doctrines of the *imago dei* and sin, the ultimate irony. Taken as a whole, the disciplines that explore humanity are the humanities. The humanities and the sciences together make up the block of the academy known variously as the *liberal arts* or the *arts and sciences*, dating from the medieval and ancient tradition of formal education that focused on the mind and the contemplative life.

The Professions

The professions hold a hard-fought patch of ground in the academy. Whereas the liberal arts came from the monastery, the professions came from the marketplace. Business, law, medicine and nursing, teaching, social work, engineering and architecture, and similar professions were once learned in the marketplace by apprentices studying or working with a master. People learned a profession through practice. We still speak of "practicing" law and medicine. The professions have tended to be regarded by the liberal arts as second-class disciplines in the academy because they lack the focus and method of the liberal arts. By their very nature, the professions have what to the liberal arts constitutes a fatal flaw: they are actually not disciplines at all. They focus on a task, but they are interdisciplinary in their approach.

A nurse must learn biology, chemistry, math, sociology, psychology, communication arts, and a variety of other disciplines that go into the day-to-day activity of being a nurse. Nurses must understand the relationship between the various disciplines that contribute to nursing. Whether with understanding or not, nurses must know how to use these various disciplines in the care of sick people. While the disciplines concentrate on the unique and discrete qualities that set them apart from one another, nursing must pull the disciplines back together into a functioning whole.

Each of the professions involves the integration of a number of disciplines. Professional life does not enjoy the luxury of examining a single aspect of knowledge divorced from the rest of knowledge. Nevertheless, the professions involve practice in the world more than they involve theoretical precision. The teaching profession, for example, requires that teachers have a broad knowledge of all the liberal arts disciplines as well as how to help people learn. They must know not only content about psychology but also how to call upon what they know to help students. The same can be said of their knowledge of sociology. Even within the body of education courses, students will study the *history* of education and the *philosophy* of education, as well as other courses built on other disciplines.

The profession of architecture involves the design of buildings, yet this profession is not a pure discipline. Architects must master geometry and other areas of math. They must know physics, not only for the strength of building design but also for acoustics and light. They must understand psychology because structures either positively or negatively affect the mental state of those who inhabit them. They must have an understanding of art and design because buildings and their place in the community have an aesthetic aspect. Engineering involves many of these same aspects, yet with more emphasis on the application of the sciences and less emphasis on the aesthetic.

Social work involves helping people. The course of study for a person preparing for a career in social work involves a strong dose of the humanities. Psychology and sociology provide background for understanding the mental and social context of clients. Political science provides a framework for understanding governmental agencies and policies related to social welfare. Unlike the social sciences that study people, however, social work becomes involved in the lives of people, more like the artist who engages a canvas or a mound of clay. In that sense, social work becomes the artistic and personal expression of the social sciences that have been reintegrated.

Some professions focus their attention on educational experiences beyond the undergraduate degree. The older, if not the oldest, professions require a college education as a prerequisite to commencing study for a profession. In law, medicine, and ministry, mastery of the breadth of disciplines is necessary to undertake the profession. These professions depend on the body of knowledge, intellectual tools, and insights of the disciplines to train their guild members for work in the modern world.

The Professional Caveat

While the professions, by their very nature, involve the integration of other disciplines, they have also grown susceptible to the fragmenting tendency of modern life. We experience this fragmentation and specialization of the professions on a day-to-day basis. I first became aware of it a few years ago when my family's doctor retired. In a hundred years, my family had only two doctors: a father and the son of his old age. When it came time to seek a new family doctor, we found that no such thing existed anymore. Everyone specialized. The closest thing we could find was an internist who would then refer us to other specialists as the need arose.

Specialization has come to all professions in one way or other. Professionals choose their specialty of practice. Nurses focus on areas within a hospital, such as cardiac care or newborns. They may focus on community care or become a nurse practitioner. Teachers specialize according to discipline as well as age level or special needs. Business has developed true disciplines, such as marketing, management, and accounting. Lawyers specialize in such areas as corporate law, labor law, civil law, domestic relations, and criminal law. Though the United States does not have the formal distinction between barristers and solicitors that the legal profession has in the United Kingdom, we do make the distinction in preference and practice. Some lawyers specialize in the courtroom while others avoid it like the plague!

Conclusion

This brief survey has illustrated the extent to which disciplines share common concerns. In contrast to Stephen Jay Gould's argument that science and religion belong to non-overlapping magisteria (NOMA), it appears that virtually all disciplines overlap with at least one other discipline, and usually more. Not only science but also every discipline and family of disciplines overlaps with religion in their fields of concern. The fact that psychology and sociology utilize different methods and focus on different dimensions in their study of people does not invalidate or jeopardize either discipline.

From time to time, one would expect that the disciplines would mutually inform one another. If not, they have grown too introspective.

Whether or not God exists, the academy must deal with the problems of introspection and isolation. By withdrawing from or avoiding the dialogue, we only restrict the kind of insightful conversation that may help us come to a new breakthrough in our own disciplines.

Further Reading

Few books have been written in this area, but two commend themselves as helpful in beginning to think about how a discipline may relate to the basic matters of Christian faith:

Dockery, David S., and Gregory Alan Thornbury, eds. *Shaping a Christian Worldview: The Foundations of Christian Higher Education.* Nashville: Broadman & Holman, 2002.

Palmer, Michael D., ed. *Elements of a Christian Worldview.* Springfield, Mo.: Logion, 1998.

7

Interdisciplinary
Dialogue

The explosion of knowledge that has occurred during the modern period has come in part through the discipline of focusing narrowly on specific questions. The law of unintended consequences in this situation, however, has led to a fragmentation of knowledge. Despite initiatives by many schools to introduce interdisciplinary programs and the positive encouragement by faculties for such programs, interdisciplinary study holds an ambiguous place within the academy. The normal drive for full status within the academy would typically lead to establishing a major and, ultimately, advanced degrees in interdisciplinary studies. The problem with this drive toward self-realization lies in the very nature of interdisciplinary studies. In order to be interdisciplinary, one must first have a discipline of one's own to relate to another discipline. More cautious faculty members remain suspiciously concerned about the free exchange of ignorance and the absence of a body of knowledge.

The mistake of this approach to interdisciplinary study lies in viewing it as a discipline, the traditional route to respectability within the academy, rather than as a method. By viewing interdisciplinary studies as a discipline that students study, one arrives at the ultimate absurdity in fragmentation. The very approach designed to stem the tide of fragmentation becomes the means of finally ridding the academy of content. Slice a pie in thin enough pieces, and nothing remains but air. (For readers from chemistry and physics, this statement belongs to the poetic and should not be understood as a statement about chemical or atomic bonding.)

133

By regarding interdisciplinary study as a method, however, knowledge and understanding may be advanced. Such a method involves dialogue between two or more disciplines. Each retains its body of knowledge and unique perspective. These are the resources that each contributes to the conversation. The purpose of the conversation is not the blending or, the ultimate horror, "watering down" of the disciplines. Instead, the conversations aim at gaining broader insights that would not have been possible from the perspective of one discipline alone.

Years ago my violin teacher seasoned his string instruction and conducting by endlessly referring to history, which enriched his understanding, appreciation, and interpretation of music. My college geology professor seasoned his lectures with poetry. When we studied coastline geography, he quoted from Tennyson's "Crossing the Bar." When we studied the phenomenon of frost heaving in cold climates, he recited Robert Frost's "Mending Wall": "Good fences make good neighbors."[1] One might substitute the term *collaboration* for *interdisciplinary study*, but that would almost suggest a cessation of the traditional cutthroat turf competition that usually exists between departments on campus. In industry, however, some corporations have discovered that an interdisciplinary approach to problem solving, rather than a segmented approach, leads more quickly to a solution.[2] Great breakthroughs often come with the pooling of a critical mass of insight, knowledge, and understanding.

One of the greatest benefits of interdisciplinary conversation is its promotion of a discipline's self-examination. Each discipline exists as a freestanding culture within the universe of the academy. Each has its own private language and rituals. Each has its own values: absolute values in a relativistic universe. Even the most rabid relativists will cling, "to the death," to the absolute values of their discipline. It is possible to do this because people accept cultural norms uncritically. Beliefs and practices of a culture belong to the realm of "what everybody knows." In fact, they belong to the culture of the discipline so much that we do not notice them, or if we do notice them we keep it to ourselves. Whether we conceive of our disciplines individually as a professional association, a guild, a private club, the old-boy network, a monopoly, or the Mafia—going against the grain is simply not done.

A helpful approach to interdisciplinary study begins with recognizing the strengths of individual disciplines and the contributions they make to knowledge. This recognition may involve an understanding of how the disciplines relate to and inform one another. Sir Arthur Peacocke, a biochemist and theologian for many years at Oxford University and winner of the Templeton Prize, has devised a helpful diagram for conceiving the relationship between academic disciplines (see fig. 7.1).[3]

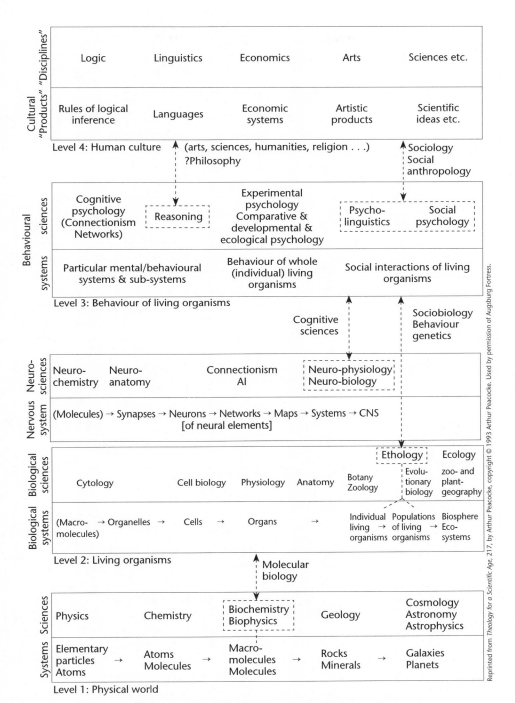

Figure 7.1. Peacocke's Model of Systems and Disciplines

He uses a hierarchical approach based on four levels of examination: (1) physical world, (2) living organisms, (3) behavior of living organisms, and (4) human culture. Within the first three levels of examination, Peacocke identifies the systems of each level with the sciences that examine those systems. For the fourth level, human culture, Peacocke identifies cultural "products" and their corresponding disciplines that study those products. As might be expected from a biologist, Peacocke's approach corresponds to an evolutionary understanding of the world. As might be expected from a theologian, Peacocke's approach corresponds to a teleological understanding of the world, in which humans play the key role within nature.

Within the first level of the physical world, Peacocke describes the relationship between the disciplines as though they might form a spectrum from the micro to the macro. Moving from the micro level, he describes the systems and their sciences as (1) elementary particles and atoms (physics), (2) atoms and molecules (chemistry), (3) molecules and macromolecules (biochemistry and biophysics), (4) minerals and rocks (geology), and (5) planets and galaxies (astronomy, cosmology, and astrophysics). At the second degree of complexity, which deals with molecules and macromolecules, Peacocke introduces molecular biology as the link between the systems of the physical world and the systems of living organisms.

Within the second level of living organisms, Peacocke identifies two kinds of systems: biological systems and the nervous system. Biological systems lead to the study of the nervous system. Sciences that examine biological systems are the biological sciences, and sciences that examine the nervous system are the neurosciences. Moving from the micro to the macro level, biological systems and sciences that examine them are (1) macromolecules and organelles (cytology), (2) cells (cell biology), (3) organs (physiology and anatomy), (4) individual living organisms (botany and zoology), (5) populations of living organisms (evolutionary biology), and (6) biosphere ecosystems (ecology, zoo and plant geography). The nervous system and its sciences are (1) molecules (neurochemistry), (2) synapses (neuroanatomy), (3) neurons (neurology), (4) networks, maps, systems, central nervous system (connectionism, artificial intelligence). Linking the second level (living organisms) with the third level (behavior of living organisms), Peacocke notes two areas of relation. From the biological sciences, he identifies ethology as the link to behavioral systems through sociobiology and behavior genetics. From the neurosciences, he identifies neurophysiology and neurobiology as the link to the behavioral systems through the cognitive sciences.

Within the third level, behavior of living organisms, Peacocke identifies behavioral systems and behavioral sciences. The systems and their sciences are (1) particular mental/behavioral systems and subsystems (cognitive psychology, connectionalism networks), (2) behavior of whole (individual) living organisms (experimental, comparative, developmental, and ecological psychology), (3) social interactions of living organisms (psycholinguistics, social psychology).

Peacocke's model helps in understanding that a relationship exists between spheres of interest in the academy, but its hierarchical nature does not exhaust the ways of relating. The disciplines certainly relate to one another in a hierarchy of information. In terms of function, however, perhaps other models provide greater insight. Within management theory, one model for the organization of a business is the hierarchical model. Another model, however, calls for a "flat" system that allows for collaboration more easily between and across business divisions. Another way of conceiving the relationship between areas of the academy might be a complex matrix in which each part relates to other parts, like the spokes of a geodesic dome (see fig. 7.2).

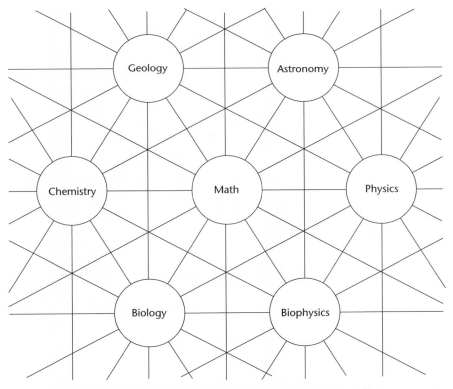

Figure 7.2. Poe's Relational Model of Academic Disciplines

One can easily recognize that physics provides the foundational information on which the entire academy rests, because everything in the universe rests upon the subatomic world. Carl Sagan used to say of this world, or cosmos, "The Cosmos is all that is or ever was or ever will be."[4] Having arrived at this foundational knowledge, however, we must ask how physics does its work if it is the foundation for all other knowledge. Physics depends on mathematics, which only appears as a final ornament on the great hierarchy of knowledge. Is mathematics the final foundation for knowledge? Before we answer, we must ponder how mathematics came into being. Does it exist in the universal world of forms, or does it arise as a mental construct? Is it an aspect of logic, communication, economics, psychology, sociology, or something else? Mathematics works, so it passes the pragmatic test, but we do not know why it works. We may accept it by pragmatism, by tradition, or by faith, but all of these leave us with uncertainty.

Understanding Our Own Disciplines

For several years I have employed a brief instrument to stimulate seminar and conference discussion about the place of religious faith in the academy. The instrument does not deal with faith as such; it simply explores how disciplines relate to one another. (This instrument has not been used in an attempt to carry out a serious research program on the subject. Most participants have allowed me to keep copies of their responses, but the responses fall under the category of qualitative, not quantitative, research.)

The effort to understand better our own disciplines is helped by understanding how they fit into the broader academy and how they relate to other specific disciplines. Generally speaking, faith intersects an academic discipline at the point where it asks its most fundamental questions. Faith intersects where a discipline appropriates its most fundamental assumptions, from whatever source they may come. Faith intersects at the point where a discipline adopts a philosophical position to guide it or to provide a structure for its theories, data, and explorations. Faith intersects where a discipline establishes its core values, upon whatever basis they are founded. One could argue that faith is the fundamental basis for all human knowledge, without which rationalism and empiricism could not function.

To begin the interdisciplinary dialogue, consider these simple questions from my survey instrument:

1. With what is your discipline concerned?
2. What characterizes the methodology of your discipline?

3. On what other disciplines does your discipline build? To what other disciplines does your discipline contribute? Give specific examples.
4. What are the values on which your discipline is based? At what point do these values come into conflict with other disciplines? List the values. Give specific examples of conflict you have seen.
5. Over what values within your discipline do members of your discipline disagree?
6. What is the philosophical basis for your discipline's values? What is the origin of the values? In what context did the values emerge?
7. When did your discipline come to be taught as a separate discipline within the academy? Was it part of another discipline earlier?

The instrument's value lies in its benefit for generating discussion about the faith dimension within disciplines. Unfortunately, the integration of faith and learning as an exercise often takes the form of importing into a discipline something that is not already present. An interdisciplinary approach, in contrast, strives for the recognition of critical issues within a discipline that actually involve faith but are often neglected.

With What Is Your Discipline Concerned?

Chapter 6 explored the specific areas of interest for many of the disciplines within the academy. Each discipline has a body of knowledge and in some cases a skill that they protect, expand, and pass on. The body of knowledge has come through great effort and often not without sacrifice. Each discipline has its own body of heroes or "saints." The established disciplines have been around long enough that everyone knows what they involve. Such is the nature of culture. Culture involves "what everyone knows," whether they do or not. What everyone knows tends to go unexamined. Sidney Brenner, one of the 2002 winners of the Nobel Prize in physiology/medicine, suggests that creativity in a discipline comes when we do not know too much about the subject. When we have not been "brought up in it," we are less likely to appropriate what is, after all, not so.[5]

Few disciplines have normative, universally accepted definitions for themselves. Those who write textbooks will invariably define the subject in some way, but few disciplines ever take a vote. The value of my survey instrument in this instance does not lie in its ability to discover accurate technical definitions for the disciplines. Instead, it reveals ways that those who practice the discipline think about it and feel about it on any Tuesday afternoon. Regardless of the official party line, how the discipline grows or changes depends on how those involved in it think and feel. The instrument functions more like a Rorschach test. The representatives of most disciplines involved in the survey reveal wide variability in how they understand their disciplines. The notable exception comes in the sciences. All chemistry professors used the phrase *matter-energy relationships.* All biology professors used the phrase *study of life.* Beyond these scientific areas, however, faculty members reveal a variety of preferences for how they think about their disciplines, sometimes extending to the idiosyncratic.

Faculty members may have a vague conception of other disciplines within the academy. The old core curriculum provided some basis for grasping a broader collection of knowledge, but the variability within disciplines has changed what some disciplines outside the sciences actually do. Some art faculty believe that their discipline is concerned with beauty while others scorn the very idea of beauty. English professors have been notorious in recent years for vehement debates about the nature of their discipline. Professors in other disciplines who took their college English courses in the 1960s, however, may have difficulty understanding the change that has taken place; young faculty members who took their English courses in the early 1990s will have fundamentally different conceptions of literature than do their elders. The difference is not simply one of changing interpretations of text; the difference lies in debating whether the text has any meaning at all, other than what the reader gives it.

What we begin to see is that radical interdisciplinary study has now been taking place for several decades, but not necessarily from a critical perspective. Members of one discipline may borrow tools from another discipline without ever having been trained in the proper methodological use of those tools. This happens when historians do sociology, sociologists do hermeneutics, and literary scholars undertake psychology. The list goes on and on.

What Characterizes the Methodology of Your Discipline?

The greatest advance in knowledge probably began with Sir Francis Bacon's argument that the acquisition of knowledge cannot blossom through reliance on ancient philosophy or tradition.[6] Instead, he proposed a systematic experimental method that involved trial and error. His initial thoughts on what has come to be known as the *scientific method* were published as *Novum Organum* in 1620. *Novum Organum,* or *New Organon,* was a takeoff on Aristotle's treatise on rational thinking, *Organon.* Bacon proposed replacing Aristotle's method of deductive reasoning from unquestionably true premises with a new method of inductive reasoning, which is based on raw evidence found in nature. Robert Boyle (1627–91) further refined the scientific method in his experiments on gases.

In response to the methodology survey question, one biophysicist remarked that the scientific method has not changed much since the 1600s–1700s. He went on to claim that "some disciplines change methodologies all the time." This casual remark represents an interdisciplinary observation. It involves no judgment or condemnation, but simply suggests that the sciences hit upon a highly successful method of study that may be employed in a variety of efforts to understand nature. It also suggests that other disciplines have been less successful in identifying an equally valuable method. Success of the scientific method, however, has led to other disciplines' effort to adapt it to their work, with mixed success.

As might be expected from an instrument of this kind, many of the respondents from the social sciences indicate that they employ the scientific method. When discussing responses in a seminar setting, professors from the "hard" sciences sit politely as they hear their colleagues say that they use the scientific method. They do not refer to the social sciences as "pseudosciences" in public. Instead, they speak of them as "soft" sciences, which is code for pseudosciences. In the background lies the biophysicist's casual remark, "Some disciplines change methodologies all the time." The science faculty seems to observe the rest of the academy's methodological chaos with quiet reserve and detached amusement. At least, many disciplines experience their work that way. Much more likely, the majority of disciplines have been intimidated by the scientific method's astounding success and have sought to shroud themselves in its mystique.

The social sciences have appropriated, quite successfully, some features of the scientific method. The scientific method allows social scientists to organize data. Variables that social scientists deal with are too great, however, to establish the kind of cause-and-effect precision that the natural sciences strive to achieve. They may merely identify "risk factors" that correlate with certain probabilities. The social sciences have not achieved the predictive power of the natural sciences. The social sciences can take heart, however. In quantum physics, prediction is futile and probability reigns. Even medicine, which in the twentieth century tended to see itself as a science rather than a profession, has to stand shoulder to shoulder with stock analysts in terms of prediction. Probability allows the physician to know that a certain number, on average, out of every hundred people will suffer a heart attack, but the physician does not know which people in the hundred will actually have a heart attack. It then becomes a matter of correlating risk factors and giving advice.

If we were to turn back to Peacocke's model in figure 7.1, we would observe that the scientific method works with relative precision at the lowest levels of exploring the physical world, but that its effectiveness diminishes as the subject of study becomes more "social." Yet the cloud remains. Modern people tend to think that *real* knowledge is *scientific* knowledge. The preference for empirical knowledge has overshadowed all other forms of knowing within the academy.

Fascination with the scientific method became a feature of theological scholarship early in the modern period and continues to the present. Whether conservative or liberal, theologians have embraced the scientific method as the road to real truth. Charles Finney thought he had discovered the laws of revival. With his dispensational scheme, C. I. Scofield believed he had determined the scientific way to study the Bible. A. T. Robertson, one of the leading Greek grammarians of the twentieth century, self-consciously sought to write a scientific Greek grammar. In discussing the study of New Testament syntax, Robertson claimed, "But, all in all, it is more scientific to gather the facts of usage first and then interpret these facts. This interpretation is scientific syntax, while the facts of usage are themselves syntax."[7]

In the last two hundred years, an unfortunate association has grown up between the scientific method and naturalistic philosophy. Naturalism is not innate to the scientific method developed by Christians. By extension one may argue that faith does not inhibit scientific progress. In recent years, a number of prominent Christians in the sciences have assumed that they must adopt a stance of "methodological naturalism," thinking this approach will prevent bias on their part. What they fail to see is that naturalism is a bias. Naturalism was the philosophical perspective of Hume, incorporated into biology by Darwin, and borrowed from biology by the social sciences and the humanities. What Bacon sought to accomplish was freedom from the old enslavement to philosophical ideas. The association of naturalism with the scientific method prejudges the data to conform to the philosophical paradigm.

On What Other Disciplines Does Your Discipline Build?

The problem of methodology becomes more critical when we explore the extent to which disciplines borrow from one another, contribute to one another, or look to one another for a foundation. Sociology is a relatively recent member of the academy. Not surprisingly, it borrows from a number of other disciplines to acquire tools for considering its subject. Among these disciplines we find economics, history, political science, anthropology, psychology, and statistics. To say that sociology borrows from these disciplines today, however, minimizes the nature of the complex borrowing, for most of these disciplines were developing as new disciplines in the nineteenth century, alongside sociology. To say that one or the other of these disciplines had a ten- or fifteen-year head start does not mean much in the context of a five-thousand-year cultural tradition. They influenced one another even as they began to emerge as distinct disciplines. Unlike those in the natural sciences, in which a single theory emerges as the most helpful way to understand an aspect of the physical world, rival theories in the social sciences hammer away at one another, gather allies, and battle away some more. Theories have adherents that then fall out of fashion, but they do not have the same standing within the social sciences that they have within the natural sciences.

Rival theories exist in the natural sciences until evidence suggests the most likely alternative, and then members of the guild (except those most emotionally attached to the discredited theory) shift their allegiance. Theories come and go in the natural sciences, but they tend to be viewed with a more tentative perspective. A possible exception may exist with respect to biology. While exploring these issues with a group of scholars meeting in Cambridge, England, one chemistry professor from Cornell University observed that "biologists worship Darwin in a way that physicists and chemists do not regard Newton and Fermi." Whether or not the observation is true, many chemists and physicists perceive it to be so.

Part of the difference between the physical sciences and biology may lie in how these respective sciences have developed their own cultures since they separated from the old, general field of natural philosophy, when everyone dabbled in everything. Bacon assumed that his method of absolute objectivity was free of bias and emotion, and that it would lead to absolute certainty. Descartes and Pascal challenged this method, but with Einstein's overturning of Newtonian physics in his theories of relativity, the emergence of quantum theory, and the strange world of chaos theory, Bacon's old assumptions have proved flawed. Chemistry and physics have become much less dogmatic as they have learned more about the universe. Biology has not yet had a similar experience in its study of life. In terms of their experimental base, chemistry and physics are two hundred years ahead of biology. Darwin is biology's Newton. The shock will come when biology meets its Einstein and Bohr.

We can see the difference between the sciences by comparing two of the most prominent theories of modern times: Darwin's theory of evolution by natural selection and the big bang theory. The big bang theory, simply stated, describes the universe as an ever-expanding space that started from an extremely dense mass a long time ago. The theory makes no attempt to explain what caused the expansion; it merely deals with the observable phenomenon. Darwin's theory, however, goes beyond describing the phenomenon of change in life forms over time. It goes on to make a significant metaphysical claim that the scientific method cannot investigate. Darwin's theory claims that the cause behind the phenomenon is natural selection. Not all biologists mingle this philosophical position with their science, but many biologists do not realize that they have mingled a philosophical position with their science either. It simply goes with the territory, and it goes unnoticed. It is part of the received cultural tradition of the discipline from within. The value of interdisciplinary dialogue in this situation comes in the form of a helpful and well-intended remark from a physical scientist: "Your slip is showing."

The reliance of one discipline on others appears most clearly in the professions that focus on a task. The task may be social work, medicine, nursing, teaching, engineering, or law. The task, however, requires the weaving together of various realms of knowledge to form a seamless fabric. For these disciplines, knowledge must move from theory to practice, and it must do so in relation to other fields.

Social work involves the application of sociology, psychology, economics, political science, biology, and philosophy. In turn, it contributes to nursing, teaching, religion, political science, and economics. Nursing builds on sociology, psychology, biology, chemistry, education, anthropology, mathematics, communications, and medicine. It reciprocates with many of the same disciplines. Teaching (or education) requires psychology, sociology, philosophy, history, communication arts, and anthropology for its discipline, yet it relies upon every other discipline for its content. In turn, teaching may contribute to every other field as one of the primary bases for transmitting and preserving the disciplines and their content. In similar fashion, all professions intersect many realms of knowledge for the solution of particular problems.

The same kind of interdependence operates within the humanities. Although the humanities have a much older tradition in the academic practice of their crafts, in the late modern period the humanities have tended to operate like the social sciences and the professions in the way they perceive themselves and their task. The humanities have borrowed heavily from one another as well as from the natural sciences and social sciences. In many respects the humanities have gone through an identity crisis over their actual task. Language study now involves anthropology, geography, philosophy, physiology, history, art, and psychology. Literature study now involves history, economics, anthropology, political science, sociology, psychology, rhetoric, art, and philosophy. History now involves a consideration of economics, psychology, political science, sociology, anthropology, and philosophy. Philosophy began a wrenching transformation during the modern period and now draws from the natural sciences, linguistics, psychology, sociology, and political science.

A work of this kind assumes that the reader has a general familiarity with the academy, such that a detailed description of how disciplines build on one another will not be necessary. These discussions have not gone on in secret. Yet a brief expansion on how this dynamic has affected philosophy may be helpful. At the beginning of the modern period, all that we now call *science* was a part of the discipline of philosophy and was referred to as *natural philosophy*. Even as science broke away and established its own methodology after Bacon (d. 1626), philosophers continued to be interested in questions arising from nature, as we see in the work of Immanuel Kant (d. 1804). The skepticism of Descartes (d. 1650) and Pascal (d. 1662), however, led to a new understanding of the task of philosophy, as seen in the existential philosophers following Kierkegaard (d. 1855), who had a more psychological orientation.

The scientific stream of experimentation, however, contributed to another stream of philosophy that developed in Vienna and came to be known as *logical positivism* and, later, *scientific empiricism*. In essence, this stream of thought moved the scientific method from *a* way of knowing to *the only* way of knowing. In this regard, one can speak meaningfully only about something that may be verified empirically. Otherwise, it is literally nonsense. Ludwig Wittgenstein (d. 1951) left positivism to create a new approach to philosophy known as *linguistic analysis*, which blends linguistics with social, psychological, and anthropological analysis. Wittgenstein argued that words like *God* have important social, psychological, and cultural meaning but have no cognitive meaning.

In the case of philosophy, we can see that developments within the natural sciences influenced new directions in philosophy. This new direction, however, began to influence other fields as well. C. S. Lewis studied philosophy at Oxford before he came back to do a second course in medieval and Renaissance English literature. With this background he had a unique perspective on a sudden and dramatic shift that took place in the study of literature in England as a result of Wittgenstein's new philosophy. Wittgenstein had begun to introduce this new philosophy to his students at Cambridge in the years 1933–35. Wittgenstein's theories were published after his death as *Philosophical Investigations* (1953). In the meantime, however, Wittgenstein's students circulated transcripts of his lectures as the "Blue Book" and the "Brown Book," and these books had a profound influence on how philosophers began to conceive their task. In particular, Wittgenstein influenced John Wisdom of Cambridge and A. J. Ayer of Oxford. These philosophers popularized Wittgenstein's ideas long before *Philosophical Investigations* was published. In an article published in 1938, Wisdom remarked that the point of philosophical statements "is the illumination of the ultimate structure of facts, i.e. the relations between different categories of being or (we must be in the mode) the relations between different sub-languages within a language."[8] By 1943 C. S. Lewis found that his young college students had already accepted the new philosophy as fact in their reading of literature. Linguistic analysis not only had changed the philosophers' understanding of their task, but also had begun to change the nature of literary study. Lewis discovered that his students had studied an elementary English textbook that incorporated the new philosophy in its teaching of literature. Alec King and Martin Ketley wrote *The Control of Language* as an introduction to the study of literature, yet it builds on a philosophical foundation it treats as fact. Lewis quotes the offending reference to Coleridge's experience at a waterfall that caught his attention:

> When the man said *That is sublime*, he appeared to be making a remark about the waterfall. . . . Actually . . . he was not making a remark about the waterfall, but a remark about his own feelings. What he was saying was really *I have feelings associated in my mind with the word "Sublime,"* or shortly, *I have sublime feelings.* . . . This confusion is continually present in language as we use it. We appear to be saying something very important about something: and actually we are only saying something about our own feelings.[9]

Lewis understood that children who read words in a textbook will take them as authoritative. The lesson teaches, not about literature, but about an understanding of all of life. A philosophical interpretation of the nature of reality and humanity has been slipped under the door in the guise of one discipline when, in fact, it is quite another discipline. Lewis observed:

> The very power of [King and Ketley] depends on the fact that they are dealing with a boy: a boy who thinks he is "doing" his "English prep" and has no notion that ethics, theology, and politics are all at stake. It is not a theory they put into his mind, but an assumption, which ten years hence, its origin forgotten and its presence unconscious, will condition him to take one side in a controversy which he has never recognized as a controversy at all. The authors themselves, I suspect, hardly know what they are doing to the boy, and he cannot know what is being done to him.[10]

This situation represents the kind of dependence that occurs between disciplines when the content of one discipline is appropriated uncritically by members of another discipline. It is also important to note that the appropriation occurs with the assumption that the teaching of one discipline is an established fact rather than a discussion in progress. When this happens, the nature of a discipline may change as a result of external forces, rather than as a result of the scholarship within the discipline itself.

On What Values Is Your Discipline Based?

While every discipline has some body of knowledge with which it deals and some methodology by which it examines its subject, it also has some core values that provide the stimulus for concern with the subject in the first place. These values may extend to the guidance of the methodology. Some values are seen as applying to the broad scholarly enterprise, almost as a binding force that unites faculty across disciplines. Such concepts as truth, justice, and integrity appear on surveys from people who teach in different areas.

As I write these words, a group of campus faculty members are meeting in the room beneath mine to discuss the issue of plagiarism in our new technological environment. Why should plagiarism be of concern to faculty? What value does this issue concern? Many students fail to see why professors make such a big deal over it. Is it wrong, or is it simply not helpful? Is it an ethical issue, a pragmatic issue, both, or neither? If I do not learn because I cheat, whose business is that but mine? If something bigger is at stake, who decides what that is? If the stigma of cheating is just a community issue, why not change the community's opinion? If it is an issue of integrity, what constitutes integrity? If it is a matter of justice for those who worked hard, why should anyone be concerned about justice? Where does the idea of justice come from? If it is just a social construct, why should I be bound by it? If it is for the good of the whole, why should I care about the whole? If it leads to the survival of the group, why should I care about the group? Is there any ultimate origin of values, or do all values represent the attempt by one group to exercise power over others?

The issue of power is addressed by sociology. A variety of social theories have developed as an aid to understand the exercise of power. Theories that focus on power offer an explanation for the common values held by a group. The relationship between sociology and social work illustrates how a discipline that builds on another discipline may appropriate conflicting values. Social work began in the nineteenth century as the expression of concern for those in need during the evangelical awakenings and in the emerging urban life of the Roman Catholic Church in North America. It began to emerge as an academic discipline alongside sociology in the late nineteenth and early twentieth centuries. Social work has clung tenaciously to its values: the worth and dignity of the individual, social and economic justice, and self-determination. As long as social work was rooted in Christian faith, it had a basis for its core values. As the profession became disengaged from its roots and identified more social theory for its foundation, however, social work lost the basis for the core values it continued to affirm. Social theory rooted in Darwinian naturalism has no place for the kinds of innate values held by social work.[11]

Without belaboring the point by examining every discipline, perhaps these examples will serve to illustrate the way in which disciplines borrow from one another. In the process of borrowing, unintended consequences result. While we borrow some aspects of another discipline intentionally, we also acquire presuppositions, philosophical perspectives, and values that lie embedded in the content of the discipline. As Lewis suggested, we may be totally unaware of the controversy surrounding the theories that underwent great debate within a discipline. We have not participated in that debate and may be oblivious to the issues at stake.

What Is the Philosophical Basis for Your Discipline?

Everyone has a philosophy, although few realize it. Many people have tangled philosophical messes by which they live conflicted lives full of self-contradiction. Others live consistent lives in keeping with a philosophical position with which they may be quite unaware. Life's clichés reflect these perspectives: "There's more to life than meets the eye" reflects an idealist perspective. "Seeing is believing" reflects a real-ist or materialist perspective. "You can't argue with success" reflects a pragmatic perspective. "If it looks like a duck, walks like a duck, and quacks like a duck . . ." reflects a rationalistic, empirical perspective.

Philosophy might be understood as how we think about things. Using a metaphor from this technological age, we can liken philosophy to a software program that organizes mental data. Different programs have been written to organize the same data, but they do it in different ways. WordPerfect and Microsoft Word are two popular word-processing pro-grams that organize letters and characters on a screen. They go about this organization in different ways, however, and champions of each program believe that the one they use is the only way to go. People who switch programs discover that they cannot do some things with one program that they could do with the other. The program simply does not include some tasks. It is not that the program does not do the tasks in the same way; it simply does not do them at all.

Philosophy works in a similar way. It sets the agenda for what people are capable of thinking about, as well as how they think about what they think about. The data or subject matter of an academic discipline may remain the same, but how people think about the discipline may vary widely depending on their philosophical perspective. Most disciplines can be viewed from any number of possible philosophical perspectives. The danger comes when we equate a particular philosophical perspective with a discipline. In the history of science, this great equation occurred once when Western thinkers equated knowledge of the natural world with Aristotelian philosophy. In the Soviet system in recent years, all disciplines were required to equate their knowledge with the Marxist-Leninist philosophy of history. This proved to be a major challenge for physics.

As a discipline, history illustrates the impact of philosophy on what the discipline chooses to notice from the data. Those outside the field might even be tempted to view history as something anyone can do, a bit like a hobby. A simplistic view of history might be that it is merely the study of the past. The caricature of history comes in the picture of a high school student charged with memorizing a list of dates. For many people, history is little more than an exercise in putting the data in the right chronological order. Behind this facade of simplicity, however, lies a disturbing question: Which data does one put in chronological order? Further, with all the data of the past, how does one decide which data is of sufficient interest to set it apart as significant? With the rise of feminist awareness, African-American scholarship, and non-Western critiques of Western thought, another question has arisen: Who determines which data to select? The answers to these and similar questions reveal the underlying philosophy by which historians undertake their work.

In *The Idea of History,* a critical study of the history of the philosophy of history, R. G. Collingwood pointed out that even those who think about the philosophy of history disagree about what they mean by the term. Voltaire meant critical history, history that went beyond merely repeating the old stories. Hegel meant a universal understanding of history as a whole. For the nineteenth-century positivists, *history* meant the discovery of the facts of history and the discovery of natural laws that govern history.[12] For Collingwood, the philosophy of history involved an inquiry into the nature of history as a special kind of knowledge. Benedetto Croce, the Italian philosopher of history and opponent of fascism, argued that history was not merely "a variety of knowledge, but it is knowledge itself."[13] For Croce the chronicles and accounts of past happenings were not history but historical material. History involved asking questions related to the *requirements of life*, the main values of spiritual existence: moral, economic, aesthetic, and intellectual.[14] In short, history is a means of thinking about the problems of the present. Wilhelm Dilthey, the German philosopher and historian, repudiated any attempt to find meaning in history outside the human mind, which organizes the events of experience. In this regard, Dilthey labored to make human studies distinct from scientific studies.[15] The emphasis on the internal world of ideas, however, makes history a largely subjective enterprise.

Other approaches to the philosophy of history have sought to find the meaning of history in other loci. Hegel viewed history as a cosmic process moving toward culmination in an upward spiral, unlike nature that merely repeats itself. Hegel described this spiral as a dialectic progression from thesis to antithesis to synthesis, which became the new thesis. History is logical in its progression and, therefore, all events are historically necessary. The notion of determinism, so popular in scientific thought at the time, comes to mind. For Hegel, the meaning of history revealed itself in the emergence of the state, a political vision. Karl Marx adapted Hegel's philosophy of history to discover a different meaning found in economics. In both cases, reductionism occurred.

The positivist school of the philosophy of history would have a profound impact on New Testament studies. In an attempt to determine the facts of history, positivists rejected the views of authorities as they pressed for empirical data. The miraculous events of the New Testament attested by many witnesses could not have happened; therefore, one was left to understand how such stories could have emerged in the first place. Collingwood provides a stinging critique of the new method of historiography that continues to this day in New Testament studies, notably in the Jesus Seminar: "A radical historical skepticism resulted not from the use of critical methods but from a combination of those methods with uncriticized and unnoticed positivistic assumptions."[16]

Some historians have adopted a philosophy of history that views history in cycles. Oswald Spengler, an early-twentieth-century German historian, described history in terms of distinct cultures with unique expressions that nonetheless go through identical stages of life in a discernable cyclical pattern. In *The Decline of the West*, Spengler adopts the terminology of biology to describe the morphology of civilizations. Each civilization follows a predictable life process of "childhood, youth, manhood and old age" in succession.[17] Spengler argues for a natural, inevitable cycle from the vitality of youthful culture to the decay of worn-out civilization, which may persist in its forms but exists as little more than a rotting corpse. He offers China, India, and the Islamic world as examples of this phenomenon. Arnold Toynbee offered an alternative cyclical philosophy of history in his massive *Study of History*. Toynbee did not have quite the deterministic view of Spengler, for he explored civilizations that he regarded as arrested in infancy (i.e., Eskimo and Polynesian). Rather than holding to a deterministic inevitability, Toynbee explored how civilizations responded to challenges through their willingness to follow a creative leader.

The historian's philosophy of history provides the *Weltanschauung*, the *Gestalt*, the worldview, the paradigm, the template through which the historian sees the patterns and interprets the meaning of the past. It is not difficult for history to become confused with, and then identified as, the particular philosophical approach in vogue at the time. In this scant survey we can see that philosophy influences history, and that the scientific method has influenced philosophy. History, in its turn, has influenced New Testament studies. These influences usually go unrecognized, as adherents of one philosophical perspective or another cling to their view of the discipline in an ideological battle.

How does one's philosophy of history appear in an actual text? Christopher Hill gained a well-earned reputation as one of the twentieth century's most important historians of English Puritanism and the English Civil War. In *The World Turned Upside Down*, Hill remarked:

> History has to be rewritten in every generation, because although the past does not change, the present does; each generation asks new questions of the past, and finds new areas of sympathy as it re-lives different aspects of the experiences of its predecessors. . . .
>
> The historical narrative, the main outline of events, is given. No amount of detailed working over the evidence is going to change the factual essentials of the story. But the interpretation will vary with our attitudes, with our lives in the present. So interpretation is not only possible but necessary.[18]

In short, history has great propagandist value in the advance of one's ideology.

Theology is not exempt from the influence of philosophical thought that filters its consideration of the divine, the spiritual, the nature of the universe, the nature of Scripture, or any other theme. Rudolf Bultmann, one of the great Greek scholars of the twentieth century, gained more fame as a theologian than as a grammarian. He developed a method of biblical interpretation, demythologizing, that allowed him to retain his discipline while conforming it to a naturalistic worldview. Bultmann explained:

> The whole conception of the world which is presupposed in the preaching of Jesus as in the New Testament generally is mythological; i.e., the

conception of the world as being structured in three stories, heaven, earth and hell; the conception of the intervention of supernatural powers in the course of events; and the conception of miracles, especially the conception of the intervention of supernatural powers in the inner life of the soul, the conception that men can be tempted and corrupted by the devil and possessed by evil spirits. This conception of the world we call mythological because it is different from the conception of the world which has been formed and developed by science since its inception in ancient Greece and which has been accepted by all modern men. In this conception of the world the cause-and-effect nexus is fundamental. Although modern physical theories take account of chance in the chain of cause and effect in subatomic phenomena, our daily living, purposes and actions are not affected. In any case, modern science does not believe that the course of nature can be interrupted or, so to speak, perforated, by supernatural powers.[19]

Bultmann adopted a naturalistic philosophy of nature that forced him to reinterpret, or demythologize, all of his religion.

Every discipline undergoes a similar influence from philosophy, although it may not be as involved or entail as many alternative philosophical options. The professions have been molded by philosophical perspectives. Though John Dewey has been rigorously critiqued, his pragmatic philosophy of education probably still dominates in the United States. Dewey sought to hold philosophers to the same methodology as modern science: experience. In simplest terms, Dewey's experimentalism, or pragmatism, teaches that whatever works is true. Moreover, his philosophy of experimentalism, or pragmatism, is built on a foundation of assumed naturalism. A person who goes through an educational process guided by Dewey's philosophy may not be taught or hear a lecture about Dewey's pragmatism, but he or she will have learned it all the same.

Marketing has grown into one of the most important areas of modern life. It has a place within the academy and a major role in society. It borrows from economics, psychology, sociology, anthropology, mathematics, and statistics. Where does it find its philosophical foundation? Where does it learn to think about what it does? Steve Strombeck, former professor of marketing at Union University, guided me through his sober analysis of the philosophical underpinnings of marketing. It is a pragmatic discipline that strives for results. Its pragmatism is driven by a rigid empiricism that regards the numbers as truth. It may view other disciplines as a waste if they do not help the market function better. Since the knowledge valued by marketing changes constantly, history has no value.

Conclusion

The purpose of this chapter has been to explore the variety of ways in which the various disciplines influence one another, either directly or indirectly, intentionally or unintentionally. The subject deserves a major study, however; this exercise was little more than suggestive. Nonetheless, it does at least suggest the extent of influence that usually takes place uncritically. It suggests the extent to which aspects of almost every discipline may not actually have anything whatsoever to do with that discipline. It suggests the extent to which all disciplines are susceptible to the domination of a philosophical perspective. It raises the question of humane values in a naturalistic universe.

Last year a great debate erupted in a faculty meeting at my school. The issue is not important, but the dynamics are relevant to this discussion. A report was stated in a way that seemed to have tremendous philosophical and theological implications for some members of the faculty. After the debate had gone on for a few minutes, the committee member who had drafted the document explained that it had to be stated thus because the Modern Language Association (MLA) said so. We often accept the style guides or the prevailing attitudes of a discipline even though we do not participate in the discussion that led to the new standard. The basis for the establishment of the position, however, may be far from scientific, much like Bismarck's quip that "the making of laws is like the making of sausages—the less you know about the process, the more you respect the result." Prevailing MLA standards are based on the current values of those in the position to influence or control their adoption. The ends may be political, social, or purely idiosyncratic as well as the desired logic and simplicity of language. We may complain about changing our language patterns as a result of a change in MLA standards, but we tend to accept them nonetheless. At least this process is public and trumpeted. How often have we accepted the judgments on philosophical issues hidden in the ethos of other disciplines?

Why take so much time and space in a book that supposedly deals with faith? Because these are the points at which the issues of faith arise in the pursuit of knowledge. Faith does not stand opposed to knowledge and scholarship. It may, however, stand in conflict with some philosophical interpretations of the nature of knowledge and reality. It is important to recognize the playing field. Susan Jacob, dean of the school of nursing at Union University, has observed that in recent years several nursing textbooks have appeared that focus on alternative healing of an occult variety. Ralph Leverett, professor of special education and director of Union University's Center for Educational Practice, has observed that for philosophical reasons some education textbooks now have a muddied view of multiple intelligence. Do we recognize when our disciplines have been altered by philosophical influences from other disciplines?

Further Reading

Two books provide a readable and understandable introduction to several of the major rival philosophies that challenge Christianity in the marketplace. One need not have a background in philosophy to find these volumes helpful:

Cunningham, Richard B. *The Christian Faith and Its Contemporary Rivals.* Nashville: Broadman, 1988.
Sire, James W. *The Universe Next Door: A Basic Worldview Catalog,* 3d ed. Downers Grove, Ill.: InterVarsity, 1997.

8

Asking the Critical Questions

$\mathbf{F}$red McCormick lived next to me in graduate school. He was an artist who became a Christian and decided that he wanted to be a "Christian" artist. He told me that his mother once said to him, "Just remember, Fred, that there is more to Christian art than landscapes sprinkled with apostles." Many Christians in higher education shrink from the notion of teaching and writing as a "Christian" scholar for fear that it will mean sprinkling their research and lectures with apostles. Others shrink from attempting to engage their discipline as a person of faith because they have seen others' efforts that seemed vacuous at best. A worst-case scenario might be found in the well-meaning mathematics professor who presents the following problem: Jesus had five loaves and two fishes. Into how many pieces must he divide each fish in order to feed five thousand men?

In fact, a fair amount of what people represent to be the integration of faith and learning really is not. It may be appropriate in its context, but it is something other than the intellectual engagement of an academic discipline with the insights and understandings of faith.

The Devotional Approach

In the devotional approach to faith and learning, the two exist alongside each other. The content of the academic discipline, however, functions as a basis for providing life lessons or illustrations of biblical

155

truth. Analogy plays a strong role in this relationship. An example of this approach appears in an article dealing with Christian colleges. The article, which appeared in *The Chronicle of Higher Education*, quotes a student from a Christian college noted for its emphasis on the integration of faith and learning:

> Just as the plants in my ecosite are growing well, despite the fact that they are not in the spotlight, I too can grow in Christ even while I am not center stage. The difference is that plants and insects have a more limited capability to adapt to different environment [*sic*] and niches, while humans are much more capable with help of the Lord Jesus Christ.[1]

The statement deals with biology, but only as an analogy to describe the Christian life and the believer's relationship to Christ. Faith does not inform science, and science does not inform faith. Rather, they stand alongside each other metaphorically. The statement is not a statement of faith and learning, but a statement of faith alone. Within a Christian institution, this approach has validity as an expression of piety and devotion in the midst of life. It should not, however, be mistaken for the intellectual task of grappling with the faith implications of how people approach their disciplines. The question of faith and learning in this statement would involve what the student means by "adapt."

The Over-Under Approach

In some approaches, faith stands over disciplines in determining their content. In these cases faith usually involves a fairly thorough predetermined understanding about what kind of knowledge may be possible or impossible based on a particular reading of the Bible. This approach usually leads to the rejection of ideas or their practical application. An example of this approach would be the rejection of blood transfusions by Jehovah's Witnesses based on their interpretation of the biblical prohibition against drinking blood. Another example would be the rejection of big bang cosmology or geological conclusions about an old earth based on Archbishop James Ussher's (1581–1656) calculations for the age of the universe.

The problem with placing religion over the other disciplines lies in a failure to recognize the extent to which Christianity always involves interpreting the primary data of biblical revelation through a matrix of influences. In both cases cited, those who reject a particular field of learning do so on the basis of a textual interpretation rather than a clear article of faith, such as the resurrection or the incarnation. This critique should not imply that faith will not or should not reject some views and applications of knowledge. But it does suggest that an approach more self-aware than the over-under approach will be more beneficial for faith seeking understanding.

In other approaches, the disciplines stand over faith in determining what cognitive meaning is possible for faith. In these cases, the disciplines limit options for religious knowledge as well as possible conceptions of God. An example of this approach surfaced at a conference on science and religion held in Chicago in 2000.[2] While the speakers stressed the importance of a dialogical approach, they also stressed that the sciences should have priority in the conversation. On the surface, this demand is reasonable. After all, science is so much more scientific. Upon closer examination, however, we may detect the fatal flaw.

If we want science to have priority over religion, we must then ask, "Which science?" Scientific knowledge is a moving target, always changing. Whenever religion has built itself on a scientific foundation, it has paid the price. In the late Middle Ages, the church allowed scientific understanding to guide theology. Copernicus, Kepler, and Galileo did not conflict with the creeds of Christian faith; they conflicted with the dogma of the best science of the day: Aristotle and Ptolemy. In other words, every discipline can easily fall victim to what C. S. Lewis described as "chronological snobbery," by which he meant the view that prevailing ideas of the moment were the final truth.[3] Every discipline has its current fashion that replaced the old, out-of-date way of thinking. Though we can look back and see the endless stream of discarded ideas, we have great difficulty emotionally dealing with the idea that the current fashion could ever pass away. We are reluctant to recognize the extent to which emotion plays a part in our work.

In a reciprocal approach, however, both parties in the conversation extend mutual respect by recognizing the validity of the other's realm. A true dialogue involves a degree of humility that recognizes the limitations and methodological problems common to all disciplines. This humility involves the ability to distinguish between God, God's revelation, and human attempts to understand and interpret revelation. This humility also involves the recognition that knowledge in all the disciplines is a shadow that constantly moves across the face of human experience.

Critical Engagement

Within the academy, one of the games we play is what Wittgenstein called *language games*. Among people interested in the appropriate presence of faith in the academy, it is not surprising to find that no small amount of energy has gone into arriving at the most appropriate way to discuss this presence. Many people choose to speak of the integration of faith and learning. C. S. Lewis did not care for this choice of words because it suggested that the Christian has brought something into the discipline that was not already there. Whatever terminology one chooses to use, the enterprise certainly involves discovering the presence of faith issues within a discipline. This discovery process uses a skill to which most academic people aspire: asking critical questions.

I did not have a philosophy course in undergraduate school. When I took my first philosophy course in graduate school, I studied with an articulate, urbane, prematurely silver-haired, sophisticated professor who continually told us that we needed to learn to ask the critical questions. Whenever he made this statement, I sat poised to jot them down in my notes, yet he never gave us the list of critical questions. Instead, he seemed to badger students and pick on them mercilessly during class discussions. He had little use for glittering generalities or appeals to "what everybody knows" to substantiate an argument. He once asked me to declare my presuppositions as I was presenting a paper in his class. I announced that I had no presuppositions in writing the paper; I was purely objective. What followed remains vague in my memory, no doubt due to some psychological defense mechanism, but by the end of the hour he had managed to dismantle both the paper and me. He never did give the class that "list" of critical questions, yet by the end of the semester I had begun to ask them.

Asking critical questions is an acquired skill that develops in conversation with others. Unfortunately, some who master the skill use it as a weapon in a malicious effort to humiliate others. It can degenerate into a rhetorical debating technique designed to throw an opponent (or academic rival) off guard and put them in the worst possible light. In its best role, however, critical questioning becomes a tool to advance the thought and understanding of colleagues who are willing to discover error in their own ways of thinking. Once when leading a preaching workshop for pastors in Minnesota, I suggested the importance of having a critical understanding of how one interprets the Bible. One of the pastors quickly responded that he never interprets the Bible; he just preaches the truth.

Harold Heie has developed examples of what he refers to as *integrative questions* for a variety of disciplines. In some cases the questions of faith arise from the discipline, and in other cases the question of faith is brought to the discipline. Allowing the question to arise from the discipline and then exploring its implications would be a more appropriate approach in a secular environment. In a Christian institution, however, one has the luxury of being able to bring more pointed questions of faith to the disciplines.

Biology: To what extent, if any, should genetic engineering be used to enhance human well-being?

English: What are the similarities and differences in interpreting biblical texts and other literature?

Sociology/Social Work: To what extent are social problems caused by inadequacies in societal structures or by individual or group irresponsibility?

Business: What social responsibility, if any, does business enterprise have toward its employees and the geographical region in which the business is located?

Political Science: What is the role of forgiveness in international relations?

Criminal Justice: To what extent should the penal system be retributive or restorative, or both?

Fine Arts: What are the limits, if any, on the freedom for human creative expression?

History: How do alternative views on the "direction of history" (e.g., linear, cyclical, teleological) fit or not fit with the Christian narrative?

Computer Science: What are the ethical implications for use of the internet?

Economics: What is the relationship between the quest for profitability and the Christian call for compassion and justice?

Education: What is the relationship between subject-centered and student-centered teaching pedagogies in light of a Christian perspective on personhood?

Physics: What are the similarities and differences between the use of models in scientific inquiry and the use of models in theological inquiry?

Sports Medicine: What are the limits, if any, on allowable means for enhancing athletic performance?

Communications: What is the potential for finding common ground through dialogue when the conversationalists are embedded in different traditions?

Mathematics: Are mathematical principles created or discovered?[4]

Another approach to critical engagement can come through a dialogical process. When Jimmy H. Davis and I wrote our first book on science and religion, we used the dialogical approach to organize the book.[5] As a professor of chemistry, he represented the perspective of the sciences. As a professor of faith and culture, I represented the perspective of religion. As discussed in chapter 6, different disciplines frequently have a concern for the same area of study, but they treat different aspects of the area. We could have asked what science thinks about the Genesis account of creation. We could have asked what religion thinks about Darwin's theory of natural selection. Instead, we chose to ask open-ended questions that would lead to deeper engagement. We also tried to make the questions as simple as possible. Simplicity has the advantage of avoiding inflammatory bias while at the same time penetrating the fundamental presuppositions we hold.

Our first question, "What can we know and how do we know it?" has implications for virtually every discipline, although the stakes are higher in some disciplines than in others. This question opens the discussion on epistemology or the philosophy of knowledge. Science and religion rely on different ways of knowing, yet not exclusively so. We normally think of science as knowledge through sensory experience (empiricism) or logical calculation (rationalism). In his famous essay *Eureka* (1848), Edgar Allan Poe argued that science must acknowledge the extent to which scientific advances have come through neither of these two processes. Instead, some of the greatest advances have come through intuition. His essay would remain unappreciated as his most *un*important work for more than a hundred years, but then science caught up with Poe. In his essay he argued that the universe had begun from an original, primordial speck. He went on to expound the big bang theory. In comparing Poe's description of the origin of the universe with the current prevailing cosmology, several differences emerge. These differences, however, are of the sort between Copernicus and Kepler. The point to be made is that a poet and literary critic who studied languages at the University of Virginia arrived intuitively at an understanding of the universe that physicists had failed to grasp. Embedded within his argument was a means of illustrating the power of intuition.

Questions of epistemology are central to the enterprise of faith and learning. Is religious knowledge legitimate? Is it real? While these sorts of questions were asked of religious knowledge throughout the modern era, the question has now turned on empiricism and rationalism. Extreme skepticism asks if we can know anything. In an age of quantum uncertainty and cultural ambivalence, a relativistic attitude toward knowledge has affected many disciplines, from physics to literature.

Such an attitude poses problems for the validity of the scholarly enterprise in all disciplines.

Our second question, "What kind of universe exists?" strikes at the heart of both physical and metaphysical (spiritual) reality. Different cultures have different perspectives on this question. Even the scientific world has different perspectives on the question. The question has subdivisions. Cosmology refers to the current state of the universe, while cosmogony refers to the origin of the universe. The Western scientific tradition, from Aristotle until the twentieth century, regarded the universe as static and without beginning. During the second half of the twentieth century, the old view was replaced by a view that the universe had a beginning and has been in a state of expansion ever since.

Within Hindu culture, the physical world is the expression of deity, much in the way that a smile is an expression of inner feeling. Within Islamic culture, everything that happens occurs as the direct will of God; therefore, the scientific notion of independent "laws of nature" does not have the same currency as in western Europe. Within Zen Buddhist culture, the world is an illusion that does not really exist; thus, there is no physical world to examine. The physical illusion merely detracts from ultimate reality. Within the old Marxist-Leninist culture of the Soviet Union, no ultimate reality existed apart from the material world.

How people understand the universe will affect how they think about the world in which they live. Their view forms the starting point for how all other knowledge fits together. It becomes the mold into which they pour what they know. The rest of knowledge must conform to this mold, which represents a primary organizing principle. Everyone with the intellectual capacity to reflect on such matters has a fundamental presupposition about the nature of the universe, including whether it involves a metaphysical and a physical dimension. Modern Americans are accustomed to thinking more in terms of the physical universe; people in the Orient tend to think more in terms of the metaphysical. A Westerner may not believe that the spiritual world exists, but an Easterner may not believe that the physical world of empirical experience exists.

Our third question, "Where did we come from?" focuses on the origin of life, but it also raises other questions about meaning and purpose in life. Most arguments about the nature and origin of life are not based on this question. This subject may be the battleground, but the actual differences of opinion, the weapons and tactics of the battle, depend on what we can know and how we know it, and on what kind of universe exists. In other words, the great debates of life hinge on the simplest of questions that accumulate into complex issues. We hold to extensive and profound presuppositions about reality, and we carry these with us into other conversations. We build our views on what we assume about life. How one deals with life's great moral and ethical issues, which have arisen largely through the scholarly work of the academy, will depend on a person's views on knowledge and the nature of the universe. Critical questions probe the foundations for presuppositions and explore the legitimacy of uncritical presuppositions. Critical questioning also probes the merits of the prevailing popular hierarchy of these views of knowledge.

What Does It Mean to Be Human?

The purpose of this chapter, if it has not yet become apparent, is to illustrate how asking critical questions exposes the religious themes already present in every discipline. While some questions arise with respect to only one or two disciplines, some questions cross the boundaries of disciplines. We saw this dynamic in the discussion of interdisciplinary dialogue in chapter 7. After writing two broad books on science and religion, Jimmy Davis and I decided that we wanted our next book to focus quite narrowly on a single subject that we could treat thoroughly: we wanted to explore the meaning of life. In asking what it means to be human, however, we suddenly realized that every discipline has a stake in the question. Every discipline has its own perspective on the question and something to contribute to the answer. It is not a subject that can be conceded to biology or genetics. In the early 1970s, one frequently heard that the issue of abortion was a private question between a woman and her doctor. That being the case, exactly what does the doctor have to say on the matter?

In as little as five or ten minutes, Dr. Davis and I thought of a variety of issues that concern different disciplines in relation to the question "What does it mean to be human?"

Art—why people make art
Biology—the genetic code and human freedom
Chemistry—the chemical building blocks of life
Communications—the animal that fails to communicate
Economics—greed and reciprocity
Ethics—the animal that kills its own kind
History—the animal that tells its own story
Literature—the animal that has to hear stories
Music—the animal that must sing and make melody
Philosophy—the rational animal

Political science—the animal that seeks and exerts power and
influence

Psychology—the animal that hides within itself

Religion—the animal that talks to what it cannot see

Sociology—the animal that creates social structures

Social work—the animal that cares about those least fit for survival

Sports and recreation—the animal that organizes games

This brief list illustrates that a simple question may have far-reaching
implications. A reductionist approach to one's discipline may tend to
defer the abortion question to a woman and her doctor, as though life
were merely a medical question. If one assumes the materialist understanding of the universe, then one may adopt Darwin's explanation of
life as merely natural selection. Under this theory, every dimension of
human life has some basis for survival but no transcendent meaning.
In exploring the critical questions that arise from a discipline, we often
move beneath the question at hand to the underlying presuppositions
that lead to a materialistic interpretation of the data rather than to some
other interpretation. The Christian need not surrender the field when
raw data allows for a variety of interpretations, all of which involve
some basic religious position. Even materialism defines itself negatively with respect to the prevailing view of the human race by denying
non-material realities.

The Natural Sciences

In the exploration of the relationship between the doctrines of the
Christian faith and the academic disciplines in chapter 6, we observed
that every discipline has some primary relationship to a doctrine of the
Christian faith in terms of its primary subject matter. In simplistic terms,
we may say that the natural sciences relate to the doctrine of creation. It
would be a mistake, however, to think that all critical questions of faith
and science will involve the doctrine of creation. In *Science and Faith*,
Dr. Davis and I moved beyond the foundational issues of epistemology
and cosmology to questions raised by virtue of recent scientific advances
in quantum mechanics and chaos theory.

As physicists gained the ability to probe the depths of the atom,
they discovered something that came as a great shock. The atom was
not composed of billiard balls running along wire rings around a solid
center, as the models portrayed. Depending on what the physicist was
trying to find, the interior of the atom appeared to be either continu-

ous waves or discrete particles. To make matters worse, instead of neat orbits like Aristotle's perfect circles, electrons appeared to have a range within which they moved, an inner orbit and an outer orbit. While the electron moves from the inner to the outer orbit and back again, it does not travel. In other words, it leaps from one orbit to the other, but it does not appear in the space between the inner and outer range. This phenomenon raises enormous questions about the nature of the universe (cosmology). The phenomenon also raises questions about the nature of knowledge (epistemology) because what the observer could observe depended on what he or she was looking for and the method of observation. The observer could detect the speed of the electron, but not its location. On the other hand, the observer could detect the location of the electron, but not its speed. Furthermore, the most the observer could hope for is mathematical probability rather than absolute certainty. If the world of quantum mechanics seems strange to the reader, take comfort in the fact that it seemed strange to Einstein as well.

How does one interpret the data of quantum mechanics? It depends on what one believes about the nature of the universe. Niels Bohr, who carried out the initial research on quantum mechanics, became a devotee of Hinduism, and he interpreted the data from that perspective: the world only appears to be here; it is created by the observer. The data, however, does not demand Bohr's interpretation. From a Christian perspective, the wave-particle phenomenon is not so surprising in a universe presided over by one who is fully God and fully human. Ideas do have consequences, as Richard Weaver suggested. The idea of a creator God who became incarnate has profound implications for what kind of universe exists. Alfred North Whitehead, not a professing Christian, argued that modern science emerged in the West precisely because the Christian faith provided for a tangible world that could be known. Rather than inhibit scientific discovery, the foundational teachings of Christianity make scientific discovery possible. Other worldviews call into question the possibility of knowledge about something that may not be there after all.

Besides shaking the scientific notion of certainty that had placed such faith in empiricism, quantum theory also dashed the dogma of determinism. In its extreme form, the concept of cause and effect had grown to view the universe as a place in which all events were determined by events that had preceded them, thus disallowing personal freedom. At the quantum level, this determinism broke down and the universe opened up. There was no place for God in a deterministic universe, but could God have a place in an open universe? Is a quantum universe one in which God can interact with nature?

What are the implications of an open universe for a notion of God's sovereignty?

The point of this discussion is that more than the discipline of physics is involved in interpreting the data of quantum mechanics. The discipline of physics makes it possible to collect the data. Previous discoveries of physics form a framework for understanding the new data, but at some point questions about the data must be raised. Raising questions from a Christian perspective is no less scientific than raising questions from a Hindu, materialistic, or Aristotelian perspective. Einstein actually altered his data to conform to an Aristotelian understanding of a static universe.

Chaos theory has also challenged the conventional understanding of the nature of the universe. For most of the modern period, the project of science involved discovering and describing the laws of nature. These laws provided scientists with great predictive power under controlled laboratory conditions. The laws were universal: heat rises, water evaporates at a certain temperature and condenses at another, changes in barometric pressure create air movement, and so forth. Put them all together, however, and it becomes impossible to predict the weather with reliable accuracy beyond the short term. In retrospect, one may describe how the laws of nature operated to create a specific weather condition, but so many variables exist that the phenomenon cannot be predicted in advance.

In such a situation we may ask the critical question Does life have a goal or purpose? Or, make it more generic: Does the universe have a goal or purpose? Put another way, we may ask, Does chaos suggest a closed, deterministic universe of cause and effect, or an open universe in which God might operate without violating any of nature's laws? Data by itself does not demand a naturalistic answer. If one brings naturalistic assumptions to the data, however, then naturalistic answers will follow.

One of the foundational teachings of the Christian faith involves the return of Christ and the end of time and of the physical universe as we know it. Just as scientific data allows for various interpretations, so the basic teachings of faith allow for different interpretations. The return of Christ has produced many false interpretations, but the data of faith remains. The Christian faith assumes a goal or purpose for nature as a whole and life in particular. This brief review illustrates that while a discipline or family of disciplines (the natural sciences) may have one primary doctrine to which it corresponds (creation), it may also interact with many other doctrines (eschatology, incarnation, sovereignty of God).

The Social Sciences

Because they grow out of the primary doctrine of the *imago dei*, the questions that arise in the social sciences will be quite different from the questions of the natural sciences. In exploring the varied dimensions of psychology, sociology, history, political science, and economics, questions arise that relate to many other foundational teachings of the Christian faith. The social sciences have in common their object of study: humanity. These disciplines explore both the heights and the depths of humanity. Well-trained and competent scholars in one of the social science disciplines will discover the data of their study regardless of their presuppositions about the nature of knowledge and the nature of the universe. How they interpret the data, however, will vary greatly, depending on what they believe about knowledge and nature.

An additional issue comes to the social sciences that the natural sciences do not have to consider (though they often do): How do we explain the problem of evil? A naturalist or materialist will answer this question, based not on the data but on their presuppositions about materialism or naturalism. What has gone wrong with human history? What causes people to break down at the psychological and social levels? What is it about political and economic systems that leads to failure? The Christian perspective brings with it the concept of sin. Dare social scientists consider the possibility of sin as a reality in their interpretation of the data? Why would we consider this idea invalid when compared to other ideas that come from worldview presuppositions rather than from empirical data?

Instead of subatomic particles, the social scientist deals with people and their institutions, yet some questions have a familiar ring. Does history have a goal or purpose (eschatology)? Is God involved in history (sovereignty)? What is the solution to the human problem (soteriology, incarnation, pneumatology)? In one sense people are much more accessible objects of study than electrons, but in a more profound way we are more elusive than the electron we cannot track from one orbit to the next. What is it about the assumptions of social sciences that makes social scientists less willing than natural scientists to consider the transcendent (epistemology)? As the ultimate chaos system, humanity remains veiled in unpredictability. This being the case, the social sciences lack the predictive power of chemistry and physics. Possibly for this reason, the social sciences tend to adopt a materialistic philosophy of the nature of humanity. In attempting to "get a handle on" humanity, materialism helps to reduce people to objects. Such reductionism, however, creates a blinder that would prevent a scholar from recognizing the transcendent if transcendence actually exists.

The Arts and Humanities

When we move from the social sciences to the humanities, we move
from the study of human behavior to the study of human communication. Ironically, many scholars within this family of disciplines have
given up on attaching meaning to human communication. Whereas
chemistry and physics have standard methodologies that correspond to
a consensus about what they "do," the humanities lack such a consensus about methodology or purpose. Even the decision about whether a
discipline belongs in the humanities or the social sciences hinges on the
confusion over what these disciplines do and how they do it. Is history a
social science or a humanity? The answer to this question has profound
religious implications regardless of one's religion or lack thereof.

Perhaps the humanities should be considered alongside the arts as
twins in the liberal arts curriculum. They may be siblings of the sciences, but they are more like each other than their scientific siblings.
The arts and humanities face a crisis in Western culture largely related
to the absence of a clear purpose and method. Unfortunately, students
of these disciplines and broader society recognize this problem, which
is not unlike the awareness that the emperor has no clothes. On the
lips of a freshman confronted with the core curriculum, it sounds like,
"Why do I have to take *that?*" Detached from any transcendent value, it
becomes increasingly difficult to make a case for the arts and humanities in a secular, pragmatic society. These disciplines (of which I am
a member) tend to sound like salaries in search of a job description.
Science did not develop in cultures that failed to affirm a physical dimension to reality. The arts and humanities depend on the affirmation
of a transcendent dimension of reality. Western culture now lies in the
crosshairs of a bizarre paradox: the sciences have begun to question
the reality of the physical world under the influence of some Eastern
interpretations of quantum mechanics, while the humanities have begun
to reject the reality of transcendence. Those who see this paradox have
the responsibility to point out that the emperor has no clothes, before
he catches his death of cold.

Within the field of literature, confusion of methodology suggests the
crisis in the academy. Various methodologies represent entirely different visions for the purpose of studying literature. Among the many
voices, we find both feminist criticism and deconstruction. Although the
feminist approach may come as a shock to traditionalists, it nonetheless has strong value commitments. These commitments appear to be
nonnegotiable. One might venture to call them *absolutes*. Deconstructionism, on the other hand, dismisses the notion of absolutes. Feminist
criticism, like Marxist criticism, is rooted in a political/social struggle;

deconstructionism is rooted in a philosophical position. Psychological criticism, rooted in the work of Freud, attempts to analyze literature in terms of the psychological explanation of behaviors present in the story. In other words, the principles of interpretation in these forms of criticism do not arise from the discipline of literature but are imported into it from other disciplines. The questions one asks of the text depend on the presuppositional starting point of the method of interpretation, and a Christian has a larger critical toolbox than any of these methods of interpretation.[6]

Each of these approaches gives a partial, and flawed, picture. They all tend to deny the insights of one another. A Christian can ask the same kinds of questions of the text but without the same restriction of options that these ideological approaches impose on their adherents. In the absence of a discipline-wide consensus about the nature of literary criticism, Christian literary critics may ask broader questions: for example, Why must people tell stories? and Why must people hear stories? Is storytelling merely a survival mechanism of the species, or does it reveal something more about what it means to be human?

Philosophy has suffered from the same sort of malaise that has afflicted literary studies, though it began earlier and influenced the development of deconstructionism in literary criticism. Once natural philosophy peeled off to become science and moral philosophy peeled off to become ethics, philosophy has had to struggle over its task. From its preeminent place in the academy, it has been relegated to a minor position. In antiquity, philosophy always had a divided opinion as to its task and method. During the Middle Ages, however, a cultural consensus grew up about the *right* way to approach philosophy. For more than five hundred years, the Christian West took Augustine's lead and followed Plato. A period of conflict arose in the late Middle Ages, but for another period of five hundred years, the emerging modern world favored the empirically oriented philosophy of Aristotle, following the lead of Thomas Aquinas.

For some years, the modern cultural consensus has been softening, if not collapsing. Some say we now live in a postmodern world. At least we live in a world that is seeking to find its way. If anything has been noted in this book, it is the importance of philosophical presuppositions and the way disciplines may be influenced by unstated philosophical ideas. Philosophy, more than any other discipline, provides the tools for asking the critical questions. Unfortunately, many of those teaching in higher education today have not been exposed to enough philosophy even to understand the logical or epistemological issues at stake within their own disciplines. This deficiency in education leaves one susceptible to the uncritical acceptance of philosophical ideas or logical fallacies that may creep into the tradition of a discipline.

Philosophers know how to ask the critical questions, and Christian philosophers have made some of the strongest contributions to the project of engaging the secular academy with the Christian faith perspective. People like William Lane Craig, Nicholas Wolterstorff, Eleonore Stump, Richard Swinburne, and Alvin Plantinga represent the sort of Christian philosopher who has earned a place as a recognized figure in the secular academy. These scholars are representative but by no means exhaust the list of prominent Christian philosophers who have standing among secular philosophers. L. Joseph Rosas III, the Kierkegaard scholar, has suggested why Christians have succeeded so well in finding a place within philosophy:

> Where philosophy has an advantage is that its critical skepticism causes it to challenge any truth claim, thereby allowing it to be open to ultimate truth claims. The scientific method has no special privilege. All truth claims are admitted to the table of critical inquiry.[7]

With philosophy in a state of disarray, Christian philosophers have had a remarkable opportunity to make a contribution and give direction to the course of inquiry. Other Christians who teach in the humanities may take encouragement and follow the example of their colleagues in philosophy. During periods of imprecision, great opportunities open up for charting a new course.

Art and music differ from other humanities in terms of what they do. While art and music may involve historical and critical study, the focus of these disciplines for most people involves the production of art and music. For the musician, production may involve composition and/or performance. Do these disciplines still involve critical questions? What makes art or music "Christian"? Can we speak of anything distinctive about Christian art and music when Christians in Africa, Asia, and South America produce works informed by their own cultures that bear little resemblance to one another? Or do Christian art and music become indigenous as they bring distinctively Christian themes, attitudes, and perspectives into the art forms of a culture? Until quite recently art and music could not be separated from the religious perspective of a culture. The separation has only occurred in the West in the last two hundred years. What happens to art when it does not have a spiritual foundation? What distinctive attitudes and perspectives of artists affect how they produce their work? Is it possible to speak of art and music as good or bad, and if so, why?

The study of languages may appear to have no faith implications whatsoever, but it would be a serious misapprehension to think so. My eighth-grade Latin teacher, Mrs. Mabel Lever, drilled into our young minds that in translation, we translate not words but ideas. Languages reflect the cultures in which they develop. Language philosophers like Heidegger and Wittgenstein have made much of the limitations of language, but also of the sense in which language embodies the very ethos of a culture. The Hebrew language does not use time-based verb tenses like English past, present, and future tenses. Instead, Hebrew is concerned with the quality of action, whether it is complete, incomplete, or continuous. The English language devises new words for whatever it wants to express. It may borrow from other languages, mix metaphors, shuffle existing words, and murder logic, but it comes up with new words. German, on the other hand, combines existing words to create new words. The new words are virtual sentences or phrases. For instance, speedy is *geschwind,* speed is *Geschwindigkeit,* speeding is *Geschwindigkeitsübertretung.*

Languages embody the values and mental processes of a people. When the values change, the language changes. The last great change in the English language occurred in the seventeenth century, when the formal and informal second-person pronoun collapsed into one word: *you.* The French continue to maintain a distinction between what in English used to be *ye* and *thou.*

When I first studied Koine Greek (the Greek of the Hellenistic period), my Greek professor ranted incessantly about the aorist tense. Elementary textbooks will commonly explain that the aorist tense expresses punctiliar, or point-in-time, action. In fact, it expresses indefinite action. Pedagogists like to speak of it as point action because it is easier for beginners to remember. The word *aorist* is formed of the Greek *a,* known as the alpha privative because it negates the word that follows it, and the Greek word *horizō,* which means "boundary, limit." So, *aorist tense* means "action without boundary or limit," quite the opposite of punctiliar action. In my study of Greek and Hebrew, I discovered that the languages are the gate into the mind-set or worldview of the ancient cultures.

If language study involves only the memorization of vocabulary and rules of grammar, it has little to do with faith. If this is all it entails, however, it probably has little to do with education either. It would explain why so few Americans can speak or read another language besides English. At a time when language programs are suffering in major and minor institutions around the country, Christian linguists asking profound questions about the nature and power of language to house a worldview may provide the creativity to reinvigorate language study.

Theology presents an intriguing case among the humanities. What can one say about it, since after all, theology is about faith? The intriguing situation with theology is that it was among the first disciplines to distance itself from faith. Theology began to adopt empiricism as the standard for knowledge in the late seventeenth century. From then on, scholars labored to arrive at the scientific way to understand the Bible and religion. Not all theologians followed this path, of course. Calvin laid out an approach to theology that, in its stress on specific revelation, left no place for the physical world in the revelatory activity of God. The project to integrate faith and culture has received its greatest impetus in recent years from the Reformed tradition. Yet, ironically, the Reformed tradition has played an equally important role in the empirical, natural theology tradition of separating the spiritual realm of faith from the physical world of learning. Segments of the Reformed tradition capitulated to empiricism, notably followers of Barth and Bultmann. Barth came to regard the Bible as a record of revelatory experiences, while Bultmann regarded the Bible as an expression of the faith experiences in the life of the early church. Each adopted a form of radical separation between the world of faith and the world of human experience.

Biblical criticism has tended to track developments in literary criticism, though usually adopting new methods just as they were passing from the scene in literary circles. Theological method has mirrored approaches to historical study that tend to focus on sociological and political issues in vogue at the time. Projects such as the Jesus Seminar have proceeded from presuppositions that regard the Bible as essentially a cultural document. This methodology searches for a reason why the early church would insert statements into the story of Jesus that suggest he knew the future. The assumption is that people cannot know the future; therefore, Jesus could not have predicted his death or the destruction of Herod's temple in Jerusalem.

Theology has struggled with the same secularizing trends that have affected every other discipline of the academy. Not all theologians have embraced naturalistic assumptions. Persistent are the alternative approaches to theological study holding a theory of knowledge that allows for specific, cognitive revelation from God. Among Catholic, Protestant, and Orthodox theologians, a sizeable group has clung to the orthodox faith. Different assumptions lead to different critical questions, with one group seeking to understand the faith and another seeking to understand the phenomenon of faith. In the United States, evangelical theologians have largely withdrawn from the secular academy to carry on their conversations among themselves. This leaves the larger discipline without a dissenting voice to raise the critical questions. Naturalistic assumptions have become such a common part of the theological community that they are seen as an essential aspect of what it means to be scholarly. Unfortunately, the community fails to recognize that these assumptions merely represent presuppositions brought to the discipline before the work begins. Evangelical scholars may raise the critical questions in the safety of the evangelical community, with its evangelical gatherings of scholars and evangelical publishing houses and evangelical journals, but those who know how to ask the critical questions have a responsibility to find a way to ask those who need to hear them.

The Professions

As detailed in chapters 6 and 7, the professions are interdisciplinary in nature. They draw upon the findings, skills, and methods of many disciplines in order to do what they do. The professions are action oriented: they involve the application of knowledge to concrete situations. Is it possible to assimilate the prevailing presuppositions of other disciplines when borrowing so broadly? Like music and art, the professions are primarily concerned with performance, although expectations have led the academy to develop comparable scholarly activities apart from performance. In the end the greatest philosophical lure for the professions is pragmatism: what works. Critical thought has lost the day when the most serious critical question is, How can you argue with success?

We should not be surprised if the professions are driven by pragmatism, especially if the other disciplines offer no more attractive option. The other disciplines have the luxury of contemplating many ideas as theories, but when those ideas reach the professions, they translate into practical results. Deeply embedded philosophical ideas borrowed from other disciplines by the professions will eventually emerge with practical implications. Likewise, logical inconsistencies can result when the presuppositions of some philosophical positions conflict with the stated values of a profession. This kind of conflict can be seen particularly in the caring professions, such as medicine, nursing, and social work. Philosophical or political agendas that have become identified with a discipline become indistinguishable from that discipline when it is appropriated by a profession. An example of this logical contradiction in values can be observed in the nursing profession when nurses are encouraged both to view abortion as merely a matter of choice for a woman who has control over her own body and to see prenatal care as a right of the unborn child.[8] This crisis of conflicting values has come to such a fevered pitch that many medical schools have begun to drop the Hippocratic oath from the medical degree ceremony. Likewise, in the social-work profession, the core value of the inherent dignity and worth of all people has no basis in a naturalistic world. In recent years, however, social work has reversed the secularizing trend of modernity to once again recognize the importance of the spiritual dimension of life.[9]

We should not be surprised by the ethics or lack of ethics found in business, law, and politics if students who enter these fields learned through the process of higher education that the spiritual domain and the physical domain do not intersect. If spiritual matters are private affairs, they have no place in the marketplace. If higher education frees students of the encumbrance of ultimate values, we should not be surprised when they act upon the ideas they have been taught by the academy.

When we move from the classical disciplines to the professions, we move from ideas to their consequences. If professors within the professions borrow from the insights and knowledge gained from other disciplines, they must also do the work of critiquing current thought to distinguish knowledge from philosophical presupposition. Some professions, like education, intentionally examine the philosophical foundations of their profession. This examination, however, needs to equip students to examine the foundations of ideas they will be called upon to teach for the next fifty years.

Conclusion

This chapter has stressed the importance of recognizing and understanding the presuppositions and assumptions embedded in the theories and methodologies prevalent in the disciplines of the academy. Sometimes these presuppositions are cultural (e.g., Minnesotans are smarter than Iowans). Sometimes they are philosophical (e.g., empiricism is the final test of truth or knowledge). They can be social (e.g., a woman's place is in the home). They are often economic (e.g., business is the business of America). Sometimes they are noble (e.g., all men are created equal). Too often they are tawdry (e.g., the public be damned!). The first responsibility of a Christian scholar to his or her discipline is to offer the discipline a critique of its prevailing presuppositions. This responsibility is a service to the academy because it leads to a clarification of the discipline's work.

This exploration of foundational biases and presuppositions by no means exhausts the meaning of faith and learning. It is a bare beginning, but it is a necessary beginning. If this critical issue is understood, then the critical questions that engage faith and culture will begin to flow. Without this basic understanding, little can happen. We may know intuitively that something is wrong without being quite sure of the problem. If a new idea surfaces in the discipline that seems to conflict with one of the basic assertions of faith, it is time for some of the most basic critical questions that we learn as children: Why? Why not? Who says? This exercise also compels us to understand the essential message of the gospel so that we can learn to distinguish the layers of interpretation and cultural ornamentation that we may have confused for true faith. In this sense, the dialogue between faith and academic discipline may give us enough insight to reject a false teaching that had become a stumbling block.

The careful reader may have also noted that disciplines are organized in this chapter differently from previous chapters. The organization is close but not quite the same. This minor variation reflects differences between how institutions regard the disciplines. Is history a social science or a humanity, and for that matter, why can we move a discipline from one academic family to another? Does this movement represent a vagueness of the subject matter or a shift in the values of those who handle the subject, or something else? What does this say about the discipline's subject matter and the method of investigation? What does this say about the nature of the academy? Some in the academy see organizational structures as practical matters that do not affect the substance of education, but they are mistaken. It is not enough to ask the critical questions of our own discipline. If Sullivan was correct and form does indeed follow function, we must ask critical questions of the entire function of higher education.

Further Reading

Several important resources give further insight into how a variety of scholars in a variety of disciplines go about asking the critical questions:

Books & Culture (www.booksandculture.com)
First Things (www.firstthings.com)
Mars Hill Audio Journal (www.marshillaudio.org)
Touchstone (www.touchstonemag.com)

Because they enable interaction and conversation, personal relationships and networks provide some of the most stimulation in considering the critical questions of one's discipline. Three ministries in particular are dedicated to fostering such relationships and networks through their conferences and other meetings:

C. S. Lewis Foundation (www.cslewis.org)
The Wilberforce Forum (www.wilberforce.org)
InterVarsity Faculty Ministry (www.intervarsity.org/grad/index.html)

A listing of discipline-specific organizations for Christian faculty in higher education is found in the appendix.

Two books illustrate ways to go about asking the critical questions:

Garber, Steven. *The Fabric of Faithfulness: Weaving Together Belief and Behavior during the University Years.* Downers Grove, Ill.: InterVarsity, 1996.

Sire, James W. *Habits of the Mind: Intellectual Life as a Christian Calling.* Downers Grove, Ill.: InterVarsity, 2000.

Garber's book is written primarily for students, but it is a valuable guide for anyone who has neglected this area of life. Sire's book is written for the Christian faculty member, although others who take the intellectual life seriously will also benefit from it.

9

Etcetera

Christians in higher education face the same dilemma as Christians in every other walk of life: How do I live out my life in Christ on a day-to-day basis? Likewise, Christians in higher education face the same challenge as Christians who face persecution: How do I remain faithful in my witness to Christ when it may cost me? The cost of following Christ in the academy is not as high as following Christ in China or Saudi Arabia, of course, but it is tangible. Believers who work in higher education face the same problem as believers in business, law, manufacturing, farming, politics, and medicine. Teachers may wonder why they should take risks for their faith when no one else does.

Within the academy certain traditional realms of conflict, prejudice, or superiority persist. Every society has a hierarchy, and the academy has its social pecking order. The sciences look down on the social sciences. The liberal arts look down on the professions. The faculty looks down on the support staff. The administration looks down on the faculty. It is the way of the world. In the business world the office staff is in conflict with the sales staff. In corrections the security staff is in conflict with the rehabilitation staff. Even among inmates, con artists look down on bank robbers, who look down on petty thieves, and everyone looks down on sex offenders. Jealousy, envy, strife, pride—these are the way of the world.

Christian institutions mirror this reality as much as prisons. If the correlation of faith with other realms of knowledge were merely an intel-

lectual issue, it would be quite simple. But Christianity is not a gnostic
religion. It involves emotions, social relationships, character, and much
more. Any effort to deal with the cognitive issue of faith in the academy
must also deal with the broader spiritual dynamics.

Alongside the crumbling image of naturalism, a renewed interest in
spirit, or soul, has emerged among some disciplines of the academy as
an aspect of the postmodern climate. Few are willing to go so far as to
be interested in religion, but they are on a slippery slope. The problem
for conversation lies in the multiple meanings people attach to words
like *spirit* and *soul,* or even *God.* To many people, spirit and soul are synonymous with a ghost or personality within people. Among the ancient
Hebrews, however, *soul* referred to the totality of a person, including
body and spirit. God breathed the breath (spirit) of life into the body
and it became a living soul. *Spirit* referred to that personal aspect in-
volving the will, intellect, emotions, character, talents and abilities, and
vitality itself. In various measure, all disciplines deal with these issues.
Attempting to separate the sacred from the profane does no good. From
a biblical perspective, or from the perspective of most religions of the
world, all of life and all of creation are sacred. Though some disciplines
relate more specifically to certain domains of the human spirit than
others, most of the disciplines deal with spiritual issues.

Since Descartes managed to separate mind (spirit) and body, the
stream of Western cultural life has followed his example. Pascal followed
suit by separating intellect from emotion as though they were two different things, rather than aspects of the human spirit. This fragmentation
of what it means to be human made it possible for people to become
preoccupied with certain kinds of knowledge while viewing other kinds
of knowledge with suspicion.

Faith is not an inferior form of knowledge so much as it is a way of
integrating many ways of knowing. It forms an umbrella that brings
the totality of human knowledge back together. The body provides the
sensory experience needed for empirical knowledge, but it only becomes
knowledge when appropriated by the mind. The mind, however, has
come to mean only the kind of reason that involves just one kind of
cognition, rational logic, which in turn too easily descends to rationalism. The tendency is to discredit emotion, character, and imagination
as legitimate ways of knowing. Character is associated with natural law
and conscience. Natural law is an unpopular concept because it implies
a lawgiver. Reason seems much more dependable until we realize that
reason cannot be separated from the emotions that affect how we look
at life and evaluate data. Neither can we separate reason from character,
which has the capacity to lie to ourselves and to others. In other words,
the totality of our spiritual being affects our knowledge. Those who real-

ize this dynamic and admit they are spiritual beings have a remarkable advantage in doing scholarly work. If "pride goes before destruction" (Prov. 16:18 NIV), a flawed character can have devastating effects on a person. Our spirits can blind us to the truth. Perhaps this dynamic is why truth has seemed such a mythological concept in recent years.

Many Christians lead fragmented lives as they cling to their faith in private but ignore it in the public square. Presented with a choice to believe the Bible or modern learning, they are not quite sure what to do. Somehow they believe the Bible part of the time and modern learning part of the time, but it is a struggle. Many decide to choose between the two and become either zealous fundamentalists or zealous atheists. They must be zealous and rabid to justify giving up such a huge part of themselves. It is a tragic situation, one that has arisen largely because of the modern world's attempt to make the Bible conform to modern notions of knowledge. For the Bible to be truly valid, it must be scientific. Both its defenders and its opponents hold this view. It is the curse of the Enlightenment that has darkened the Western intellect. Confusion arises when people read of ancient cosmologies in the Bible. Must we choose between believing these cosmologies or the modern cosmologies? It becomes even more difficult for those who realize that the Bible contains several cosmologies!

The Western will to judge the Bible as a scientific book blinds the mind, blocking the understanding that the Bible does not teach Egyptian, Babylonian, or Greek cosmology but, rather, speaks to people who held these understandings. In other words, those who abandon modern learning and adopt an ancient concept of nature have failed to understand that the Bible does not teach these concepts. Rather, it speaks to people who believed these concepts. The person who has rejected the Bible and its God in order to cling to the knowledge of the modern world has struck a poor bargain. What has he or she gained but a phantom?

We may ridicule the cosmologies of the ancients, but they are no more out of date than Einstein with his attempt to retain Aristotle's constant universe. If we want a scientific understanding of the universe, why would we think that the present view is the end of the matter? Experience should tell us that we are still wrong. So what good is the Bible? It speaks to the spiritual domain and how it relates to the physical domain.

Many Christians long for the halcyon days of yore when faith and learning were one. They imagine an ideal age in which all of these matters were settled and all of society enjoyed a pastoral orthodoxy without dissent or error. For many, this ideal age took place with the medieval synthesis.[1] Of course, this was the age in which superstition and debauchery afflicted the church and dissent was settled by the Inquisition. It was the age in which the greatest ambition of science was to discover the philosopher's stone. It was an age in which Christian princes bludgeoned one another to death in the name of Jesus. C. S. Lewis pushed the problem back to Thomas Aquinas and his love of Aristotle, whom Lewis blames for dividing things. Of course, if we push it back before Thomas, we are left in a world dominated by Platonic thought. No matter how far back we go, some sort of truncation prevailed.

Even in the best of times, people have depended on some philosophical or cultural scheme to govern their religion. We could go back to New Testament times, when the Pharisees (oriented toward the heavenly) and the Sadducees (oriented toward the earthly) contended. Each side had part of the truth, just as Plato and Aristotle each had part of the truth. The incarnation and resurrection affirm both dimensions of the truth and will not allow us to choose one over and against the other. Himself God and man, Christ affirms both the physical and the spiritual realms as well as the dynamic relationship between the two.

The incarnation may help describe why we might have such a problem with thinking of the relationship between faith and the disciplines. People may cry out for God to show himself, declaring that if they could only see God, they would believe and love him. Suppose God shows himself. Suppose he takes on flesh and dwells among us so that we can behold his glory. Do we say, "Now I see God," or do we say, "He is just a man"? The problem is that if God does something in the physical world, it can be described according to the laws of nature. If it can be observed with the senses, it conforms to the laws of physics. Of course, this situation dramatizes the significance of Christ's incarnation. A dynamic union of deity and humanity took place such that Christ was both fully man and fully God.

The incarnation does not permit the dichotomy of body and spirit. Nonetheless, we tend to think that if we can see, taste, smell, touch, or hear something, it cannot be the work of God. We ask to see God, but if he shows himself we say that it cannot be God because we see him. The problem of relating faith and the disciplines is similar because virtually every spiritual issue may be described by one or more disciplines phenomenologically or in some other way. In other words, higher education is concerned with spiritual matters, even if it only recognizes the physical expression of those matters. Ironically, educators may be interested in making sense of data without having any interest in knowing the truth of the data.

For centuries truth was understood as something that transcends mere facts, or observable phenomena. During the modern period, however, people became entranced with their ability to discover new facts, like a child with a new toy. In that fascination, we began to identify truth with observable facts and identified this cult of observation with the values of our culture. When the great disenchantment occurred and we began to realize that the facts were only interpretations of observations guided by modern cultural values, we had lost touch with the meaning of truth and did not know how to get it back. Thus, we have the postmodern critique of modernity, but it is a hopeless critique. It is a lament. Our culture traded truth for facts and in the end discovered that it had neither. The postmodern culture would trade facts for information that does not submit itself to any criteria for evaluation. Critical thought no longer has a basis if such a trend continues to its logical conclusion. Of course, faith brought the critique to modernity decades before the postmodern prophets appeared. And faith offers a way forward that would allow us to hold on to the observable physical world of phenomena while having access to a transcendent world of value.

The ability to grapple with the intersection of faith and academic disciplines is a critical intellectual issue, but the decision to grapple at all is a spiritual issue. A sense of inadequacy will keep us from doing it. The academy excels in instilling a sense of inadequacy in its members (an attitude of encouragement is not the tone of the faculty lounge), but the feeling of inadequacy is a spiritual attitude we choose to take upon ourselves. However ill we may be treated by others, no one can place the mantle of inadequacy upon us.

A sense of fear may prevent us from grappling with the issues of faith as they relate to our disciplines, and the academy makes sure that we always have much to fear. We courageously defend our academic freedom against those who do not threaten us while we bully our weaker colleagues into submission through the power of academic politics. The academy offers much to fear, but is that a reason to fear or to give fear the ultimate role in determining our behavior?

Perhaps we do not grapple with the faith issues because we want to remain objective. This concept of objectivity seems to go against the purpose of embracing objectivity. To be objective, it is necessary to be self-conscious of one's prejudices in order to ensure that they do not distort the outcome of our study. To predetermine not to consider the place of faith is to refuse to be objective.

Some teachers do not want to grapple with faith issues lest their personal opinions influence their students. This is my favorite. I first encountered it as a student in college. Following the spring riots of 1970, the president of the university convened a retreat of faculty and student leaders to consider university reforms. Many of the suggestions were aimed at making the university a more substantial place of learning. I served on a task force that sought to expose students to the rich offerings of fine arts brought to campus. Our student committee brought Dame Margot Fontaine to dance *Cinderella* and Dame Judith Anderson to perform *Hamlet*. We brought cellist Leonard Rose and guitarist Carlos Montoya, as well as the Broadway casts of *1776* and *Company*. Task force members lamented the low attendance at such fabulous events but could not think of anything to do about it. I suggested that the faculty call attention to events they knew about. Our distinguished Shakespearean scholar laughed and said the idea was out of the question. He would never consider influencing the tastes of his students.

I was furious. A faculty member may know about the cultural event of a lifetime that I could attend for free, but he would not tell me because it might influence me to consider going? This particular faculty member did not want me to have the option. He considered my state of ignorance superior to a state of informed options. I had contempt for the internationally known and venerated Shakespearean scholar at the time, and I still do not think much of this attitude when applied to religion either.

The decision of whether or not to deal with religion is not purely cognitive, no matter how we may have convinced ourselves or rationalized that it is. The decision is spiritual and involves the intellect as well as the emotions, the character, and the will, if not more. Several years ago I was engaged in a conversation with an eminent Cambridge physicist and an equally eminent Oxford biologist about the relationship of God to time. Is God inside time or outside time, or something else altogether? Both scientists gave reasons why God is inside time and thus does not know the future. Each reason was incomplete, however, so I continued to ask the follow-up questions that critical inquiry demands until we finally came to the "real" reason. After a long stream of rational discussion, both men gave the same answer: God does not know the future because "I am uncomfortable with that idea." In other words, their intellect voiced the answer, but their emotion had decided the matter. If there is no transcendent reality, we may turn the whole matter over to the psychology department. If we believe there is a transcendent reality, however, we need to discuss the matter with the psychology department as we seek to understand the spiritual dimensions of knowledge.

We have the tendency to believe that if we can give a physical description of something, we have captured the totality of its objective or literal or factual meaning. In his poem "Fog," Carl Sandburg writes that fog comes "on little cat feet." Surely he must be mistaken, drunk, or mad. Would it not be better to cite the barometric pressure, wind velocity, temperature, and relative humidity? Our love affair with facts may dull us to the fact that there is more to fog than meets the eye. Scientific measurement can tell us certain things about reality, but poetry can tell us things that are real, things measurement can never reveal. We should know this about our sensory experience. My vision tells me some things about the world, but it can never tell me about music. In some wondrous way our minds correlate our different sensory experiences to give a full picture. Or is it just our brains that do the correlating? Who is to say? And on what basis? Which discipline has the final say? And which disciplines have a right to take part in the discussion? Which discipline will sit out the conversation altogether?

For some surprising reasons, various Christians in higher education prefer not to think about what their faith has to do with their teaching. In some cases Christians have segmented their life of faith from their life of scholarship in reaction to what they see as bad theology masquerading as scholarship. In other cases Christians have segmented their life of faith from their life of scholarship because they have accepted the perspective of bad philosophy masquerading as scholarship. Neither case justifies quitting the field. In both situations Christians have the obligation to examine their own situation to determine what factors have led to their passivity in this matter. Today, when religion is more alive in the classroom than it has been in a hundred years, it is not a matter of proselytizing or imposing religion on the discipline. Rather, it is a matter of exploring the religious themes already present in the content of the discipline and allowing the Christian perspective to be one of the options considered in the discussion.

Some will say that they already have too much to do without having to undertake the process of learning philosophy and theology. But, as we have seen, even if God did not exist, a person would still have to understand philosophy in order to teach his or her subject in the present world. Once people claim faith in the Lord Jesus Christ, their obligation already exists to understand what they have taken upon themselves. In the end, all intellectual discussion becomes a rather quiet spiritual matter between a believer and Christ, with far-reaching implications.

Further Reading

Dallas Willard, a respected professor of philosophy at the University of Southern California, has written several helpful books that deal with the spiritual dynamics of the Christian life and the practical implications of following one's vocation as a Christian. Of particular help are the following:

Willard, Dallas. *The Divine Conspiracy: Rediscovering Our Hidden Life in God.* San Francisco: HarperSanFrancisco, 1998.

———. *The Spirit of the Disciplines.* San Francisco: HarperSanFrancisco, 1988.

Dietrich Bonhoeffer, a professor in Germany during the rise of the Third Reich, wrote one of the classics of Christian literature in 1937 as he reflected on the role a disciple of Christ must play in society:

Bonhoeffer, Dietrich. *The Cost of Discipleship*. New York: Touchstone, 1995.

Appendix

Christian Scholarly and Academic Societies

The following compilation was developed by the C. S. Lewis Foundation (www.cslewis.org).

North America

1. Affiliation of Christian Biologists
contact: Dr. Larry Seward, President
John Brown University
2000 West University Street
Siloam Springs, AR 72761-2121
email: lseward@acc.jbu.edu

2. Affiliation of Christian Geologists
contact: Dr. Stephen O. Moshier
Wheaton College
Wheaton, IL 60187
email: stephen.o.moshier@wheaton.edu

3. American Scientific Affiliation
contact: Dr. Donald Munro, Executive Director
P.O. Box 668
Ipswich, MA 01983
ph.: 508-356-5656
fax: 508-356-4375
email: asa@newl.com

4. American Society of Church History
contact: Executive Secretary
P.O. Box 8517
Red Bank, NJ 07701
ph.: 732-345-1787
fax: 732-345-1788
email: aschnoff@aol.com
web site: www.churchhistory.org

5. American Society of Missiology
contact: Dr. Darrell Guder
Columbia Theological Seminary
P.O. Box 520
Decatur, GA 30031-0520
ph.: 404-687-4584
fax: 404-684-4656
email: asm.office@ptsem.edu

6. American Theological Society-Midwest
contact: Paul Parker
Amherst College
Amherst, MA 01002-5000
ph.: 413-542-2000

7. Association of Christian Collegiate Media
contact: Dr. Doug Tarpley
Regent University
1650 Diagonal Road
Alexandria, VA 22314
ph.: 703-837-1912
email: dougtar@regent.edu

8. Association of Christian Economists
contact: Dr. John Mason, Executive
   Secretary
Gordon College
255 Grapevine Road
Wenham, MA 01984
ph.: 508-927-2300
fax: 508-524-3704
email: mason@faith.gordon.edu

9. Association of Christian Engineers and Scientists
contact: Orvin and Carol Olson
P.O. Box 25246
Portland, OR 97225
ph.: 503-228-0779

10. Association of Christian Librarians
contact: Nancy Olson
P.O. Box 4
Cedarville, OH 45314
ph.: 217-732-3168
fax: 217-732-3785
email: execdir@acl.org
web site: www.acl.org

11. Association of Christians in Mathematical Sciences
contact: Dr. Robert Brabenec
Department of Mathematics
Wheaton College
Wheaton, IL 60187
ph.: 708-820-1560
fax: 708-752-5996
email: robert.l.brabenec@wheaton
   .edu

12. Association of Christians Teaching Sociology
contact: Dr. Russell Heddendorf
Sociology Department
Covenant College
14049 Scenic Highway
Lookout Mountain, GA 30750
ph.: 706-820-1560
fax: 706-820-0672
email: heddendorf@covenant.edu

13. Association of Theological Schools
contact: Daniel Aleshire, Executive
   Director
10 Summit Park Drive
Pittsburgh, PA 15275-1103
ph.: 412-788-6505
fax: 412-788-6510
email: ats@ats.edu

14. Canadian Evangelical Theological Association
contact: Mr. David T. Priestley
Edmonton Baptist Seminary
11525-23 Avenue
Edmonton, Alberta
Canada T6J 4T3
ph.: 780-431-5249
email: David.Priestley@nabcebs.ab
.ca

15. Canadian Society of Christian Philosophers
contact: Jim Gerrie
Department of Philosophy
University of Guelph
Guelph, ON N1G 2W1
ph.: 519-824-4120, ext. 4243
email: jgerrie@hwcn.org
web site: www.geocities.com/cscp99

16. Christian Association for Psychological Studies
contact: Dr. Randolph K. Sanders,
  Executive Director
P.O. Box 310400
New Braunfels, TX 78131-0400
ph.: 830-629-2277
fax: 830-629-2342
email: capsintl@compuvision.net
web site: www.caps.net

17. Christian Business Faculty Association
contact: Don Daake, chair
Business Department
Olivet Nazarene University
240 East Marsile
Bourbonnais, IL 60914
ph.: 815-939-5137
fax: 815-928-5454
email: ddaake@olivet.edu
web site: www.cbfa.org

18. Christian Educators Association, International
contact: Forrest L. Turpen
P.O. Box 41300
Pasadena, CA 91114
ph.: 818-798-1124 *or* 818-798-2346

19. Christian Fellowship of Art Music Composers
contact: Dr. Mark Hijleh, President
School of Music
Houghton College
One Willard Avenue
Houghton, NY 14744
ph.: 716-567-9424
web site: www.ccel.org

20. Christian Foresters Fellowship
contact: Prof. Dennis Lynch
Department of Forest Sciences
Colorado State University
Fort Collins, CO 80523
ph.: 970-491-6333
fax: 970-491-6754
email: denny@cnr.colostate.edu

21. Christian Legal Society
contact: Samuel B. Casey, Executive
  Director
4208 Evergreen Lane, Suite 222
Annandale, VA 22003
ph.: 703-642-1070
fax: 703-642-1075
email: clrf@mindspring.com *or*
  CLSHQ@clsnet.org
web site: www.christianlegalsociety
  .org

22. Christian Medical and Dental Society
contact: Dr. David Stevens, Executive
  Director
Christian Medical and Dental Society
501 5th Street
P.O. Box 5
Bristol, TN 37621-0005
ph.: 800-804-0658
fax: 423-844-1005
email: mbruce@emory.edu (Amelia
  Bruce)

**23. Christian Nuclear Fellowship
(Nuclear Science &
Technology)**
contact: V. O. Uotinen
9102 Oakland Circle
Lynchburg, VA 24502
ph.: 804-237-3294
email: vic@rivermont.org

**24. Christian Performing Artists'
Fellowship**
contact: Patrick Kavanaugh, Executive Director
10523 Main Street, Suite 31
Fairfax, VA 22030
email: cpaf@erols.com

**25. Christian Pharmacists
Fellowship International**
contact: Allan Sharp, Administrative
Director
P.O. Box 1717
501 Fifth Street
Bristol, TN 37621-1717
ph.: 423-764-6000
fax: 423-764-4490
email: asharp@cpfi.org
web site: www.cpfi.org

26. Christian Sociological Society
contact: Dr. Thomas Hood
University of Tennessee
911 McClung Tower
Knoxville, TN 37996-0490
ph.: 865-974-7023
fax: 865-974-7013
email: tomhood@utk.edu

**27. Christian Theological Research
Fellowship**
contact: Elmer Colyer
University of Dubuque
2000 University Avenue
Dubuque, IA 52001
ph.: 319-589-3389
fax: 319-589-3682
email: ecolyer@univ.dbq.edu
web site: home.apu.edu/~CTRF/

28. Christian Veterinary Mission
contact: Dr. Kit Flowers
19303 Fremont Avenue North
Seattle, WA 98133
ph.: 206-546-7569
email: kflowers@cvmusa.org
web site: christianvetmission.org

29. Christians in Political Science
contact: Prof. Mel Hailey, Treasurer
Abilene Christian University
P.O. Box 28276
Abilene, TX 79699
ph.: 915-674-2095
email: haileyM@nicanor.acu.edu

**30. Christians in the Arts
Networking**
contact: Phillip Charles Griffith II,
Executive Director
P.O. Box 242
Arlington, MA 02174
ph.: 617-646-1541
fax: 617-646-7725
email: canhq@aol.com

31. Christians in the Visual Arts
contact: Sandra Bowden
P.O. Box 18117
Minneapolis, MN 55418-0117
ph.: 612-378-0606
email: sandbowden@aol.com *or*
sandrabowden@attbi.com
web site: www.uu.edu/class/civa/
civaweb

32. Christians in Theatre Arts
contact: Dale Savidge
P.O. Box 26471
Greenville, SC 29616
ph.: 864-271-2116
email: exec@cita.org
web site: www.cita.org

33. Conference on Christianity and Literature
contact: Dr. Robert Snyder
Department of English
State University of Georgia
Carrollton, GA 30118-2200
ph.: 770-836-6512
fax: 770-830-2334
email: rsnyder@westga.edu
web site: www.acu.edu/academics/
   english/ccl

34. Conference on Faith and History
contact: Dr. Richard V. Pierard
Department of History
Gordon College
255 Grapevine Road
Wenham, MA 01984
ph.: 812-237-2707
fax: 812-466-2535
email: hipier@ruby.indstate.edu
web site: www.huntington.edu/cfh

35. Engineering Ministries International
contact: Christy Taylor
110 South Weber, Suite 102
Colorado Springs, CO 80903
ph.: 719-633-2078
fax: 719-633-2970
email: ctaylor@emiusa.org
web site: www.emiusa.org

36. Evangelical Missiological Society
contact: Dr. Norman Allison
Director of School of World Mission
Toccoa Falls College
Toccoa Falls, GA 30598
ph.: 706-886-6831
fax: 706-282-6008
email: nallison@tfc.edu
web site: www.missiology.org/EMS

37. Evangelical Philosophical Society
contact: Paul F. Pardi
Biola University
c/o Philosophia Christi
13800 Biola Avenue
La Mirada, CA 90638-0001
email: philchristi@biola.edu

38. Evangelical Theological Society
contact: James A. Borland, Secretary/
   Treasurer
200 Russell Woods Drive
Lynchburg, VA 24502-3530
ph.: 434-237-5309
email: jaborland@aol.com *or*
   jborland@liberty.edu
web site: www.etsjets.org

39. Fellowship of Artists for Cultural Evangelism (FACE)
contact: Eugene and Mary Lou Tof-
   fen, Codirectors
1605 East Elizabeth Street
Pasadena, CA 91104
ph.: 818-398-2445
fax: 818-398-2263
email: Art4FACE@aol.com

40. Fellowship of Christian Librarians & Information Specialists (FOCLIS)
contact: Dr. Paul Snezek
Buswell Memorial Library
Wheaton College
Wheaton, IL 60187
ph.: 630-752-5101
fax: 630-752-5855
email: paul.snezek@wheaton.edu

41. Health Physics Society Christian Fellowship
contact: Dr. Steve Sims
1002 Northview Drive
Lenior City, TN 37771
ph.: 423-574-6692
email: czs@ornl.gov

42. Institute for Biblical Research
contact: Dr. Michael Holmes
Bethel College
3900 Bethel Drive
St. Paul, MN 55112
email: holmic@bethel.edu
web site: www.eisenbrauns.com/
   ECOM/_11YONE8KT.HTM

**43. Institute for the Study of
   American Evangelicals**
contact: Edith Blumhofer
Wheaton College
Wheaton, IL 60187-5593
ph.: 630-752-5437
email: isae@wheaton.edu
web site: www.wheaton.edu/isae

**44. Network of Christian
   Anthropologists**
contact: Darrell Whiteman, School of
   World Mission
Asbury Theological Seminary
204 North Lexington Avenue
Wilmore, KY 40390
ph.: 859-858-2215
email: Darrell_Whiteman@asbury
   seminary.edu

**45. NeuroScience Christian
   Fellowship**
contact: Dr. Kenneth J. Dormer
University of Oklahoma
Health Science Center
P.O. Box 26901
Oklahoma City, OK 73190
ph.: 405-271-2334
fax: 405-271-3181
email: Ken-Dormer@ouhsc.edu *or*
   Kenneth-Dormer@uok.edu

**46. North American Association of
   Christians in Social Work**
contact: Rick Chamiec-Case, MSW,
   MAR, Executive Director
P.O. Box 121
Botsford, CT 06404-0121
ph.: 203-270-8780
email: info@nacsw.org
web site: www.nacsw.org

**47. North American Christian
   Foreign Language Association**
contact: Kathryn McConnell
Point Loma Nazarene University
3900 Lomaland Drive
San Diego, CA 92106
email: kmcconnell@ptloma.edu
web site: www.spu.edu/orgs/nacfla

**48. North American Professors of
   Christian Education**
contact: Dennis Williams, Executive
   Administrator
The Southern Baptist Theological
   Seminary
2825 Lexington Road
Louisville, KY 40280
ph.: 502-897-4813
fax: 502-897-4004
email: celead@sbts.edu
web site: www.napce.org

49. Nurses Christian Fellowship
contact: Linda Kunz
P.O. Box 7895
6400 Schroeder Road
Madison, WI 73707-7895
email: ncf@ivcf.org
web site: www.intervarsity.org/ncf/
   ncfindex.html

**50. Religious Communication
   Association**
contact: Becky Johns, Executive Secretary
Department of Communication
Weber State University
3750 Harrison Boulevard
Ogden, UT 84408
ph.: 801-626-7455
email: bjohns@weber.edu
web site: gcc.bradley.edu/com/
   faculty/lamoureux/rsca/index.html

51. Society of Biblical Literature
contact: Kent Harold Richards, Executive Director
The Luce Center
825 Houston Mill Road, Suite 350
Atlanta, GA 30329
ph.: 404-727-3100
fax: 404-727-3112
email: kent.richards@sbl-site.org
web site: sbl-site.org

52. Society of Christian Philosophers
contact: Dr. Kelly J. Clark, Secretary/Treasurer
Calvin College
Department of Philosophy
3201 Burton Street S.E.
Grand Rapids, MI 49546
ph.: 616-957-6421
fax: 616-957-8551
email: kclark@calvin.edu
web site: www.siu.edu/~scp

53. Wesleyan Theological Society
contact: William Kostlevy, Secretary/Treasurer
B. L. Fisher Library
Asbury Theological Seminary
204 North Lexington Avenue
Wilmore, KY 40390
email: bill_kostlevy@ats.wilmore.ky.us

United Kingdom

1. Agricultural Christian Fellowship
contact: Christopher Jones
Manor Farm
West Hadden
Northampton NN6 7AQ
ph.: 0178-851-0866
fax: 0178-851-1026
email: ukfoodgroup@ukfg.org.uk
web site: www.agriculturalchristian
fellowship.org.uk

2. Association of Christian Teachers
contact: ACT
94A London Road, St. Albans
Hertfordshire AL1 1NX
England
ph.: 0172-784-0298
fax: 0172-784-8966
email: act@christian-teachers.org
web site: www.christian-teachers.org/act

3. Association of Christians in Higher Education
contact: Alan Hewerdine
38 De Montfort Street
Leicester LE1 7GP
England
ph.: 0116-255-1700
fax: 0116-255-5672
email: ache@uccf.org.uk

4. Christian Dental Fellowship
email: cdfadmin@btinternet.com
web site: www.cdf-uk.org

5. Christian Engineers Association
contact: A. John Baden Fuller, Chairman
CEA, Christians at Work
P.O. Box 1746
Rugby CV21 3ZS
email: NatDirector@Christiansat
work.org.uk
web site: www.christiansatwork.org.uk/CEA

6. Christian Literary Studies Group
contact: Dr. Roger Kojecky
email: secretary@clsg.org
web site: www.clsg.org

7. Christian Medical Fellowship
Partnership House
157 Waterloo Road
London SE1 8XN
ph.: 0207-928-4694
fax: 0207-620-2453
email: admin@cmf.org.uk
web site: www.cmf.org.uk

8. Christian Nurses and Midwives
contact: CNM
38 West Avenue Road
London E17 9SE
ph.: 0794-180-0637
email: info@cnm.org.uk
web site: www.cnm.org.uk

9. Christians in Architecture and Planning
contact: Andrew Patrick Mullion
11 Shakespeare Road
Wimborne BH21 1N2
England
email: info@capsite.org.uk

10. Christians in Science
contact: Dr. Caroline Berry
4 Sackville Close
Sevenoaks
Kent TN13 3QD
ph.: 0173-245-1907
fax: 0173-246-4253
email: cberry@centrenet.co.uk (Caroline Berry)
web site: www.cis.org.uk

11. Lawyers Christian Fellowship
contact: 29 Church Lane
Temple Normanton
Chesterfield S42 5DB
ph.: 0124-685-6783
email: admin@lawcf.org
web site: www.lawcf.org

12. Librarians' Christian Fellowship
contact: Graham Hedges, secretary
34 Thurlestone Avenue
Seven Kings
Ilford Essex IG3 9DU
email: secretary@librarianscf.org.uk
web site: www.librarianscf.org.uk

13. Social Workers' Christian Fellowship
c/o Truedata Subscriptions
23 Park Road, Ilkeston
Derbyshire DE7 5DA
web site: www.swcf.org.uk

14. Study Group on Christianity and History
contact: David Killingray
1 Trelawny Way, Bembridge
Isle of Wight PO35 5YE
email: pmd@uccf.org.uk *or*
　　d.killingray@gold.ac.uk

15. Veterinary Christian Fellowship
contact: Anthony Smith, president
5 Bruges Close, Chippenham
Wilts SN15 3SG
email: anthony@vcf.org.uk
web site: www.vcf.org

16. Workwise
contact: Tim Vickers
LICC, St. Peter's Church, Vere Street
London W1M 9HP
email: timvickers@workwise.org.uk

Notes

Foreword

1. Trans. M. Kuschnitzky and J. M. Cameron (Chicago: Regnery, 1951).
2. Chicago: University of Chicago Press, 1996.

Chapter 1: A Personal Introduction

1. Tertullian, *Apology* 46, in *The Ante-Nicene Fathers*, ed. A. Roberts and J. Donaldson (Grand Rapids: Eerdmans, n.d.), 3:51.
2. Tertullian, *The Prescription against Heretics* 7, in ibid., 3:246.
3. American Scientific Affiliation, *Annual Report*, 1999, 17–18.

Chapter 2: The Religious Spectrum in Higher Education

1. www.ccmanet.org/ccma/index.
2. www.gbhem.org/asp/campusmin.asp.
3. www.pcusa.org/links/campus.
4. www.pcanet.org/general/history.
5. www.ivcf.org/aboutiv/purpose.
6. www.ivcf.org/aboutiv/history.
7. www.intervarsitygle.org.
8. www.home.navigators.org/us/collegiate/index.
9. www.uscm.org/aboutus/index.
10. See George M. Marsden, *The Soul of the American University: From Protestant Establishment to Established Nonbelief* (New York: Oxford University Press, 1994); idem, *The Outrageous Idea of Christian Scholarship* (New York: Oxford University Press, 1997); James Tunstead Burtchaell, *The Dying of the Light: The Disengagement of Colleges and Universities from Their Christian Churches* (Grand Rapids: Eerdmans, 1998).
11. William F. Buckley Jr., *God and Man at Yale* (Washington: Regnery, 1978).

12. See National Center for Education Statistics, *Digest of Education Statistics, 2000, NCES 2001-034,* by Thomas D. Snyder; production manager, Charlene M. Hoffman (Washington, D.C.: U.S. Department of Education, 2001), table 180.

13. William Willimon and Thomas H. Naylor, *The Abandoned Generation: Rethinking Higher Education* (Grand Rapids: Eerdmans, 1995).

14. David S. Dockery, "Integrating Faith and Learning: An Unapologetic Case for Christian Higher Education" (Center for Faculty Development, Union University, Jackson, Tenn.).

15. Personal correspondence, March 18, March 27, and May 4, 2002. I am indebted to Dr. Heie for preparing a brief summary of his position, from which I have drawn extensively in presenting his model.

16. David Guthrie, *Student Affairs Reconsidered* (Lanham, Md.: University Press of America, 1997). I am indebted to Kimberly Thornbury, dean of students at Union University, for bringing this work to my attention.

17. See Larry Lyon and Michael Beaty, "Integration, Secularization, and the Two-Spheres View at Religious Colleges: Comparing Baylor University with the University of Notre Dame and Georgetown College," *Christian Scholar's Review* 29 (fall 1999): 73–112.

18. Ibid., 74 n. 3.

19. Ibid., 74.

20. David Sloan, *Faith and Knowledge: Mainline Protestantism and American Higher Education* (Louisville: Westminster/John Knox, 1994), vii–xiv, 111–49; Christopher Jencks and David Riesman, *The Academic Revolution* (Garden City, N.Y.: Doubleday, 1968), 322.

21. Lyon and Beaty, "Integration, Secularization," 100–101.

22. Ibid., 95.

23. Ibid., 97.

24. Ibid., 98. Lyon and Beaty assess this attitude toward religion in light of the work of Robert Wuthnow: "Wuthnow has explained this lack of religious belief by noting that 'social scientists and humanists study religion itself and therefore encounter conflicting Paradigms,' whereas the natural sciences are often more insulated from religious concerns. Wuthnow further speculates that since social scientists and humanists are in fields with low levels of codification, a certain amount of boundary-defining 'posturing' is likely and that a significant part of that posturing is being irreligious." See Robert Wuthnow, *The Struggle for America's Soul: Evangelicals, Liberals, and Secularism* (Grand Rapids: Eerdmans, 1989), 150.

25. Lyon and Beaty, "Integration, Secularization," 81.

26. Ibid., 82.

27. Ibid., 83–84.

28. Ibid., 85.

29. Ibid., 100.

30. Richard T. Hughes and William B. Adrian, eds., *Models for Christian Higher Education: Strategies for Success in the Twenty-First Century* (Grand Rapids: Eerdmans, 1997), 2.

31. The authors often differ about the groupings and elements of the different traditions. For instance, the editors place Messiah College within the group of Wesleyan schools largely because it has grown in prominence and needed to be included somewhere. Harold Heie, when describing his former school in his theological essay on the evangelical/interdenominational tradition, places Messiah within that group (p. 259). The editors place Seattle Pacific with Wheaton as an evangelical/interdenominational school, while John E. and Susie C. Stanley, in their theological essay, place it in the Wesleyan/Holiness tradition (p. 325). The chapter on Wheaton as an evangelical/interdenominational school presents the Reformed approach to faith and learning. The editors combine Baptist and Church of Christ traditions in the same section, though they provide only two theological

essays for this section. Finally, they altogether omit Methodists, the second-largest Protestant group in the country.

32. In his theological narrative, Harold Heie follows the typology used by David W. Bebbington in *Evangelicalism in Modern Britain: A History from the 1730s to the 1980s* (London: Allen & Unwin, 1989).

33. This separatism extends back to the earliest beginnings of Baptists, when they separated from the Church of England and later separated from the Separatists. Liberals and fundamentalists, conservatives and moderates—all seem to share this separatist tendency, which helps to separate Baptists from other denominational groups. Baptist churches tend to multiply by division, and denominational groups (both north and south, black and white) tend to split and form new groups.

34. James Tunstead Burtchaell, *The Dying of the Light: The Disengagement of Colleges and Universities from Their Christian Churches* (Grand Rapids: Eerdmans, 1998), 826.

35. Ibid., 827.

36. Ibid., 828.

37. The University of Richmond disengaged from the General Association of Virginia Baptists when a donor offered them a large bequest if they would cease to be a Baptist school.

38. Burtchaell, *Dying of the Light*, 829.

39. Ibid., 830.

40. Ibid., 833.

41. Ibid., 834.

42. Ibid., 836.

43. Ibid.

44. Ibid., 839.

45. Ibid., 842.

46. Burtchaell's description of this process may be found in ibid., 838–43.

47. C. S. Lewis, "Christian Apologetics," in *God in the Dock: Essays on Theology and Ethics*, ed. W. Hooper (Grand Rapids: Eerdmans, 1970), 93.

Chapter 3: The Challenges of Higher Education

1. For readers unfamiliar with this farming term, the stack pole is driven into the ground, and the new-mown hay is piled around it to form a haystack. The pole keeps the hay in place through the winter, allowing the cattle to feed.

2. Newbigin develops this idea in two books: *Foolishness to the Greeks* (Grand Rapids: Eerdmans, 1986) and *The Gospel in a Pluralistic Society* (Grand Rapids: Eerdmans, 1990).

3. Elizabeth F. Farrell, "California Poet Laureate Admits to Lie on Résumé," *The Chronicle of Higher Education* 49.12 (November 15, 2002): A15.

4. Florence Olsen, "Historian Resigns after Report Questions His Gun Research," *The Chronicle of Higher Education* 49.11 (November 8, 2002): A17.

5. Scott Smallwood, "Crossing the Line," *The Chronicle of Higher Education* 49.9 (October 25, 2002): A8–10.

6. Jeffrey R. Young, "Public-College Tuition Jumps at Highest Rate in 10 Years," *The Chronicle of Higher Education* 49.10 (November 1, 2002): A35.

7. Clara M. Lovett, "Tough Times for Colleges Demand Structural Changes. . . ," *The Chronicle of Higher Education* 49.8 (October 18, 2002): B12.

8. Florence Olsen, "MIT's Open Window," *The Chronicle of Higher Education* 49.15 (December 6, 2002): A31. The Web site for the OpenCourseWare project is http://www.ocw.mit.edu.

9. Scott Carlson, "Students and Faculty Members Turn First to Online Library Materials, Study Finds," *The Chronicle of Higher Education* 49.8 (October 18, 2002): A37.

10. Florence Olsen, "Phoenix Rises," *The Chronicle of Higher Education* 49.10 (November 11, 2002): A29.

11. Welch Suggs, "How Gears Turn at a Sports Factory," *The Chronicle of Higher Education* 49.14 (November 29, 2002): A34. In 2002, Ohio State had an athletic budget of $79 million.

12. Welch Suggs, "Gardner-Webb President, Enmeshed in Sports Scandal, Resigns," *The Chronicle of Higher Education* 49.9 (October 25, 2002): A41.

13. C. S. Lewis, *The Abolition of Man* (New York: Macmillan, 1947).

14. C. S. Lewis, *Mere Christianity* (San Francisco: HarperSanFrancisco, 2001), 121.

Chapter 4: From Modernity to Postmodernity

1. A major portion of the first half of this chapter originally appeared as the article "The Institutions of American Culture after the Counter-Culture" in the on-line journal *Findings Online*. See www.wilberforce.org/WilberforceForum/ChannelRoot/Features/FindingsOnline.

2. Richard M. Weaver, *Ideas Have Consequences* (Chicago: University of Chicago Press, 1948), 176.

3. An essay of this sort tends to make broad general statements that do not apply to all situations in particular. With more than 3,900 institutions of higher learning in the United States, several hundred could cling to their responsibility for character development and not invalidate this generalization. Identifying and recognizing character-building schools is one of the projects of the John Templeton Foundation, which affirms institutions that continue to accept some responsibility in this area.

4. "The Willowbank Report," in *Perspectives on the World Christian Movement: A Reader*, ed. Ralph D. Winter and Steven C. Hawthorne (Pasadena, Calif.: William Carey Library, 1981), 509. This report came from a consultation on "Gospel and Culture" sponsored by the Lausanne Committee for World Evangelization in 1978.

5. Alfred H. Kelly and Winfred A. Harbison, *The American Constitution: Its Origins and Development*, 4th ed. (New York: Norton, 1970), 1043.

6. Alexander Hamilton, John Jay, and James Madison, "The Federalist No. 81," in *The Federalist: A Commentary on the Constitution of the United States*, intro. by Edward Mead Earle (New York: Modern Library, 1937), 523.

7. Idem, "The Federalist No. 78," ibid., 510.

8. Ibid., 510–11.

9. Michael Moffatt, *Coming of Age in New Jersey: College and American Culture* (New Brunswick, N.J.: Rutgers University Press, 1989), quoted in Bryan Strong, Christine DeVault, and Barbara W. Sayad, *The Marriage and Family Experience: Intimate Relationships in a Changing Society*, 7th ed. (Belmont, Calif.: Wadsworth, 1998), 206.

10. Strong et al., *Marriage and Family Experience*, 244. These estimates come from the Centers for Disease Control.

11. L. Kann et al., "Youth Risk Behavior Surveillance—United States, 1999," in *Morbidity and Mortality Weekly Reports* 45 (CDC Surveillance Summaries, June 1999, no. SS-4), quoted in Nijole V. Benokraitis, *Marriages and Families: Changes, Choices, and Constraints*, 4th ed. (Upper Saddle River, N.J.: Prentice Hall, 2002), 149.

12. K. S. Miller et al., "Adolescent Sexual Behavior in Two Ethnic Minority Samples: The Role of Family Variables," *Journal of Marriage and the Family* 61 (February 1999): 85–98; K. A. Rodgers, "Parenting Processes Related to Sexual Risk-Taking: Behaviors of Adolescent Males and Females," *Journal of Marriage and the Family* 61 (February

1999): 99–109; F. Perkins et al., "An Ecological, Risk-Factor Examination of Adolescents' Sexual Activity in Three Ethnic Groups," *Journal of Marriage and the Family* 60 (August 1998): 660–73; M. Upchurch et al., "Neighborhood and Family Contexts of Adolescent Sexual Activity," *Journal of Marriage and the Family* 61 (November 1999): 920–33; L. B. Whitbeck, "Early Adolescent Sexual Activity," *Journal of Marriage and the Family* 61 (November 1999): 934–46; L. D. Lindberg, "Teen Risk-Taking: A Statistical Portrait" (Washington, D.C.: Urban Institute, 2000). Quoted in Benokraitis, *Marriages and Families*, 150.

13. E. Sorenson and C. Zibman, "Child Support Offers Some Protection Against Poverty" (Washington, D.C.: Urban Institute), quoted in Benokraitis, *Marriages and Families*, 410.

14. Strong et al., *Marriage and Family Experience*, 491.

15. For a more detailed discussion of the opportunities afforded by the postmodern vacuum, see Harry Lee Poe, *Christian Witness in a Postmodern World* (Nashville: Abingdon, 2001).

16. Earl Palmer, "Education as Sabbath," in *The University through the Eyes of Faith*, ed. Steve Moore with Tim Beuthin (Indianapolis: Light and Life, 1989), 53.

17. Bear in mind that this maxim comes from Ralph Waldo Emerson.

Chapter 5: A Christian Worldview

1. Arnold Toynbee, *A Study of History*, abridged by D. C. Somerville (New York: Oxford University Press, 1953), 60–61.

2. C. S. Lewis, *Mere Christianity* (San Francisco: HarperSanFrancisco, 2001), viii–ix.

3. C. H. Dodd serves as the pivotal figure in scholarship related to the identification of the gospel message in apostolic times. Originally presented as three lectures in 1935, his small volume has become the point of departure for any serious consideration of the subject. Great disagreement has followed Dodd over whether the apostles held to a common "formula" or merely a common understanding of the gospel. See C. H. Dodd, *The Apostolic Preaching and Its Developments* (New York: Harper & Row, 1964). For a discussion of various views on the gospel, see Harry L. Poe, *The Gospel and Its Meaning* (Grand Rapids: Zondervan, 1996), 15–55.

4. *The Apostolic Fathers: Greek Texts and English Translations*, ed. and rev. M. W. Holmes, updated ed. (Grand Rapids: Baker, 1999), 165.

5. Irenaeus, *Against Heresies* 10, in *The Ante-Nicene Fathers*, ed. A. Roberts and J. Donaldson (Grand Rapids: Eerdmans, n.d.), 1:330.

6. Tertullian, *The Prescription against Heretics* 13, in ibid., 3:249.

7. Philip Schaff, ed., *The Creeds of Christendom*, rev. David S. Schaff, 6th ed. (New York: Harper & Row, 1931; reprint, Grand Rapids: Baker, 1983), 1:16–18, 24–26.

8. *The Hymnal* (New York: James Pott, 1920), ix–xi.

9. *Baptist Hymnal*, ed. Walter Hines Sims (Nashville: Convention, 1956), vii–viii.

10. Lewis, *Mere Christianity*, 59.

11. For a comprehensive discussion of how the gospel has addressed major issues of various cultures over the last two thousand years, see Poe, *The Gospel and Its Meaning*.

12. When given the option of freedom if he would only sacrifice to Caesar, Polycarp replied, "For eighty-six years I have been his servant, and he has done me no wrong. How can I blaspheme my King who saved me?"(*The Martyrdom of Polycarp* 9.3; *Apostolic Fathers*, 235). While resolving to remain loyal to Christ as the German church made accommodations to Hitler, Bonhoeffer wrote, "But there is a far greater form of suffering than this, one which bears an ineffable promise. For while it is true that only the suffering of Christ himself can atone for sin, and that his suffering and

triumph took place 'for us,' yet to some, who are not ashamed of their fellowship in his body, he vouchsafes the immeasurable grace and privilege of suffering 'for him,' as he did for them" (Dietrich Bonhoeffer, *The Cost of Discipleship*, rev. ed. [New York: Collier, 1963], 273).

Chapter 6: The Doctrines and the Disciplines

1. See Stephen Jay Gould, *Rock of Ages: Science and Religion in the Fullness of Life* (New York: Ballantine, 1999), 4.

2. I am indebted to Dr. Pickett's gracious critique of this chapter, and in particular for his suggestions that relate to the arts (emailed September 27, 2002).

3. Dr. Padelford made these remarks at a workshop for new faculty of member schools of the Council for Christian Colleges & Universities, Union University, July 28–August 1, 2001.

4. Dr. King made these remarks at a workshop for new faculty of CCCU member schools, Union University, July 28–August 1, 2001.

5. Todd Pickett, email message to author, September 27, 2002.

Chapter 7: Interdisciplinary Dialogue

1. Robert Frost, "Mending Wall," in *A Little Treasury of Modern Poetry*, ed. Oscar Williams, 3d ed. (New York: Charles Scribner's Sons, 1970), 164.

2. In an article on successful corporations, the interdisciplinary approach gained recognition: "Larson replaced J & J's single-drug research teams with a more entrepreneurial system that created interdisciplinary teams of biologists and chemists to cut drug development times. . . . J & J now has 29 compounds in early development, vs. just a half-dozen five years ago." Dean Foust, Amy Barrett, Brian Hindo, Frederick F. Jespersen, Fred Katzenberg, Mike McNamee, and Aixa M. Pascual, "The Best Performers: The Business Week 50," *Business Week* (March 25, 2002): 39.

3. A. R. Peacocke, *Theology for a Scientific Age: Being and Becoming—Natural, Divine, and Human*, enlarged ed. (Minneapolis: Fortress, 1993), 217. Peacocke's table is an elaboration of figure 8.1 in W. Bechtel and A. Abrahamsen, *Connectionism and the Mind* (Oxford: Blackwell, 1991).

4. Carl Sagan, *Cosmos* (New York: Random House, 1980). The Greek word *kosmos* does not mean what the scientific word *planet* conveys. The Greeks had no concept that would correspond to the modern idea of the universe, although by the time of Ptolemy they had a concept of a solar system.

5. These comments were made during Richard Harris's report on the Nobel Prize awards, "All Things Considered," National Public Radio, October 7, 2002.

6. For a concise discussion of the development of scientific method, see Jimmy H. Davis's narrative in Harry L. Poe and Jimmy H. Davis, *Science and Faith* (Nashville: Broadman & Holman, 2000), 3–15.

7. A. T. Robertson, *A Grammar of the New Testament* (Nashville: Broadman, 1934), 385. Robertson repeated this theme throughout his massive grammar, as in one case: "Humboldt is quoted by Oertel as saying: 'Linguistic science, as I understand it, must be based upon facts alone, and this collection must be neither one-sided nor incomplete.' So Bopp conceived also: 'A grammar in the higher scientific sense of the word must be both history and natural science.' This is not an unreasonable demand, for it is made of every other department of science" (p. 10).

8. John Wisdom, "Philosophical Perplexity," in *Philosophy and Psycho-Analysis* (Oxford: Blackwell, 1953), 37.

9. C. S. Lewis, *The Abolition of Man* (New York: Macmillan, 1947), 14.

10. Ibid., 16–17. Lewis does not refer to King and Ketley by name. Instead, he calls them Gaius and Titius and refers to their book as *The Green Book*, perhaps a jocular reference to the "Blue Book" and "Brown Book."

11. See Mary Anne Poe, "Christian Worldview and Social Work," in *Shaping a Christian Worldview*, ed. David S. Dockery and Gregory Alan Thornbury (Nashville: Broadman & Holman, 2002), 331–32.

12. R. G. Collingwood, *The Idea of History* (New York: Oxford University Press, 1956), 1.

13. Benedetto Croce, *History: Its Theory and Practice*, trans. Douglas Ainslie (New York: Russell & Russell, 1960), 32.

14. Benedetto Croce, *History as the Story of Liberty*, trans. Sylvia Sprigge (London: George Allen & Unwin, 1949), 17.

15. Wilhelm Dilthey, *Pattern and Meaning in History*, ed. H. P. Rickman (New York: Harper Torchbooks, 1962), 68–69.

16. Collingwood, *Idea of History*, 136.

17. Oswald Spengler, *The Decline of the West*, vol. 1, *Form and Actuality*, trans. Charles Francis Atkinson (New York: Knopf, 1950), 107.

18. Christopher Hill, *The World Turned Upside Down: Radical Ideas during the English Revolution* (New York: Viking, 1972), 13. When I was reading English Reformation history at Oxford, Hill was generally regarded as having Marxist leanings. Later in his introduction he remarked, "The philosophical truth of the ideas is irrelevant to the historian's purpose, though all of us have our preferences: the reader will no doubt soon discover mine" (p. 15).

19. Rudolf Bultmann, *Jesus Christ and Mythology* (New York: Scribners, 1958), 15.

Chapter 8: Asking the Critical Questions

1. Dan Carnevale, "Virtual Faith," *The Chronicle of Higher Education* 49.13 (November 22, 2002): A52.

2. "Evidence for Design: Finding New Ground for Dialogue," June 23–27, 2000. The conference was funded by the John Templeton Foundation and hosted by Chicago's Zygon Center for Religion and Science under the auspices of the Science and Religion Course Program, administered by the Center for Theology and the Natural Sciences of Berkeley.

3. C. S. Lewis, *Surprised by Joy* (New York: Harcourt, Brace, 1956), 207.

4. Harold Heie has incorporated these ideas in a recent essay: "Developing a Christian Perspective on the Nature of Mathematics," in *Teaching as an Act of Faith*, ed. Arlin C. Migliazzo (New York: Fordham University Press, 2002), 95–116.

5. See Harry L. Poe and Jimmy H. Davis, *Science and Faith: An Evangelical Dialogue* (Nashville: Broadman & Holman, 2000).

6. For a helpful discussion of how a Christian might utilize the methodologies current in literary criticism while bringing to the project the questions of faith, see Barbara McMillin, "Christian Worldview and Literature," in *Shaping a Christian Worldview*, ed. David S. Dockery and Gregory Thornbury (Nashville: Broadman & Holman, 2002), 149–61.

7. L. Joseph Rosas III, private conversation with the author, December 7, 2002.

8. I am indebted to Jill Webb, professor of nursing and director of the master's nursing program at Union University, for calling this contradiction to my attention.

9. Mary Anne Poe, "Christian Worldview and Social Work," in *Shaping a Christian Worldview*, 331–34.

Chapter 9: Etcetera

1. Gregory Thornbury has developed this theme at length in "The Reformation Epistemology of Carl F. H. Henry," in *Remaking the Modern Mind: Evangelical Foundations and the Theology of Carl F. H. Henry*, ed. David S. Dockery and Gregory A. Thornbury (Nashville: Broadman & Holman, forthcoming).

Index